Closed Encounters

CLOSED ENCOUNTERS

— LITERARY POLITICS AND PUBLIC CULTURE —

Jeffrey Wallen

University of Minnesota Press

Minneapolis

London

Copyright 1998 by the Regents of the University of Minnesota

An earlier version of chapter 7 was published as "The Poverty of Conversation," *Yale Journal of Criticism* 9, no. 2 (1996): 405–19. Reprinted by permission of the Johns Hopkins University Press.

Published by the University of Minnesota Press
111 Third Avenue South, Suite 290
Minneapolis, MN 55401–2520
http://www.upress.umn.edu

Printed in the United States of America on acid-free paper

The University of Minnesota is an equal-opportunity educator and employer.

Library of Congress Cataloging-in-Publication Data
Wallen, Jeffrey.
    Closed encounters : literary politics and public culture / Jeffrey
Wallen.
        p.   cm.
    Includes bibliographical references and index.
    ISBN 0-8166-3187-5 (alk. paper). — ISBN 0-8166-3188-3 (pbk. :
alk. paper)
        1. Criticism.   I. Title.
    PN81.W286   1998
    814'.54–dc21   98–6232

10   09   08   07   06   05   04   03   02   01   00   99   98   10 9 8 7 6 5 4 3 2 1

Contents

Introduction

FELLOW TRAVELING IN ACADEMIA

◆

[I]ch will nur Kenntnisse verbreiten, ich be-
richte nur, auch Ihnen, hohe Herren von der
Akademie, habe ich nur berichtet.
— KAFKA, "Ein Bericht für eine Akademie"

Tel est le triomphe de l'éducation jésuitique:
donner l'habitude de ne pas faire attention à
des choses plus claires que le jour.
— STENDHAL, *La Chartreuse de Parme*[1]

The goals of literary criticism have never been more ambitious. The word "intervention" is now commonly used in place of "essay," and it suggests the hope of disrupting the current state of affairs, of stepping into and transforming the balances (or imbalances) of power through the agency of one's words. The imagined arena of influence, like the circles from a stone dropped in a lake, is ever widening: professors interested in the particular object of study, the literature department, the "institution," the public sphere, society. The current revival of the term "intellectual" testifies to the desire for an impact that goes beyond the professional divisions of field and reaches, potentially, any-one interested in thinking about complex questions of cultural, social, or political significance.

Edward Said's *Culture and Imperialism*, for instance, aims to rethink the history and challenge the effects of Western imperialism, intending thereby to change the future course of relations between Western and non-Western peoples. A typical essay of literary criticism, published in a scholarly journal with a small readership, offering a new interpreta-tion of a work by Conrad or Austen, may seem more modest. Yet any postcolonial (or feminist, post-Marxist, queer, or any of the leading

1

forms of interpretation) reading of *Heart of Darkness* or *Mansfield Park* likely contains, whether articulated or not, much larger goals. For a postcolonial interpretation of a literary work makes little sense unless one has a position concerning colonialism, judgments about its continuing aftermath, and hopes for a different path in the future. The critical horizon of a typical essay, even if the critic has not thought through any goals more far-reaching than getting another article into print, is not modest at all.

Since so much is potentially at stake now in literary criticism, insofar as it addresses (at least implicitly) the essential problems of American society and offers new visions for a more democratic culture, the public battles around literary and cultural criticism have also not been modest. Such hyperbolic terms as canon wars, culture wars, even Kulturkampf, for those with an eye on another era, have been used to describe conflicts about which books students ought to read. In fighting over whether students should be assigned Toni Morrison or Ernest Hemingway, Alice Walker or Shakespeare, the real points of contention are radically different aspirations for literary education: the hope that students will become motivated, through exposure to the wrongs of the past and to nonwhite, nonbourgeois perspectives, to fight effectively against racism and oppression; or the belief that by reading canonical works, students will imbibe a common culture and learn the fundamental, unifying principles of American society. The culture wars are about the different goals and philosophies that drive competing analyses of our society; the merits of particular books or artworks are of only incidental importance.

Participating in these debates usually means choosing the proper goal for literary criticism: fighting for social justice or upholding the values of traditional humanistic study are popular choices, and one can also opt for the seeming middle ground of promoting dialogue, even "teaching the conflicts." Although each side rarely gives serious consideration to the opposing arguments, these debates are still important, especially insofar as they force us to articulate, defend, and question our values and suppositions. But such polemics take place as if choosing the proper goal, deciding what it is that one hopes one's criticism will accomplish, was really the key task. It isn't. Settling on what we want literary criticism to change, to reform, or to cure (and students offer a wonderful medium on which to project hopes of transformation) is only of consequence if one assumes that academic modes of writing about literature are direct vehicles for reaching these goals of social transformation. In the chapters that follow, I will argue that current practices of literary criticism often take us on a different path than the yellow-brick roads leading to a less "oppressive" and more equal society, or to a newly invigorated public sphere.

I don't want to joust in the culture wars; all the thrusts and ripostes deflect our attention away from looking at what criticism does. Most of the dominant forms of academic literary criticism today envision possibilities of social or political change (the attention to "gender," for example, always presupposes the potential to transform the categories and relations under analysis), but the power of criticism lies in its forms of thinking and interpretation, in what it performs and leads toward, and in what it enables us to envision and carry out. No one expects that analyzing literary works (or more broadly, "cultural texts") is a transparent or direct means for bringing about political change; at best, such ends might be achieved in a highly mediated fashion, teaching us, for instance, to read the signs of domination and power embedded in all the products of our culture. But is such a lesson really a step toward resisting domination and achieving greater democracy? Any answer depends partly on the modes of argument and analysis, on the procedures for interpretation and deducing significance, on the basic set of assumptions, and on all the other elements that make academic criticism a fairly coherent set of practices. If the argument presumes that the critic, by looking for any signs of inequality and injustice, is thereby more enlightened than all the characters in the novel and all previous readers of the novel, then the structuring premise (I judge from a position of moral superiority, because I see the unacknowledged failings of others, and my analysis therefore discredits everyone who ignores these sins) works against the claim of learning from other perspectives and providing a common path for battling the sources of inequality. This example is simplistic, but I believe that such forms of "reading for evil," which instill an ethical smugness and complacency rather than a profound questioning, are a common outcome of current pedagogy (I discuss further the consequences of "reading for evil" in chapter 6, "Criticism as Displacement"). My point, however, is that the explicit or implicit political goals that structure academic literary criticism need to be considered against the drift of the actual practices. Debates that revolve around the proper aims for criticism are a sideshow. I focus therefore on drawing out the critical strategies and forms of argument that contradict or undermine the overarching goals of political and institutional change, with the aim of stripping off some of the protective coatings that insulate critics from the effects of their own discourse.

It is hardly a new insight that academic critics in the humanities do not achieve most of the goals they envision. "Academic" is often a synonym for "not practical" or "ineffectual," and there is a whole genre of books addressing the current disparity between the vitality of academic leftism and the anemia of progressive politics in wider American society.[2] I do not want to pose the question that typically proceeds from such observations, How can we make literary (or cultural) criticism more politically effective? First, I have no great desire to see literary critics wield much greater influence, or reshape the political horizons, even if that were possible. Much academic criticism is now a form of moralism and does not reveal any deep wisdom about what types of social change are possible or desirable. More importantly, the focus on making criticism more politically "effective" (or conversely, arguing that to do so would betray its true mission) places the emphasis on what we would want criticism to do, not on how we actually think, argue, and interpret. What makes academic criticism both recognizable and consequential (and this is why I use so often the adjective "academic") is not the object of criticism (a book, movie, or cultural item) nor the goal (ending sexism, social change), but the distinctive mode of discourse (the set of assumptions, the ways of reading, the interpretive methods) — one that is not widely shared or understood by the broader populace, especially insofar as it has been shaped by poststructuralist theory. The demand that criticism become politically effective is frequently an appeal for a more familiar and digestible discourse, and it often has the effect of turning attention away from critical thinking and from a full exploration of the ramifications of the strategies we now deploy.[3]

In each of the chapters, I examine different ways in which these critical strategies do something other than carry out the underlying program of social and political change. For example, critics often now hope that their work will have a public impact. Not only do they want to bring their insights to an audience outside academia, but they also aim, more grandly, at revivifying the public sphere and creating better possibilities for public discussion. This concern for the "public" is often directly related to the "academic" work of reading texts,

since these readings frequently diagnose instances of muddled thinking, intolerance, contradictory desires, and ignorance that fester when
there is little vigorous public discussion to counter and contest the
mass-produced ideologies of consumer capitalism. And the tools of
criticism — ideology critique, exploring the difference between manifest and latent content, a knowledge of rhetoric and semiotics, and so
on — are very good for detailing the failures of civic life in our age of
sound-bite politics, corporate-controlled media, and increasing social
stratification. Typically, however, the analysis will depend on a stance
(being outside of and opposing the social mainstream) and on strategies (debunking the opinions of others by exposing the dismal forces
that have produced them) that disqualify anyone from participating in
discussion who has different views and has not yet been enlightened
to the fact that their beliefs reflect the imperatives of the dominant
culture. Such practices hardly lay a solid foundation for public dialogue; what enables us to make an academically persuasive argument
works to disable the envisaged solution. The strategies for making the
argument often block the goal of a vital public sphere far more than
do the constraints that are usually invoked, such as addressing a small
community of literature professors or using literary texts as the basis
for social criticism (in chapter 4, "Why I'd Rather Be Talking to a TV
Camera," I explore further some of the contradictions between academic modes of argument and the lofty aims toward which they are
directed).

For the most part, I am not trying to perform the usual tactic of
pointing out the flaws in prior interpretations and then offering my
own superior version. I find many of the analyses of the impoverishment of the public sphere compelling, even when I think the critical
strategies lead away from the proposed solutions. Moreover, the contradictions between the methods and the underlying goals are often
not "internal" to the arguments themselves (an example of an "internal" contradiction, which I discuss in chapter 7, "The Poverty of
Conversation," would be when one appeals to an ideal of conversation to attack one's opponents but then undermines this ideal through
one's own rhetoric). It is not at all simply a matter of overcoming
hypocrisy. For instance, central to much contemporary criticism have
been a critique of the notion of "truth" (and of truths as universal
foundations for knowledge) and also an attack against many of the
notions that accompany an ideology of truth (objectivity, neutrality,

disinterestedness, and so on). The philosophical claim, in the work of Richard Rorty (or very differently, in that of Stanley Fish), is that we should "call 'true'...whatever the outcome of undistorted communication happens to be."[4] I find this post-Nietzschean argument largely convincing (even if I think that many problems in critical theory stem from poor readings of Nietzsche).[5] The social consequence of this critique is that we should therefore embrace persuasion (or "freely arrived at agreement") rather than universal and absolute truths as the basis of democratic society. In more utopian writers, the hope is also to free us from believing that we can know the truth, to open us to other "truths" and other perspectives, to expand our horizons through contact with other cultures, and to increase exponentially human awareness. All well and good; these hopes are admirable, and Rorty's analysis of truth and contingency is not hypocritical — his arguments are not based on dogmatic assertion, religious revelation, or other claims (for example, the authority of the argument is directly proportional to the "marginality" of the critic) that undermine the concept of persuasion.

I will argue, however (in "Political Correctness: The Revenge of the Liberals" and "Is Academic Freedom in Trouble?"), that the critique of truth and the promotion of persuasion often lead to a climate in which "undistorted communication" (or the "free and open encounter" of differing views that Rorty embraces) becomes much *less* likely. The philosophical critique of the idea of "truth" also undermines the foundations of liberalism and knocks the ground out from under the institutional structures that serve to protect persuasion from coercion or to distinguish a conflict of opinions from a struggle of interests. A consequence of Rorty's claim that "truth is made rather than found" is the discrediting of the notions and institutional habits (such as freedom of inquiry or seeking an objective stance when evaluating the ideas of others) that have been considered necessary for the "pursuit of truth." It is often argued that since the "pursuit of truth" does not describe anything real, but is only a convenient fiction that masks power and stifles conflict between competing interests, we need no longer be restrained by any of these notions and traditions from exercising our own power and pursuing our own interests. Unfortunately, this does not lead to "free and open" conflict by clearing away the misguided principles that have hindered debate. The upshot is more likely to be that since we now recognize that "everything is political" and "whose discourse prevails makes all the difference" (that is, since "persuasion" is so important), we need either to restrict persuasion to the realm of the nonoffensive (people might be harmed by the wrong words or ideas) or to control the outcome. In addition, any ideal of striving to consider different opinions in the hope of discerning those with the most merit, or of creating new and better ideas through this interchange of opinion, can be trumped whenever necessary: such ideals merely conceal a struggle of interests. As the dean of faculty where I teach put it, the First Amendment was written by rich white male slaveholders (this was the capstone in her argument against a measure before the faculty supporting freedom of expression at our college — a measure that failed).[6] The notion that "truth is made rather than found" becomes a handy tool to debunk the ideas of those enshrined as the "founders" of our traditions.

Critiques of liberalism often aim at demystifying the functions of various discourses and institutions in late capitalist society in order to help the disempowered recognize their class and group interests, and understand hegemony so that they can resist it. But these techniques of stripping away the rhetoric of freedom and democracy to expose exploitation and injustice, which frame our view of conflict as a struggle of interests masked by a superficial contest of ideas, are likely instead to give those in power all the greater license to act on their desires. When corporations have no other obligations than pursuing their "interests," the results are not pretty. What orients several of my chapters is a critique of the critique of liberalism.[7] I emphasize that the poststructuralist and postmodernist critiques of autonomy, individuality, and other related notions underlying political liberalism do not lead to the envisaged egalitarian and democratic society and sometimes yield instead a further diminishment of freedom, since they undercut the traditional protections of liberty. In addition to the disparity between critical practice and envisioned goal, I also focus on the pressure points where critics of liberalism seek to justify, legitimate, and defend their roles, since we usually find here reinvocations of a "discredited" liberal discourse, such as a renewed appeal for participation in public discussion.[8]

◆

Teaching at Hampshire College has made me especially attuned to the ways in which the hopes of applying critical insights for political ends go awry. It was actually for the failure to apply criticism for the right purposes — a failure to "educate for social justice" and to offer the appropriate Third World challenge to the canon — that another colleague and I were denied reappointment. Beyond watching all the contradictions, such as professors and administrators pledging support for dialogue, diversity, and academic freedom while doing everything to suppress them (the language of liberalism always returns when academics must sport a "public face," talking to the media or other outsiders), I was forced to reassess the effects of the different theories that constituted the topology of my professional landscape. I faced the need to defend myself institutionally and publicly (media coverage was a major factor in my ultimately successful appeal, and I became a participant in the political correctness battles of 1990–91), which required invoking commonly shared principles and beliefs that I felt were being violated. This was not all that hard to do, yet every appeal to academic freedom, toleration, and the liberty to choose how and what to teach felt like a step outside my professional identity and a betrayal of my critical training. Appealing to a widely held "foundational" principle is quite different from teasing out its polemical character, its agonistic functions, and its ambiguities — much less exposing its oppressive, exploitative, and ruinous features, as the next generation of graduate students have learned to do. The latter forms of "critical" argument challenge any appeal to foundational principles as naively deluded. The tension here not only is around my person — I need to rely on and also to deconstruct "principles" to keep my job — but arises whenever the negative critique requires some new basis on which to build public consent. In several of the following chapters, I focus on moments when academics seek to "go public," in order to bring out the tensions between the discourses that prevail within academia and those that are employed when seeking public support.

Even more problematic for me was watching such ideas as "There is *only* a perspective seeing, *only* a perspective 'knowing'" (Nietzsche) return as an institutional policy that one must advocate the proper (oppositional, Third World) perspective in the classroom.[9] Most academics do not have to confront such perverse institutionalizations of their criticism, in which a (seemingly) liberatory insight is reduced to an institutional demand to promote a "marginal" perspective against a "dominant" one. I do not want to claim that critical theory in the wake of Nietzsche is responsible for a narrow-mindedness and intolerance that come largely out of an ethos of institutional loyalty ("Cherish or perish" is the unofficial motto where I teach), yet I do want to suggest that these contradictions at Hampshire (between a call for diversity of perspectives and an enforced restriction of view-points)[10] are exemplary and a magnification of tendencies that are kept more in check elsewhere. At most universities, the autonomy of departments, the lessened sense of mission (Hampshire was founded as a "progressive," "alternative" college), the greater range of political viewpoints (at Hampshire, everyone is on the "Left"), or the lack of an administration pledged to "educating for social justice" inhibit the drive to institutionalize new critical insights in an effort to achieve social change.[11]

Academic critics frequently overlook or ignore the consequences of institutionalizing their ideas, even as they aim for social trans-formation. The translation of the insight that the teacherly pose of impartiality, nonpartisanship, or objectivity is constricting, even false, into the institutional promotion of "advocacy in the classroom" does not yield the desired result of a more honest, open, and conflictual dia-logue. In order for "advocacy" to work as envisioned — as a productive engagement of different opinions — all the protections, functions, and assumptions about a liberal sphere of dialogue would have to be in place. But the new sphere is open only to those who agree to play one of the desired roles, once the theoretical critique of nonpartisan-ship comes to define what is pedagogically acceptable. Anyone who is unwilling to adopt a stance of advocacy can then be fired on the grounds of professional incompetence: they are obviously not aware of current knowledge and are therefore poor teachers, stifled by the mys-tifications of bourgeois liberalism. Critiques of liberalism often founder on the contradiction of attacking the frameworks that are necessary to support the dialogues on which they still continue to place great hopes (I analyze these tensions at length in "The Poverty of Conversation").

In the last several years, critics have been paying substantial atten-tion to the importance of the "institution" for interpretative practices. Samuel Weber in *Institution and Interpretation* explored "the operative forces that shape and limit interpretive practices," and he attended especially to the "instituting process" as well as the "instituted or-ganization"; and Gerald Graff, in *Professing Literature: An Institutional History*, situated recent controversies about the teaching of litera-ture within the history of academic literary studies in the United

States.[12] There are many analyses of the discriminatory and exclusionary characteristics of institutions, and recent works investigate how the pressures of professionalism, the job market, and the star system impact the forms of thinking and the succession of theories that constitute contemporary literary criticism. These writings are essential for understanding the ways in which literary study is not an unmediated relation between reader and text and also for learning more about the contexts and constraints within which we work and about the character of and differences between institutions. I want to shift the focus to a related but different set of questions. Rather than looking at how "institutions" affect interpretations, I want to ask how our interpretations — our critical strategies and our conceptual frameworks — affect our institutions. (What might it mean to deploy a "Foucauldian" critique as the basis for a new policy or as the groundwork for a "new conversation"?) Are these interpretative practices compatible with the desired institutional effects? (What happens when a deconstructive or psychoanalytic literary analysis is not only applied to social categories but transported and directed at institutional change?) What are the disparities between an academic and a public voice? (How does a claim of "speaking from the margins" have a very different force within the discipline of literary studies than externally, in other settings?)

Posing questions about the contradictions in the work of others, examining how texts "perform" something other than their apparent intention, or looking at interpretations in relation to institutions are all part of what we are trained to do, yet it has been very awkward for me to write about these questions. In 1991, during the height of the media interest in political correctness, I found on several occasions that invitations to speak came with the expectation that I would fill a certain role (such as attacking those who had been chosen to exemplify the Left and the current trends of academic thinking and lining up with the conservatives, defenders of tradition and liberty). I tried my best to argue that these configurations of Left and Right had little to do with the issues of "political correctness" at Hampshire College, and more importantly, I explained that this insistence on determining "Which side are you on?" only blinds us from understanding anything further about the ramifications and the possibilities of critical arguments. Yet I was struggling against much more than the televisual desire for confrontation, which requires that "dialogue" be a matter of clear oppositions. The goals of social change, and the new strategies of reading texts for their political tendencies, also place a constant emphasis on determining the *position* of the speaker and on judging arguments largely on the basis of who (apparently) is being supported or attacked.

Much more than my personal discomfort at feeling pushed into the "wrong" position is at stake here: searching every essay for the politics or the subject position of the author filters out any play of ideas and discounts the opinions of all those who are not from the approved categories. Interpretative practices that depend upon identifying and placing the speaker not only undermine the declared goals of openness, diversity, inclusion, and public participation, but work to keep everyone in their places and to insulate us from those who hold contrary views. The desire for efficacious criticism engenders practices that short-circuit the very questioning of textuality and of institutional frameworks that academics hope their criticism will foment.

Writing these chapters has also been awkward since the audience I want to persuade is composed of those whose works I am criticizing. The critics with whom I argue — Edward Said, Gerald Graff, Richard Rorty, Stanley Fish, among others — are those whose work I find the most incisive, and from whom I have learned a great deal. I am not appealing to some other group that might provide a safe haven, such as perhaps a (very small) circle of demographically similar and like-minded colleagues, or to some imagined silent minority of clear-sighted academics, or to people who read *Harper's* and the *Atlantic Monthly*. It is much easier to gain critical leverage when one has a secure base of support; the shared assumptions of the audience provide a stable framework that can be used in judging whatever one targets. Nor am I drawing on some alternative critical space that I envision or invoking some earlier time to which I urge a return. Although several of these chapters consider the relations between academia and the public, my aim is not to ground myself in some external, public space in order to denounce the betrayals or perversities of academic critics, but rather to examine the ways in which critical discourses undercut the possibilities for public access and impact that they now require.

In the hopes of engaging a broader public and achieving a more democratic society, most forms of contemporary criticism rely, implicitly or explicitly, on notions of persuasion and dialogue. In several chapters, I therefore explore the ways in which critics fail to bring us any closer to the horizons of dialogue that they invoke or idealize. My aim in analyzing the poverty of critical conversations is both to diagnose how we might invigorate the debilitated interactions with those who have different ideas and also to think through how we might strengthen our forms of criticism. Critical strategies that envision potential interlocutors as incapable of the openness and the self-reflection necessary for critical exchange not only foreclose the possibility of dialogue, but also lead to a criticism that is self-contradictory (incapable of achieving its goal of engaging others), defensive (any contrary ideas can always be discredited), and unwilling to confront its own implications.

I do not have one comprehensive theory to explain all the disjunctions between what literary criticism does and what, at some level, it seeks to do. Recent trends in criticism do not culminate in one primary contradiction that can be captured by an oxymoronic slogan such as "tenured radicals," "illiberal education," "dogmatic wisdom," or "the revolt of the elites."[13] Instead of setting forth a new theory of interpretation, or a model of dialogue that I hope others will follow, or even a set of prescriptions for restructuring education, I hope to spur a reexamination of what we really carry out in academic literary studies. I would like to write a more conventional study, but that would require accepting the viability and the importance of academic discourse. These chapters are in some sense preliminary: questions to be addressed before going further, and before assuming the purposefulness of the frameworks within which we work.

A few of the chapters are overtly polemical and attack what I take to be unwarranted restrictions, unintended and counterproductive consequences, or just poor thinking that result from many of the current critical practices. In looking at how the rhetoric of diversity conflicts with the supposed aim of a diversity of opinion and the supposed allegiance to academic freedom (in chapter 2, "Is Academic Freedom in Trouble?"), or at how the blithe promotion of "advocacy in the classroom" can easily shut down the very debate and inquiry it is meant to enliven, I want to expose the unwillingness to see any of the problems arising out of these new and cherished notions (any of the forms of curtailment and suppression that are effects of these discourses of openness and liberation). I also want to explore the institutional forces that breed blindness and complacency. My polemical aim is not to banish politically charged or methodologically disruptive critiques; I think academic criticism is already too insular, complacent, and self-righteous. Rather, I would like to bring out the conflicts that are suppressed or ignored, despite the widespread claims for replacing the outmoded ideals of "consensus" and "pluralism" with a new respect for "conflict," "partisanship," and "dissensus." As I stated above, my point of departure might often be construed as a critique of the critique of liberalism, but my intention is not so much to defend liberalism or to argue against modes of criticism that are incompatible with liberal goals, as to push for a criticism that better recognizes the tension between its practices and its hopes and that does not seek to tailor its thinking according to whatever patterns are now deemed socially desirable.

The motivation for this book is less my frustration with what is happening in literary studies than my disappointment with what is not. The current moment ought to be the most exciting and consequential period in literary studies, now that we have an extremely broad sense both of literature and of our mission as educators, now that the restraints of tradition and the desires to downplay any conflict have been pushed aside, and now that we have an ever-expanding ferment of new theories and intellectual frameworks to employ. Entitling chapters "Criticism as Displacement" and "The Poverty of Conversation" registers my view that this is not the case. In "Criticism as Displacement," I argue that current literary analysis offers a poor vehicle for debating political issues. The interpretative frameworks that dominate literary criticism today arise from a concern with the political, social, and philosophical issues that are at the center of the most important disagreements in American society, yet the readings that flow from these frameworks confine productive discussion to a few questions about the interpretation of literary texts. Literary criticism, in the guise of engaging social and political questions, functions instead to displace political debate. We cannot pretend that these structural contradictions between the practices and the aims of criticism are merely an incidental effect or a local problem, and will quickly disappear in the next round of critical essays.

I could provide a fuller theoretical justification for my approach of analyzing the incompatibilities between the performance and the goals of criticism. I could invoke Paul de Man and rework some of his insights to ground my enterprise: "Literary theory raises the unavoidable question whether aesthetic values can be compatible with the linguistic structures that make up the entities from which these values are derived. Such questions never ceased to haunt the consciousness of writers and philosophers."[14] With the substitution of a few words, this argument could be reworded to question the compatibility between the values and the structures of contemporary criticism. De Man continues: "What is established is that their compatibility, or lack of it, has to remain an open question and that the manner in which the teaching of literature, since its beginning in the later nineteenth century, has foreclosed the question is unsound, even if motivated by the best of intentions" (25). Especially when motivated by the best of intentions, critics today fend off any questioning of their "admirable ambition to unite cognition, desire and morality in one single synthetic judgment" (25); the usual (unsound) logic is that our critical tools are means of demystification and understanding, and if we deploy them to bring about political change, these tools will certainly be compatible with our goals. I do not want to shift attention, however, to which theory would offer the best explanation for the incompatibilities that I describe. Instead, I want to put forward questions that will haunt incessantly the consciousness of academic critics.

I have divided the book into three sections: "Administering Conflict," "Facing the Public," and "Failed Encounters: Dialogue or Chatter?" In the first section, I explore problems that arise from efforts to incorporate new insights about the social and institutional bases of knowledge into the practices of the university. Inquiries establishing the mutability and constructedness of knowledge have provoked a reappraisal of our ideas about "difference" and "conflict" and require new models for mediating between conflicting viewpoints. For instance, an earlier concern for transcending differences (in a quest for knowledge that is "universal") has largely been displaced by a new respect for the differences between cultures and groups of people. This shift in paradigms poses a tremendous administrative challenge: How do we, and how does a university, make a clash of perspectives become an intellectually productive conflict? And what are to be the criteria for underwriting and the means for regulating multiple perspectives, now that the earlier norms for adjudicating difference have been rejected? In the chapters in this section, I argue that because these critiques appear to be liberating (if values and knowledge are not immutable and transcendental but "constructed," then we can transform them), there is a strong resistance to seeing any contrary effects. I use my experiences at Hampshire College as a point of departure for analyzing the constraining of thought and narrowing of outlooks that often occur when critiques of objectivity, truth, and disinterestedness are institutionalized through policies and pressures that affect curriculum, hiring, professional advancement, and teaching.

The controversies around political correctness a few years ago presented a grand opportunity for exploring questions about the institutional consequences of new critical paradigms. The fuss arose initially from a feeling by some that academic practices had become newly coercive and restrictive, often in an effort to promote a (leftist) political viewpoint (restraint, of course, is more easily felt — and resisted — when it pushes against one's own political leanings). Rather than an insightful debate about the principles of education, or about the dynamic between freedom, persuasion, and coercion in education, or about the civic obligations of the professor, we got instead either fearful stories that ridiculed academic fashions (with the intent of bringing public pressure against universities) or flattering defenses of all that we do (designed to raise the morale of professors in a horrible job market and to reassure the public that nothing is wrong). In the charged atmosphere of journalistic attack, most academics responded like porcupines: using their quills to ward off enemies and to prevent anything external from penetrating into their domain. But such a posture of denying that the views of journalists and "conservatives" may be worth considering only reinforces the divisions between academics and others and belies the desire to influence and claim solidarity with the public. This book seeks to overcome the refusal to consider that the application of new critical paradigms may have unforeseen and deleterious consequences, by stressing the dissonance between liberatory expectations and institutional effects.

Although the repercussions of academic literary criticism are mostly felt within the university, the horizon for literary and cultural analysis, I have been arguing, is largely beyond the university. The goal that justifies the enterprise is not changing the English department but transforming American cultural politics. Academic criticism now seeks to push outward, to exert a force (hence the vocabulary of resistance, oppositionality, vectors) against others, to move those who think and act differently. Articulating this "outside" as a "public" — both a generality and commonality, of which everyone (that is, all the members of a bounded entity, a city or state) can partake, and a space, in which "people assemble for the free, equal interchange of reasonable discourse" (as Terry Eagleton describes the bourgeois public sphere)[15] — is especially appealing at a time when liberals and conservatives bemoan the breakdown of community and of civic structures.

In the second section, "Facing the Public," I examine the dynamics of this turn to the public in literary criticism, and I explore what is at issue in appeals to popularize academic criticism, to speak in a "public" voice, or to cross over the boundaries that separate an academic discipline from the public sphere and from a broader audience. Again, I question whether the critical practices used to theorize and formulate the urgency of engaging a public are at all adequate for leading the way toward the goals that are envisioned. Do the academic critiques that now discuss or imagine a public help to open new dialogues with others outside universities? or pave the way for "public access" so that our analyses can reach and radicalize American culture? or disturb our complacency by opening our disciplines to public scrutiny and accountability? or begin the task of revitalizing a public sphere, in which the academic would no longer be so marginal to the larger society?[16] I focus on what I take to be the failures and the contradictions of these critiques and argue that the very strategies by which we analyze the need for public participation and theorize a public domain often have the perverse effect of positioning the "public" as necessarily always outside the realm of academic discourse and as incapable of participating in our discussions.

Another way to frame this is in terms of the conflicting conceptions of the public that are at work. One notion of the public describes a *mass*, those who are to be moved, those whose commonality lies in a common subjection to the state, to the media, and to consumer capitalism. Another version of the public is conceived in opposition to the state, as *potentially* common, and as "open": as not restricted by institutional affiliation or by belief or identity. This latter notion of the public posits a hopefulness, a possibility of participation and community to be achieved, and is not merely descriptive (as is the former). I look at how critical arguments get their force from treating the public as a mass, even as they require a more optimistic conception of the public, and plead for new possibilities of public access and participation. I also consider topics such as pornography that bring out the contours and the tensions of the borders between "academic" and "public." I seek to probe the ambivalences and the fault lines that are animated by this turn to the public.

The efforts to administer conflict within the university and to engage a public beyond it bring forth calls for a "genuinely critical dialogue," for "critical exchange and broad reflection," and for a "new conversation."[17] Dialogue is prescribed as the remedy for the insufficient contact and exchange of opinion among those who differ. In the third section, "Failed Encounters: Dialogue or Chatter?" I analyze the conflicting pressures that are placed on dialogue and explore whether literary criticism offers a vehicle for the desired conversations. In the aftermath of a critique of autonomy and truth, the emphasis on what dialogue is to achieve has shifted from "a non-coercive inquiry into what [is] at the same time correct and right," as Habermas puts it,[18] to a process of inclusion, participation, and representation. Dialogue and exchange — rather than correct interpretation or brilliant analysis — are the desiderata of a criticism that seeks to build a vital, democratic, and responsive public culture. Yet most appeals for dialogue cover over the incompatibilities between models of rational-critical debate and cross-cultural conversation and ignore the ways in which the presuppositions of what now counts as a critical argument undermine rather than foster the grounds on which the hoped-for interchanges might take place. The hopes for a politically effective criticism require an embrace of "dialogue" and "persuasion," but it does not follow that these modes of politically oriented academic criticism actually do anything to bring about new possibilities of dialogue and engagement with others.

Again, my aim is not to develop a new model in which criticism and dialogue will once more be compatible, but rather to argue for a criticism that is not fundamentally at odds with what it envisions as its tasks. An ideal of dialogue now functions as a safety net: it legitimates the political and intellectual prospects of a criticism that requires contact with others, even when these critical practices are themselves not amenable to the dialogue they now demand. The expectation that dialogue might still take place, if only people accept our presuppositions, or if only the university becomes a universal model for discourse, allows us not to face the consequences of all the failed encounters and insulates us from having to engage the understandings of others at the present moment. Literary criticism has morphed into cultural studies by absorbing all the neighboring discourses, but it still remains insular, still shielded from its desired audience. It is time, at least, to practice our high-wire acts without the protection of the nets that give us only the illusion of risk.

In a brief afterword, I question whether there is any openness to persuasion among the imagined other parties for critical dialogue, such as political conservatives, civic associations, or the media. I also question whether the state of academic criticism makes any difference at all for possibilities of social transformation through an exchange of ideas with others. Using what I witnessed at the Heritage Foundation as a point of departure, I speculate on the potential for dialogue with the political "other" and conclude that academic critics still can play an important role in shaping the expectations and the spaces for critical thinking and discussion.

⟬ *Part I* ⟭

Administering Conflict

1

Political Correctness:
The Revenge of the Liberals

◆

*The institutions were much more ambiguous
than I could have expected....*

*[T]he university...is after all only a ve-
hicle for contents in principle separable from
it....*

*Without it, all these wonderful results of
the theoretical life collapse back into the primal
slime from which they cannot re-emerge.*

— ALLAN BLOOM,
The Closing of the American Mind

Amid charges of "political correctness," universities were in the news again. Perhaps more than at any time since the Vietnam War, what was occurring on college campuses became a topic for local and national news coverage. Conflict, as was the case a generation ago, was again the central focus. The conflicts this time, however, were not between the students and the federal government or, for the most part, between the students and the university administration. Nor was a matter of national public policy — such as whether or not the United States should be engaged in fighting a war on the other side of the globe — at the heart of these controversies. Oddly, questions of seemingly "internal" interest to the universities — what is being taught, what students can and cannot say, who is being hired and fired — garnered a great deal of "external," national attention, especially in the print media. The recent controversies, as opposed to those of twenty-five years ago, were not very televisual: they did not *look* like serious or threatening confrontations.

21

Is a high level of interest, rhetoric, and passion a sign of the health of the universities, a sign that diverse viewpoints are generating a lively debate about important issues, or is it rather a sign that conflict is actually being suppressed and that only those with the "correct" positions are being allowed to speak? And does the media give voice to those who are not being listened to on campus, or rather does all the press coverage work instead to rebuke and constrain anyone who dares to step outside the boundaries of the cultural mainstream?

Derek Bok, then outgoing president of Harvard, chided the American Society of Newspaper Editors for giving too much attention to "political correctness" and added, "Whatever silly things may be said or done, there is more debate today...on campus than at any time in my memory." Alan Dershowitz, however, disagreed: "Ignore what Derek Bok told you this morning. We are producing a generation of students who do believe in political correctness.... This is the most serious issue that faces universities today. We are tolerating and teaching intolerance and hypocrisy."[1]

How do we decide whether a conflict is "healthy" or not?[2] Or whether it produces a "genuine" debate, or leads instead to the suppression of debate? Derek Bok himself seemed unsure. In the next day's paper, it was reported that in his annual report he "focused on 'serious challenges to the academic mission of American universities'" such as "'the use of academia for political ends,'" which "jeopardize[s] the 'basic values that allow universities to flourish and to command our loyalty and respect.'" The newspaper also noted that Bok "strongly criticized the 'threat of orthodoxy' from within the university" and that "he cited as an example students and faculty who have frequently expressed opinions against war, discrimination and oppression and have sometimes prompted 'deliberate attempts to harass professors, censor students, or disrupt speeches by visitors believed to hold unacceptable views.'" Also, "Bok was critical of attempts by pressure groups inside and outside the campus to 'embroil the university in political conflicts that divide, distract and ultimately weaken the institution.'"[3] It is not at all surprising that Derek Bok would speak of "lively discussions" and "debate" to one audience and describe the same phenomena as a *threat* to the well-being of the institution to another; we expect a university president to speak out of both sides of his mouth. His remarks highlight, however, the central importance of debate, politics, and conflict for thinking about the "academic mission of American universities" and the "basic values that allow universities to flourish."

Conflict in the University

At issue in all of these stories is what sort of community the university should be and which forms of conflict should be encouraged or tolerated, and which discouraged or suppressed. The conflict over political correctness (PC) is itself about the nature and purposes of conflict. Does the university have the mission of creating a more supportive, comfortable, and "enabling" environment than exists in the society at large? Should limits be set on speech that might cause harm or discomfort to others, or should all forms of speech by students and professors be allowed? In controversies over these and other issues, the people on each side predictably accuse others of stifling debate, while maintaining that they in turn are promoting a genuine dialogue.

It is never easy to make such distinctions, even though they are central to the "academic mission" and the "basic values" of the university. Conflict, by its very nature, always has the potential for suppressing conflict. In almost any conflict there is an attempt to change — and end — the conflict by overcoming one's opponent. Even the extreme point — killing one's antagonist — can be viewed, in a larger (or another) context, as furthering rather than as suppressing conflict. The customary means for distinguishing between conflict and the suppression of conflict, both within the university and more generally in liberal democracy, is by differentiating between persuasion and force. In the university, a conflict is typically deemed "healthy" or "lively" when each side seeks to persuade the other of the merits of its positions. At the other end of the spectrum, a direct intervention of state force, such as the police or National Guard, is a sign that the autonomy and the entire "mission" of the university are in jeopardy.

In any particular case, however, it is difficult to uphold a clear distinction between persuasion and force and between conflict and the suppression of conflict. Persuasion always seems to be "contaminated" by force. One reason for this is that a major tactic of persuasion is to *delegitimate* one's opponent. Thus we are rarely simply presented with two (or more) equally legitimate but opposing voices, among which we are to decide which is the most "persuasive." Stanley Fish, to take an example from the PC controversy, asserted that "the National Association of Scholars is widely known to be racist, sexist, and homophobic."[4] The implication here is that one need not even listen to these people; they discriminate and have thus forfeited the right to participate in legitimate discussion (and they should therefore be kept off hiring and promotion committees). A condition of full participation in institutional life is assumed here to be an *openness* to persuasion — not having decided in advance that blacks, women, and gays, for example, are unfit for employment — yet Fish himself seeks to prevent certain people from being heard (at least in the arenas of hiring and promotion committees). At what point does persuasion (the argument for or against a set of views) become coercion (the use of force to prevent certain views from being expressed)?

Controversies around political correctness are all about who has the right to speak. Forty years ago, it was commonly accepted that anyone who was fundamentally seeking to subvert the educational system should be expelled from the university. In its 1956 statement about "vigilance against subversion of the educational process," the AAUP (American Association of University Professors) declared:

> The academic community has a duty to defend society and itself from subversion of the educational process by dishonest tactics, including political conspiracies to deceive students and lead them unwittingly into acceptance of dogmas or false causes. Any member of the academic profession who has given reasonable evidence that he uses such tactics ... should be expelled from his position if his guilt is established by rational procedure. Instances of the use of such tactics in the past by secret Communist groups in a few institutions seem to have occurred, and vigilance against the danger of their occurrence in the future is clearly required.[5]

In the 1990s, by contrast, when even a president of Duke University will state that a "university, is, after all, meant to be a subversive institution,"[6] the imperative may almost seem to be in the opposite direction — expel those who are not subversive enough. Paradoxically, a failure to "subvert" (to challenge the canon, to fight against "institutional" forms of discrimination and oppression, to dismantle elitism, privilege, and hierarchy) can itself now be viewed as a "subversion of the educational process." In any case, "vigilance against subversion of the educational process" is still firmly at work. The "educational process" is sometimes loftily defined as giving free play to the powers of persuasion, but the ever-present threat of expulsion is used to protect the university from the persuasive power of those who might disrupt the academic "community" (in 1956, from those who engage in "political conspiracies," "dishonesty," and "deception"; today, from those with supposedly unreformed "discriminatory" attitudes). And a most effective means of persuasion is to characterize one's opponent as occupying illegitimate territory, outside the norms of the community.

Force and persuasion are always intermingling. Institutional structures regulate conflict and determine the framework within which persuasion can operate. On the one hand, the structures of the university create the space for debate, and principles such as academic freedom protect speakers from certain forms of recrimination and retribution. Yet these structures also enforce differences of authority and power, differences that undermine any belief in the unfettered reliance on persuasion in the university. The persuasive capacity of any academic discourse always also depends on the identity and position of the speaker (this becomes particularly apparent when a grade, a grant, a job, or a promotion is at stake).[7] The greater "persuasive" power of those in positions of authority does not stem solely from their greater learning, experience, or eloquence; the threat of force — such as the loss of employment or advancement — thoroughly penetrates the academic realm of persuasion.

On a more far-reaching and profound level, the entire Foucauldian project offers a strident critique of the opposition between persuasion and force; Foucault's analysis of the interpenetration of power and knowledge renders untenable any attempt to cleanly separate the two. Moreover, the recent critique of the institution (which has become especially important in literary studies) emphasizes that interpretation is never free of its institutional context and that this context is one of contending and conflicting forces — forces that necessarily exclude, marginalize, and repress. The many different critiques of the institution all give the lie to any notion of the university as a protected but fundamentally open and free field of persuasion.

Even if we could find a means for distinguishing between persuasion and force, or at least delimit a space, such as the seminar room, in which everything would be done to maximize persuasion and dialogue, and reduce force and coercion, it is not at all obvious that this would allow us either to better fulfill the "academic mission" of the university (the pursuit and the transmission of knowledge) or to bring into the open and address the conflicts that permeate the university. A different possibility — different from the notion that genuine discussion and debate are threatened by force and intimidation — but one with much more disturbing consequences for the university, is that the entire arena of discussion and debate (the realm of persuasion) is itself now a sideshow, an "empty formality," that has little to do with knowledge and that functions even to mask and displace conflict. What if the notions of openness and discussion, and of the importance of debate, now only serve to reduce conflicting opinions into chatter, into an empty contest of words?[8]

The emphasis on debate and persuasion stems from a belief in liberalism. Richard Rorty offers a contemporary philosophy of liberalism when he asserts that *truth* is "whatever the outcome of undistorted communication happens to be, whatever view wins in a free and open encounter."[9] But if the possibilities of "undistorted communication" and "free and open encounters" are discredited, and if a willingness to be persuaded and a belief in the persuadability of others are rejected, then the entire project of education through "healthy" conflict and open debate needs to be reexamined. Recent critiques of academic and political institutions have focused specifically on the ways in which communication is never "undistorted" and in which encounters always take place in contexts that restrict freedom and openness; the basic foundations of liberalism have been sharply attacked, if not completely rejected or discredited.

The University and the Media

It may seem that I've made an enormous leap — moving from a journalistic controversy to a concern for the foundations of liberalism — and that the discussion of political correctness has so far only led to a further muddying of distinctions, rather than to a means for separating genuine intellectual conflict from the usual pressures to conform to current attitudes. Moreover, such a move from an incident of media interest and outrage to a "hysterical" concern for the very foundations of liberal democracy is an all-too-common gesture of commentators from the far Right (and is not surprisingly a prominent motif in articles on political correctness). Right-wing cover boy Dinesh D'Souza argues that our universities are now engaged in a process of "illiberal education." He claims that an "academic revolution," based on the "politics of race and sex" coupled with the latest (French) fashions in literary theory, has undermined the liberal values at the core of a traditional university education.[10] I don't want to espouse the conservative agenda of preserving and consolidating power through an appeal to "traditional standards," yet I will argue that a consideration of press coverage offers a good place for beginning to theorize conflict in the university and that the controversy over political correctness brings out some of the paradoxes at the heart of many recent theories of institutions and interpretation.

Whenever an academic debate makes it into the mainstream press, it is no longer merely "academic." The reporting of such conflicts signals that something other than a "mere" difference of intellectual opinion is at stake, and the act of reporting also transforms the debate. Even when an article attempts primarily to inform readers of the intellectual content of the opposing positions (and this is rarely the case)[11] so as to allow the public also to participate in a well-informed discussion of the issue, the transgression of the institutional boundary already alters the context and thus the nature of the conflict. "Going public" with an "internal" academic dispute, either by alerting the press or by writing an article on one's own, brings new pressures to bear and requires different modes of persuasion. Appealing to another audience implies that the norms and values of a particular department or campus, or the academic community, are out of step with those of the broader public.

The media, as another major social institution, function to demarcate the borders of the university. These borders are very porous and often seem unclear, especially in the humanities, where so many boundaries are in question. The efforts to erode distinctions between popular and intellectual, and between different forms of writing, and the increasing study of the media within the university might seem to be indications that the old tensions between journalism and "belles lettres" are dissolving. Yet the constant bemoaning of the demise of the "public intellectual" provides grounds for the opposite conclusion, and almost the entire spectrum of academic writing attempts to set itself off from the "journalistic" — that which need only be read once, and at only one point in time. The continuing force of these boundaries becomes especially apparent when professors who theorize about misprision, distortion, and uncertainty complain vehemently about having their own views distorted and falsified by the press; an academic discourse presents difficult problems of translation into the public sphere of the mass media.

Any attempt to understand conflict within the university requires an awareness of and attending to institutional boundaries. Theoreticians of the "institution" (and especially of the English department) such as Gerald Graff and Stanley Fish pay too little attention to the interaction *between* institutions in their attempts to explain conflict "within" the institution. The press and the law offer two other arenas for playing out academic conflicts, and I would argue that these institutions have a significant influence even on disputes that do not end up in the hands of journalists and lawyers. And this influence occurs as much, for example, in the *differentiation* between academic and legal forms of arguments as through the legal underpinnings of the university. I will return to the role of the press in the controversy around political correctness, but here I only want to emphasize that the linking of media accounts to theoretical inquiry is an important rather than a superficial or hysterical aspect of an effort to understand academic conflict.

Truth in Conflict

For many thinkers today, conflict is inseparable from, rather than peripheral to, the notion of knowledge, and essential to the entire academic enterprise. If conflicts were viewed as temporary disagreements soon superseded by consensus once a new truth is established, or as unfortunate upheavals of differences that have no bearing on the "academic mission" of the university (and which ought to be settled or mediated by those in power), then the question of how conflict is regulated, and the whole issue of political correctness, would not be important. "Political" differences might still temporarily interfere with the process of education, but they would have no real effect on the *content* of education. But now more than ever, and especially in literary studies, there are few adherents to the notion of conflict as mere bumps on the road of knowledge. One might even say that literary theory is a theory of conflict. This conclusion does not depend on whether one agrees with Harold Bloom that literature itself is inherently agonistic — whether the *object* of theory is or is not conflictual, ambivalent, or undecidable. Rather, literary theory is a theory of conflict because it is not grounded in an object at all — not grounded in a text, a reader, a canon, or even an institution. Literary theory attempts to respond to conflict (conflicting meanings within texts, conflicting interpretations of texts); emphasize conflict (always insisting on difference); and expose conflict (revealing the mechanisms by which conflict is habitually suppressed, resisted, and ignored). All of these tasks follow from the abandonment of a "ground" for theory, and especially of the grounding of interpretation in truth.

One of the most important aspects of twentieth-century thought is the critique of *truth*. This critique has taken many forms, and its results are phrased in many different ways: the idea that truth is made rather than found; a rejection of the notion of "truth conceived in terms of the *adequatio intellectus et rei*," and thus a rejection of "the *separation* of thought from its object and the *priority* of the latter over the former"; or the conclusion that "truths" are only contingent, local, and temporary, rather than "absolute, universal, and timeless."[12] Here I only want to emphasize that this critique dislodges any *absolute* ground for resolving conflicting interpretations, since it renders problematic any autonomous, preexisting, and unchanging object to which one can appeal as the basis of interpretation. Interpretation, rather than being a somewhat steady progress toward a more "adequate" representation, becomes instead a continual contest between newer and older forms of understanding.

There are two major consequences of this critique of truth that I wish to explore. The first is the elevation of "persuasion" to a central position for interpretation. If there is no autonomous ground for truth, independent of language, then persuasion is a mechanism not only for resolving differences but for establishing "truth." This elevation of persuasion goes against a long tradition of discrediting persuasion and rhetoric as forms of expression that interfere with the search for truth. Yet as I have already begun to suggest, concurrent with the dismantling of the opposition between persuasion and truth (or the qualities traditionally deemed necessary for reaching truth, such as principle, disinterestedness, neutrality, and objectivity), there has also been a challenge to that which defines and delimits persuasion at the other end — to the separation of persuasion and force. Thus the notion of persuasion itself is very much in question, now that it has a greater interpretative load to carry.

The second consequence is the turn to the "institution" in the effort to explore further the processes of interpretation. Without an absolute and autonomous ground, interpretation necessarily depends also on its context. There are many ways to define this context — such as the range of ideas within and against which any interpretation proceeds, or the particular constellation of social, cultural, and historical forces — but the "institution" provides a particularly powerful conception for examining the way that not only ideas or discourses, but actual people and their quotidian practices, are organized and employed. Moreover, the university — the institution that pursues and disseminates "knowledge" (and the place where "we" work) — affords a special opportunity for studying the "extrinsic conditions" and forces of interpretation.[13] Thus there has been a burgeoning interest in the "institution"; the thrust of much of this critique is to emphasize that the institution is not a mere vehicle for the knowledge that it transmits.[14] But this attention to the institution is not without effect; it also changes the very context that it studies (and of course the desire for change motivates much of the attention to the institution). The critique of the institution itself thereby gains great importance, for it can affect the very structures and content of knowledge.

Both of these tendencies (the foregrounding of persuasion and the turn to the institution) aim to *legitimate* conflict. The insistence that truth is only an effect of persuasion requires an open conflict of ideas; if disagreement were always to be minimized in the name of harmony or obedience to authority, there would be no opportunity to persuade others of the "validity" of a new interpretation. An emphasis on persuasion highlights the function of conflict within the university. Examinations of the *contingency* of knowledge, and its dependence on institutional structures, also bring to light the ways in which conflict is habitually suppressed or ignored. Samuel Weber asserts, "The University universalizes, individualizes, and in the process excludes conflict as far as possible. Or rather, it delegitimizes conflict, in the name of pluralism." Weber goes further, arguing that

> an ideal of knowledge, of science, and of truth that deems these to be intrinsically conflict-free ... both reflects and supports the self-image of a society that imposes its authority precisely by

denying the legitimacy of its structural conflicts, and hence of its relation to alterity. For the admission of the constitutive importance of such relations would amount to a disavowal of the categories of universality, individualism, and consensus that form the foundation of American liberalism, and of the institutions that perpetuate it.[15]

But what happens next, once one recognizes the ineluctability of conflict? The attention to suppressed conflict always suggests other possibilities, suggests that things might have occurred, might occur, otherwise. Yet recognizing the legitimacy of structural conflict, and a "relation to alterity," in no way points toward what actions to take, what changes should be made, or what solutions, if any, might be desirable or achievable. Nor does such a recognition provide the means for a radical transformation of the university; greater insight concerning how institutions function does not free us from their constraints. The possibility of an "epistemological break" with the earlier history of the American university, severing it from its earlier modes of "knowledge," is the fantastic dream of the Left, the nightmare of the Right.

The effect of these analyses of conflict has not been simply to achieve a greater openness or to ensure the participation of those who have previously been excluded; greater toleration is no more likely an outcome than greater willingness to suppress those who disagree.[16] The foregrounding of persuasion and the critique of the institution have not only altered the regulation of conflict within the university, but have also prepared the ground for excluding others in turn — for excluding, for example, those who do *not* speak from a previously repressed position and who therefore might be in the way of desired institutional change. The epithet "political correctness" is a response to this new legitimation of exclusion (which appears in the form, ironically but necessarily, of a vocabulary of "inclusion").

Whose Discourse Prevails?

At the end of her preface to *Reader-Response Criticism*, Jane Tompkins states: "When discourse is responsible for reality and not merely a reflection of it, then whose discourse prevails makes all the difference."[17] For Tompkins the result of the conflict — "whose discourse prevails" — is of utmost importance. After all, the prevailing discourse determines not only knowledge and truth, but "reality" itself. But if this is the case, if the stakes are so high, why allow a free and open conflict? Why let one's opponents speak at all, if they might sway others to the "wrong" conclusion (a conclusion different from one's own)? The notion that "discourse is *responsible* for reality" makes little sense without the "free and open encounter" that Rorty urges — Soviet genetics under Stalin and Lysenko provides a striking example of the attempt to subordinate "reality" to the "prevailing discourse." Yet the traditional mechanisms and rationale for promoting a "free and open encounter" are precisely what are under attack here. Tompkins's conclusion that "language is the ultimate form of power," and all the ensuing corollaries, such as "all discourse is 'interested' " and "free choice is not a meaningful issue," arise directly from a critique of liberalism and its key pillar — the freedom of the individual. The insistence that persuasion is the means for determining truth and reality requires the protection of the liberal political and institutional structures whose philosophical foundations it seeks to undermine.

Contemporary critics of liberalism argue that the traditional oppositions between disinterestedness and interest, neutrality and partisanship, objective discourse and persuasion or rhetoric, and universality and contextuality are all invalid, since it can always be shown that there is no transcendental position beyond institutions and beyond language — God is dead, or at least homeless. A typical next step, and one that Tompkins takes, is to then argue that the "divorce between literature and politics" (or more broadly, aesthetics and politics) has been overcome, since the aesthetic model of "disinterestedness" (located in Matthew Arnold more often than in Kant) has been replaced by the political model of the clash between competing interests. But the invocation of "politics" does not at all provide a new model for understanding aesthetic judgment, comprehending differences of opinion, or choosing between competing interpretations; it only forces us to confront which political model we will use to regulate conflict. The liberal political model depends on the possibility of people *not* being fully bound or determined by (class, partisan, personal) interests. It is worth quoting at length Carl Schmitt, one of the most incisive thinkers on the crisis of liberalism, in order to help clarify what is at issue in the critique of liberalism:

All specifically parliamentary arrangements and norms receive their meaning first through discussion and openness. This is especially true of the fundamental principle that is still recognized constitutionally, although practically hardly still believed in today, that the representative is independent of his constituents and party; it applies to the provisions concerning freedom of speech and immunity of representatives, the openness of parliamentary proceedings, and so forth. These arrangements would be unintelligible if the principle of public discussion were no longer believed in. It is not as if one could ascribe other principles retrospectively and at will to an institution, and if its hitherto existing foundations collapse, just insert any sort of substitute arguments. . . .

Discussion means an exchange of opinion that is governed by the purpose of persuading one's opponent through argument of the truth or justice of something, or allowing oneself to be persuaded of something as true and just. Gentz — in this matter still instructed by the liberal Burke — puts it well: The characteristic of all representative constitutions (he meant modern parliament in contrast to corporative representation or the estates) is that laws arise *out of a conflict of opinions* (*not out of a struggle of interests*). To discussion belong shared convictions as premises, the willingness to be persuaded, independence of party ties, freedom from selfish interests. Most people today would regard such disinterestedness as scarcely possible.[18]

In regard to Schmitt's observations about discussion, one can emphasize that the ability to rise above "selfish interests" is *not* identical with the Kantian aesthetic notion of "disinterestedness" ("the faculty of estimating an object or a mode of representation by means of a delight or an aversion *apart from any interest*")[19] and that the "deconstruction" of all of the oppositions revolving around disinterest and interest need not result in their collapse. Nor must one be absolutely "neutral" or "objective," and certainly not disinterested, to be open to persuasion.

The power of Schmitt's critique lies not in its fairly conventional definitions of discussion, but in its prodding us to question and justify anew liberal institutions, or whatever institutional frameworks sanction persuasion, and even more profoundly, to question the meaningfulness of the entire operation of "persuasion" itself. The thrust of much recent criticism is to discredit not only the philosophical foundations of liberal thought, but the political and institutional structures of liberalism as well — to show, for example, that "justice" is not blind, but reflects the "interests" of those who have the power to administer it. Such analyses are often convincing and can work to bring about much needed change; yet if the principles and the institutions of liberalism are discredited, what is to protect the expression of opinion? If institutions merely reflect interests, why shouldn't those in power do everything possible to eliminate any threats to their interests (such as the freedom of speech of those with competing interests)?

Many of the rights and liberties for resisting institutional power (and in the university, many of the protections of freedom of inquiry, of holding dissenting opinions, and so on) are fundamentally grounded in what Schmitt calls "the principle of public discussion." But if discussion is merely a reflection of a "struggle of interests," and if the participants in this struggle do not share a "willingness to be persuaded" and a measure of freedom from "interests," who is to be persuaded? Dialogue and discussion become pointless, an empty show. The discussions of the parliamentary body become increasingly irrelevant when nothing is to be changed by the procession of speeches (a feeling that applies to the U.S. political arena today, as well as to Weimar), and similar questions about the meaningfulness of discussion in academia need to be asked. Much of what passes for debate in the university is tiresome and unilluminating precisely because of the sheer unwillingness to open oneself to persuasion and to consider antagonistic ideas seriously rather than only to dismiss them as the distorted products of false ideologies.

Not everyone sees a paradox in seeking to maintain the protections of liberal institutions while challenging their philosophical foundations. Richard Rorty argues that the founding discourse of an enterprise can, indeed always will be, separated from its historical development. He attacks the authors of The Dialectic of the Enlightenment for drawing the conclusion "that liberalism was now intellectually bankrupt, bereft of philosophical foundations, and that liberal society was morally bankrupt, bereft of social glue." Rorty continues: "Horkheimer and Adorno assumed that the terms in which those who begin a historical development described their enterprise remain the terms which describe it correctly, and then inferred that the dissolution of that terminology deprives the results of that development of the right to, or the possibility of, continued existence. This is almost never the case."[20] Thus, Rorty implies, the "continued existence" of the institutional protections of freedom of speech, or academic freedom, need not depend at all on a continued belief in the freedom of the individual or in the freedom of thought.[21] There is much to argue with here, but the main point I want to make is that the relation of the new "terminology" to the historically developed form of the "enterprise" is crucial. The dissolution of the founding terminology need not lead to the collapse of modern institutions, but neither will they necessarily continue to stand, simply out of historical momentum.

In academia, the adoption of a new terminology has certainly affected the institution. The earlier vocabulary of academic inquiry — disinterestedness, objectivity, and the pursuit of truth (and this was by no means a fixed or stable vocabulary during the last hundred years) — did not function simply to suppress, mask, or distort conflict, but rather *to regulate it*. This terminology works to give weight to certain arguments and to rule out others. The discrediting of these mechanisms for regulating conflict does not finally produce an emergence and unmasking of "genuine" conflict, in which all the previously hidden issues and agendas are now openly addressed (this idea parallels the Republican fantasy of deregulation, in which free markets and genuine competitiveness unhindered by regulation will lead to a new golden age). A "free and open encounter" cannot be achieved simply by breaking down all the apparent barriers to freedom and openness. Such a possibility also requires *protection* from the forces that would restrict such an encounter. Only in a space in which nothing is at stake — in which conflict is purely a game whose results do not matter — would such protections be unnecessary. What makes "political correctness" a complex phenomenon, however, is that it is precisely in the name of "protection" — of sheltering students from abuse, from harm, and even from threatening ideologies and insensitivity — that the "free and open" encounters of the university are being restricted.

Protection Rackets

My own interest in these questions is not entirely "academic." For nineteen months (November 1989 to May 1991) I was involved in a battle with Hampshire College over my reappointment as assistant professor of comparative literature. A few people originally objected to my reappointment on grounds that could easily be described as the determination that I was not "politically correct." I was accused among other things of not properly teaching or understanding the "Third World Expectation" and of not even being able to "think independently," since I didn't always come to the same conclusions (about the criteria for making hiring decisions) as some of my colleagues. After a labyrinthine, multilevel appeal process, I finally was reappointed.[22]

I want to discuss my own case a little further, since I think it sheds some light on the ways in which institutional discourses, and the traditions and practices of academic freedom, have indeed been affected by the challenge to liberalism and to earlier frameworks of academic inquiry. I am especially interested in exploring the thinking that lies behind the new criteria for regulating academic practices and for judging professional competence and reappointability. I think my case, though idiosyncratic in many ways, is also telling and potentially quite representative, since Hampshire College embodies (or takes to the extreme) many of the progressive tendencies in higher education: both the structural/pedagogical ones of portfolio evaluation, interdisciplinarity and team-teaching, and contract-based and student-centered education; and the ideological ones of educating for social justice, critiquing and subverting the dominant culture, and promoting advocacy in the classroom (the official motto is "Non Satis Scire" — "To know is not enough").

When I came up for my first reappointment,[23] some people felt that since they taught at an alternative institution, founded as a "progressive" challenge to traditional colleges, they had the right if not the duty to protect the mission of the college by eliminating anyone whom they viewed as a threat to the school's identity and goals. We get the paradox of a school that prides itself on encouraging diversity, the freedom to be different, and nonconformity demanding that the faculty adhere to a narrow set of views in order to carry out the college's mission. Thus some professors felt no qualms in offering justifications for voting against my reappointment that treated political, intellectual, and personal disagreement as issues of "professional competence." One professor wrote, "Jeff failed to provide any Third World challenge to the canon or to the theoretical priorities in his teaching," and another stated, "I don't think Jeff is addressing the Third World Expectation adequately in his courses." Another professor provided a fuller elaboration: "On the basis of his course work and his response to a question raised during his reappointment meeting, I seriously question his understanding of the Third World Expectation except on the most superficial, perfunctory basis. His is a conventional attitude of privelege [sic], inappropriate in a faculty member at a time when Hampshire is moving in such a different direction." A different member of the faculty offered a more impressionistic set of reasons: "Jeff feels to me encapsulated and a little distant. I had hoped for someone more dynamic, and less prone to polarizing issues in our school meetings in ways that suggest to me no [sic] an independent thinking about the issues."[24] In order to preserve the "independent thinking" of the alternative institution, anyone with differing ideas must be rooted out.

Why would a supposed failure to "provide any Third World challenge to the canon" be considered a good reason for firing someone? The operative logic in some of the votes against me was that since most education ignores Third World perspectives and thereby condones the oppression of Third World peoples, the failure to properly challenge the canon (a metonym for the dominant ideology of Western imperialism) perpetuates social injustice and is an act of complicity in oppression.[25] Being complicit in oppression may not alone be a fireable offense, but when the stated mission of the school is "to educate for social justice" (as the president declared in his inaugural speech), it is easily interpreted as a mark of bad pedagogy. Thus if one fails to teach the proper Third World writers (such as making the mistake of teaching Jorge Luis Borges), or to teach them in the right context (Richard Wright's *Black Boy* in a course on autobiography rather than as part of the African American literary tradition), or to draw the correct lessons, it will be argued that one has only a "superficial, perfunctory" understanding of the new forms of knowledge and is therefore unqualified to teach.[26] An "attitude of conventional privelege [sic]," moreover, would itself indicate a refusal or an incapacity to assimilate these new forms of understanding. One can compellingly accuse anyone with whom one disagrees of "professional incompetence" for failing to reflect certain interests, once one determines that these "interests" — such as a proper Third World perspective — are in fact now constitutive of knowledge (providing a liberation from the dulling forces of the dominant ideology).

Under the guise of challenging the myopia of previous thinkers — all those who have blithely ignored the culture and achievements of non-Western writers — a new and tighter grid of evaluation is put in place. The institutional encouragement of political correctness undermines the professional/professorial ethos of tolerating those who have different opinions and weakens the traditional safeguards of academic freedom. No one at Hampshire would claim publicly not to support academic freedom, but the toleration of opposing ideas is trumped by the stronger need to ensure that students not be exposed to thoughts that will directly or indirectly "harm" them (words that offend or teaching that fails to inoculate against oppressive ideologies). The traditional liberal beliefs in academic freedom and freedom of speech can be overridden whenever convenient, and thoughtful critiques of liberalism and of the concept of truth have been appropriated to provide the justification: we now know that these "freedoms" often shield the interests of those in power, are part of the fabric of oppressive institutions, and only help produce a false sense of "autonomy" or a misguided "quest for truth."

Once this new institutional logic is in place, it is not only the most ardent politicos who make use of it; the convenience of overriding a strong respect for the academic freedom of others often takes the petty form of "we needn't put up any longer with anyone who disagrees with us." Of course, reappointment and tenure decisions are often made on the basis of "collegiality," and whoever makes waves or disagrees is always vulnerable, but the fostering of political correctness works primarily to protect the institutionally entrenched from having to contend with any views they may find disagreeable or inconvenient.

I do not mean to suggest that everyone at Hampshire thinks and acts in the ways I have described, and I certainly do not want to give the impression that it is the most critically avant-garde or theoretically astute people who follow this path. But I do want to suggest that a transformation has occurred at Hampshire and elsewhere, from the institutional protection of dissenting views to an institutional protection from exposure to views one finds unpleasant, and that this transformation is directly related to the changing critical paradigms I have been analyzing. A legitimation of conflict, in also discrediting the mechanisms that traditionally have regulated academic conflict, can perversely lead to a narrowing of discussion and a reduction in the range of contending ideas. The promotion of "advocacy in the classroom" is another instance where a desire to widen and enrich the spectrum of thought can easily produce the opposite effect.

The New Advocates

There are many arguments I could present against "advocacy" as Louis Menand defines it: "instruction undertaken with the intention of persuading students to adopt a particular political view."[27] As suggested above, once advocacy is deemed not only legitimate but necessary for effective pedagogy, then anyone who does not practice such advocacy can be judged ineffective, uninformed, or incompetent, and therefore worthy of dismissal. Moreover, when advocacy becomes the starting point for interpretation ("I believe that U.S. imperialism oppresses Third World peoples, and my interpretation will be a step toward putting an end to such oppression"), then the study of literature often becomes a hunt simply to find such instances of oppression; any more complicated understanding of literary representation is displaced by the imperative to at least advocate something (and make one's convictions clear).

But what I want to question here is whether or not the change in the description and definition of the academic enterprise makes any difference. For this is why advocacy in the classroom has become a controversial issue (and led an alphabet soup of professional organizations in the humanities and social sciences to sponsor a conference on the topic):[28] it goes against the earlier understanding, and popular impression, that the classroom is not the place for the professor to advocate his or her own political views. Is such a separation of the classroom from the political sphere necessary for a "free search for truth and its free exposition,"[29] or does advocacy only help us to fulfill these goals?

Eighty years ago, while speaking on "science as a vocation," Max Weber articulated the view that politics does not "belong in the lecture-room on the part of the docents, and when the docent is scientifically concerned with politics, it belongs there least of all." Weber continues:

> To take a practical political stand is one thing, and to analyze political structures and party positions is another.... The words one uses in such a meeting [a political meeting about democracy] are not means of scientific analysis but means of canvassing votes and winning over others. They are not plowshares to loosen the soil of contemplative thought; they are swords against the ene-

mies: such words are weapons. It would be an outrage, however, to use words in this fashion in a lecture or in the lecture-room.... [T]he true teacher will beware of imposing from the platform any political position upon the student, whether it is expressed or suggested.[30]

The thrust of much recent scholarship is precisely to trouble such distinctions as the one between "tak[ing] a practical political stand" and "analyz[ing] political structures": critics point out that the act of analysis is not transcendental, or free from any political context, and that the decision of what (and how) to analyze is itself charged with political force. More profoundly, the work of J. L. Austin, Paul de Man, and many others calls into question any attempt to uphold strict distinctions between different ways of using words (revealing, for instance, that a seemingly "constative" description contains "performative" force).[31] Additionally, the distinction between "fact" and "value," on which Weber's notion of *Wissenschaft* depends, has been frequently challenged.[32]

What happens then when this notion of *Wissenschaft* ("science" is not an entirely adequate translation of this far-reaching term) is troubled? If the edifice on which Weber has erected his distinctions between the classroom and the political meeting is crumbling, are we free to ignore them? Surprisingly many professors seem to think so. The typical argument in defense of advocacy in the classroom is that we can still draw the line somewhere between the classroom and improper political behavior (though well beyond any limit imagined by Weber); that the line should be drawn only at the point of indoctrination and direct coercion (such as making students' grades dependent on their political views); and that the discrediting of Weber's distinctions and of his view of science has had no adverse effects on our professional behavior or has only opened up the classroom for improved discussion and debate.[33]

Louis Menand, for instance, cannot even imagine that advocacy could be a problem, except in hypothetical instances that never happen or in cases where it would be clearly wrong for other reasons (expressing a point of view the professor knows is not supported by the evidence or lecturing about political issues that are in no way germane to the stated topic of the class). He argues that honesty, professionalism, and above all a critical spirit of "disinterestedness" —

"that you should argue your views in a spirit of skepticism and self-questioning" — fully pervade the university and that the efforts to persuade students to adopt a political view take place *within* the limits of this professional ethos.[34] He also asserts that the debunking of "disinterestedness" (and of the vocabulary and the epistemological foundations on which the discourse of academic inquiry, teaching, and professionalism have been grounded) makes absolutely no difference for teaching and professorial behavior. He claims that professors will still act "in the spirit of disinterestedness," because it preserves their authority ("this authority derives from the perception of their disinterestedness" [123]), and because they find it pedagogically effective to do so.

This is an amazingly Pollyannaish view from a usually very astute critic. The logic here is that trying to persuade "students to adopt a particular political view" differs in no way at all from professors putting "across their own view about the material they teach in the classroom" (118); that professors will only attempt to persuade students to adopt their political views "in a spirit of skepticism and self-questioning"; and that the pedagogical process of scholarly inquiry, careful interpretation, and rational argument will not be affected by the goal of "winning over others," as Weber describes the political process. Would that it were so.

Menand assumes that the professional, professorial spirit he admires will continue to exist and proliferate, despite the attack on the worldview, epistemology, and methodology with which it had been habitually connected. But concomitant with a critique of Weber's *Wissenschaft,* there has also been a discrediting of some of these very habits of thinking Menand praises — skepticism, rational argument, self-questioning, "disinterestedness" — and a repudiation of the traditional professional ethos. Menand and other defenders of advocacy look to an inculcation in academic culture, a love for the traditions of the university, or an enlightened self-interest regarding the "best" forms of pedagogy and persuasion to preserve "a spirit of disinterestedness," but these institutional habits and views about what constitute effective teaching are rapidly changing. For this "spirit" to survive — and for Menand, it is the very spirit of the university — it needs to be reconnected to an elaboration of the pursuit of knowledge and a sense of intellectual integrity, grounded on a postmodern epistemological foundation.

Another Hampshire story. In a team-taught women's studies class, one of the professors was lecturing on the autobiography of Ida B. Wells. One of the very few male students asked a question that betrayed a great deal of ignorance about the racial and sexual relations of the time and that also implied that perhaps some of the black men who were lynched were not innocent of their supposed crimes. As a reply, one of the other professors in the course hissed at the student. This form of persuasion is possibly as effective as those which Menand seems to expect in the classroom, if the aim is getting a room full of students to adopt one's moral and political views. It is a response that one would expect at a political meeting, and I strongly doubt that this professor would hiss at a student who asked an ignorant, even insensitive question in her science courses. Political advocacy in the classroom breeds a new spirit in many classrooms, in which moral censoriousness replaces self-questioning.

I do not mean to suggest that those who critique Weber's epistemology, methodology, and view of science are incapable of rational argument or scholarly persuasion — quite the contrary. Nor I am arguing for a return to a Weberian notion of *Wissenschaft*. But without a recognition that in the wake of a dismantling of an earlier epistemology and methodology there are now conflicts between political advocacy in the classroom and a spirit of disinterestedness, and without a recognition that the protections of freedom provided by liberal institutions need to be connected to something more than institutional tradition alone, we will see a further shutting down of opposing views, a greater preference for words used as weapons rather than for skeptical inquiry, and more hissing and shunning of unapproved opinions.

Willing to Be Persuaded?

If the critique of liberal thought is to yield a realm of persuasion that is not more widely controlled by administrative power — and weakening such notions as academic freedom only cedes greater authority to those who have the power to demand conformity — a new vocabulary is required to legitimate institutional structures that aim to insulate persuasion from coercion, even as the notions of persuasion and coercion are being radically redefined. Of course, it is not only a question of a new terminology; there are many ways to reform liberal institutions so that they function better. Simply hoping to undermine or subvert them will not produce a freer and more open environment. Even if the elevation of persuasion is accompanied by an effort to protect the arena of discussion from forms of coercion, however, there can be no persuasion without persuadability, without a willingness to be persuaded. It is easy to challenge a notion of willingness, just as one challenges the possibility of disinterestedness. But what is the point of discussion if there is a firm unwillingness to be persuaded?

In the aftermath of the critique of oppositions such as disinterest/ interest and neutral/partisan, a new set of oppositions is often employed that, to return to Schmitt's terminology, offers only a "struggle of interests" rather than a "conflict of opinions": domination/ subordination, for example, or oppressor/victim. The exposure of "interests" functioning under the guise of disinterestedness and neutrality does not necessarily stabilize these interests; quite the contrary, it can reveal how difficult it is to know precisely which interests are at stake. The insistence, however, that everyone speaks from a position either of domination or subordination, and that one's discourse should validate one's position — that the purpose of speaking is to define (and hence to some extent to enforce) the boundaries of domination and subordination — casts a "willingness to be persuaded" as betrayal. To give up one's position (as subordinate) would only be to reinforce the structures of oppression. This is an instance of the tension between the elevation of persuasion, on the one hand, and the decline of an openness to persuasion, on the other: the "conflict of opinions" here is not dialogue or debate, since the determination to reinforce positions forecloses any possibility of exchanging ideas.

Political correctness proceeds from the claim that only certain positions have the right to be heard. Voices speaking from the wrong position — conventional privilege, tradition, Eurocentrism — are to be attacked and silenced on both moral and intellectual grounds. Morally, these positions are said to enforce structures of oppression, and intellectually, they are deemed ignorant, unaware of or blind to their own ideological assumptions. The extreme of political correctness — preventing certain people from speaking and certain opinions from being expressed — is to some extent a logical conclusion to the proposition that "whose discourse prevails makes all the difference." Yet political correctness is only a symptom of a much broader crisis of liberalism, and even without the excessive stance of stifling debate, there still remains the question of the purpose of academic conflict. Without *someone* to be persuaded, and without some communication and interchange between opposing positions, the spectacle of academic conflict is beside the point — only a diversion from more overtly political battles between competing interests that take place elsewhere.

A critique of the freedom of thought (in Tompkins's words, since "what we choose is determined by our beliefs, which we have not chosen, the notion of free choice dissolves")[35] calls into question the possibility of being persuaded through discussion, and this tendency is exacerbated by the insistence that the position from which one speaks "makes all the difference" — that the identity, more than the ideas, of the speaker is what matters. If the speakers do not share certain premises, but are divided into contending groups, there can be persuasion only within these groups, not across their borders. The pointlessness of academic discussion in the face of such obstacles to "persuadability" can be partially overcome by appealing to another audience (such as students) and through invoking a notion of community. The students, starting from ignorance of or noninterest in academic conflicts, can be persuaded (educated). They can provide a significance to these discussions by learning enough to participate in them. Gerald Graff therefore states that we need to "organize and teach the conflict" in order to make it "a productive part of the curriculum."[36] Graff hopes that the students will no longer be "outsiders" to the "academic community."[37]

Graff focuses on a key problem: how to make academic conflict more meaningful and productive. The notion of "community" again allows the university to be portrayed as a realm of persuasion, by conjuring a space — if not of "shared convictions as premises" (Schmitt), at least of a shared language (Graff) or shared institutional standards or norms (Fish) — within which persuasion is said to operate. If conflict is addressed within the institution, then the apparently unbridgeable chasm between different positions can still be deemed part of the same community. Yet within the university, the notion of community is now used more to enforce than to bridge differences, and in describing the relation to nonacademic communities, the term is frequently employed to challenge any possibility of achieving a common ground for persuasion across cultural and institutional boundaries.

The academic community sets itself off from other communities precisely by claiming a greater openness to persuasion. But since the basic persuadability of the human subject has been strongly challenged, this claim can only be supported by locating a greater denial of persuadability elsewhere, such as in the "public sphere," and especially in the media. A critique of the media — the space in which the central debates of the public sphere ought to be played out — is required in order to define a realm of manipulation of discourse and blindness to ideology, in contrast to the awareness if not freedom of the academic community. The dissolution of "the notion of free choice" is offset by the contrast with a realm that is less free and that is deluded by rather than sensitized to ideology. The academic community thus maintains its moral purity and autonomy only by imposing its separation from all others who toil in a realm of delusion — even while thereby pointing to its own "engagement" with the nonacademic world. The price of maintaining a remnant of persuadability within the university is to deny it methodologically to others.

It then becomes easy to characterize the media attention to political correctness as a right-wing backlash, since it is the "Right" that most strenuously denies the ideological thrust of its academic discourse. This perspective also justifies abdicating a role in the media debates about political correctness; after all, one's ideas will only be distorted and manipulated by the media, and in the media one can only defend a "position," rather than exchange opinions. Moreover, this greater self-awareness that sets apart the academic community requires a constant critique of the "naive" liberal beliefs in freedom, equality, and truth — the liberals, as usual, are the most easily ridiculed for deludedly hoping to forge a common ground. It is therefore no wonder that Mark Starr of *Newsweek* described the media interest in political correctness as "the revenge of the liberals."[38]

2

Is Academic Freedom in Trouble?

◆

What is the future of academic freedom? The answer is by no means obvious. An earlier consensus about the principles of academic freedom has eroded, and tenure — traditionally the primary institutional safeguard of academic freedom — is becoming a rarity in the employment conditions of the 1990s. The American Association of University Professors, which was formed in 1915 in order to promote and defend academic freedom, no longer feels secure in its mission. The previous AAUP statements of principles on academic freedom do not provide a sufficient response to the recent controversies and attacks on higher education, nor to the troubling questions posed by postmodern philosophy. No longer able to provide a clear articulation and simple defense of academic freedom, the AAUP solicited a series of essays addressing its future.[1]

The foundations of academic freedom are threatened by the twin pincers of economic and theoretical challenges to the university. Administrators argue that tenure is now an unaffordable luxury and no longer necessary in order to protect academic freedom. They assert that academic freedom — especially freedom for the professor in research, publication, and classroom teaching, but also in speaking or writing as a citizen[2] — is so deeply ingrained in the fabric of the university that it can thrive without such a strong form of economic security as tenure, and that lifetime guarantees of employment are a relic of a more placid economic environment. At the same time, many professors challenge the basic conceptual premises of academic freedom (such as Dewey's claim in his essay "Academic Freedom" that the "university is the truth-function" and the "one thing that is inherent and essential is the idea of truth"),[3] and some go on to argue that in the pursuit of equality and justice, there are now other important considerations that need to be weighed against the freedoms of individual

46

professors. Yet despite these pressures on the policies and practices of academic freedom, the most common argument today is that academic freedom is not in crisis and that no new protections from either administrative or theoretical assault are required.

There are many unfortunate examples of professors being fired for voicing their opinions, and I would argue that these cases undermine the claim that academic freedom is so assiduously protected that tenure and other contractual guarantees of academic freedom are unnecessary.[4] In this chapter, however, rather than exploring the administrative attack on employment conditions in higher education and the resulting threat to academic freedom (not to mention economic survival),[5] I want to examine the other widespread argument: that challenges to earlier paradigms of truth, knowledge, and education — paradigms that have formed the basis for traditional justifications of the need for academic freedom — pose no threat to the practice and protection of academic freedom.

Louis Menand states forthrightly that "postmodernism and multiculturalism, however these terms are defined" (and he is using these terms as shorthand for "epistemological relativism" and "the so-called politicization of the humanities"), in no way "threaten the future of academic freedom" (4, 5). I think that he is wrong; the epistemological and political dimensions of new critical practices do indeed affect the future of academic freedom. I do not want to suggest that any professor who embraces "multiculturalism" or "postmodernism" poses a threat and should be denounced, or that those who care about academic freedom should be vigilant in securing their universities from the disturbing taint of these new ideas. Such a stance is perverse and would preserve academic freedom only for the like-minded. In the first part of this chapter I will argue, however, that the goals of academic freedom and multiculturalism do often come into conflict. The promotion of multiculturalism leads to administrative attempts to instill and manage diversity, since multiculturalism implies not simply a new critical outlook, but also a blueprint for new power structures and institutional arrangements. And the administration of diversity frequently collides with the ideals of academic freedom. A refusal to acknowledge these conflicts, or a willingness to curb freedoms in order to achieve diversity, hardly bodes well for the future of academic freedom.

In the second half of the chapter, I will turn from instances of conflict between academic freedom and new critical paradigms to the more far-ranging question of whether a "postmodern" stance and "epistemological relativism" (or in Richard Rorty's version, a rejection of epistemology altogether) require a fundamental rethinking or even rejection of the principles of academic freedom. Can we still hold on to policies for protecting the pursuit of knowledge and truth in the university after we have radically challenged the very concepts of knowledge and truth? If many professors now reject the notion that the aim of their work is "the free search for truth and its free exposition" (to borrow the language of the AAUP "1940 Statement of Principles on Academic Freedom and Tenure"),[6] will principles of academic freedom, designed specifically to foster and protect such an aim, retain their efficacy? I will take issue especially with Richard Rorty's contention that philosophical debates about truth have no effect on academic freedom since they do not shape or alter the "traditions of civility" (29) or the "ethics of the academy" (32). According to Rorty, these traditions and ethics — and not philosophical convictions — are the essential bulwarks for academic freedom. I agree with Rorty that his notion of truth is not in itself incompatible with the idea or the practice of academic freedom. A different understanding of truth and a discrediting of objectivity and rationality require, however, a new justification and defense of academic freedom; "traditional standards of objectivity, truth, and rationality" will *not*, as Rorty asserts, "take care of themselves" (29).

Academic Freedom and Diversity: Congruence or Conflict?

Every college handbook has an academic freedom policy. Academic freedom is one of the most cherished notions of the American university, for it suggests that each individual professor, and the university as a whole, act as autonomous agents in the pursuit of truth. If the academician were not to be granted his or her freedom, the entire enterprise of humanistic knowledge would lose its footing. The AAUP statements, which serve as the basis for most university policies, provide a fairly narrow definition of academic freedom. One of the AAUP's central concerns is to guarantee the rights of the professor to freedom of speech when *not* acting as a professor; thus one is free to criticize U.S. government policy in off-campus political meetings without fear of institutional repercussions. But the significance of academic freedom goes far beyond the protection of the basic political rights of professors. Academic freedom is the seal that certifies that what the academy transmits and generates is a product of free thought, not coercion, and is therefore knowledge.[7]

The study of the humanities depends upon the belief that each individual is free to arrive at conclusions that are not dictated by others. An essay that its author does not believe in subjects the entire system of ideas — ideas that have value only insofar as they signify a freely arrived at "truth" — to the charge of ideology, of serving other interests, of teaching or disseminating ideas for some purpose other than that of learning or knowledge. These critiques are made all the time, particularly in terms of attacks on professionalism and on the institution, or on the ideology of the "new class" (a class defined precisely by its "knowledge" and certification),[8] yet such critiques themselves legitimate, rather than reject, the adherence to freedom and the possibility that the individual can have — must have — some relation to knowledge. For if such a critique were itself to be thought of principally as the product of discipline or coercion, it would have no value at all as a means of either understanding or transforming that which it diagnoses. If the notion of academic freedom is foreclosed from the start, what is written and taught is thereby stripped of its value.

Yet we all know that academic freedom is not only not absolute, but often severely curtailed. That is of course one reason for the discussion of academic freedom in every handbook: to assess what forms of curtailment will and will not be tolerated. The "myth" of freedom always comes up against the reality of institutional and other practices that limit, or deny, such freedom. Without a belief in academic freedom, however, academic discourses, and especially those that most ardently question autonomy and freedom, would lose their promise of knowledge. The notion of academic freedom certifies the potential value of every professor's discourse despite the intellectual and institutional forces that shape and regulate it.

Battles around academic freedom today often focus either on charges of the suppression of speech or on the alleged "abuse" of academic freedom to cloak discriminatory practices. For example, a professor might argue that a university violated her academic freedom when dismissing her in order to suppress her provocative opinions, or on the other hand, a professor denied tenure might argue that the university is invoking academic freedom only to hide its discriminatory decision-making processes from public scrutiny. Here we can see one of the basic tensions around this issue, as the defense of freedom in the first instance and the "attack" against such freedom in the second both claim that certain voices are not being heard. A shared central notion is therefore the desirability of a plurality or diversity of voices, and a key question is, How is this plurality to be defined? In the first instance, there is the claim that a voice is being suppressed because of the content of what is said; in the second, there is a claim that a voice is being suppressed because of the position or identity of the speaker. These two claims often overlap but are not synonymous. The debates in the university are rapidly shifting from an emphasis on content to a focus on positionality or identity. It is in the conflict between these two perspectives, and especially around the issue of "diversity," that some of the fiercest and most interesting battles concerning academic freedom are being waged.

"Diversity" is everywhere these days. From advertising to economics, from curricula and syllabi to the recruitment of students and teachers, from the White House even to Wall Street, everyone now stresses diversity. Yet how are we to recognize diversity, and what is the relation of academic freedom to diversity? At first, these terms seem extremely congruent. Multiplicity, the emphasis on and acknowledgment of difference, even the *diversion* implied by diversity all seem to be qualities also aligned with academic freedom, since how are we to recognize freedom if not by difference and divergence? Yet "diversity" is such a popular term because it also masks which sorts of differences are to be praised and valued, and for what reasons. The allegiance to a *diversity of opinion*, which is at the heart of traditional notions of academic freedom, and the drive for a *diversity of identities*, which underlies much curricular and institutional reform, now frequently conflict.

The notion of a diversity of opinion is central to the modern idea of the university. Whether expressed as the "marketplace of ideas," or in some other formulation, the teaching of the humanities claims not only to countenance but to require a wide range of conflicting interpretations and viewpoints. A basic premise is that there is a potential equality among all individuals (teachers and students), among all holders of ideas, and that the battle of knowledge is to be fought out between the ideas themselves. The only views to be overtly suppressed in upholding this diversity of opinion are those that are deemed to be the product of coercion (or copying), rather than freely informed judgment, and those that supposedly seek to undermine the very system of the free exchange of ideas. It is not surprising that these two grounds for exclusion are frequently marshaled against the same target. In the 1950s, there was widespread agreement that the principle of academic freedom justified, if not demanded, the dismissal of Communists from the university; it was claimed that Communists were under the authority of others and therefore could not freely hold whatever ideas they espoused.

The academic project of openly contending opinions is not tenable, however, when certain people are not allowed to have or to express opinions. The recent emphasis on a diversity of identities proceeds from the recognition that certain people have traditionally been excluded from the entire realm of academic discourse. The call for a diversity of identities — both in the curriculum and in the classroom, in terms of texts and in terms of people — is a demand to include those who have previously been excluded. Yet the ideal of a diverse environment often conflicts with the very means for measuring, achieving, and preserving this environment.

The call for diversity, for example, requires hiring faculty and staff, and recruiting students, who meet a desired profile. Certain people, then, are to be viewed as *representatives* of specific cultural identities. But the ideal of diversity is one in which class, gender, and race *no longer* have the defining impact that they are often now said to have. The educational function of diversity is not only to overcome ignorance about those with different cultural backgrounds, but also to overcome barriers to equality. If the diverse environment does not *begin* to break down these categories as determinants, the "diverse" environment becomes only the worst reflection of the traditional museum, of the monumentalization of cultural differences. Diversity always offers the possibility of contamination, of a mixing and infiltration of ingredients, but one of the first things to be contaminated is of course diversity itself.[9]

This commingling is the apparent educational purpose of diversity: learning about others helps one to overcome ignorance and prejudice and to expand and redefine the boundaries of one's own identity. But what if the identities of the "others" who have been newly imported to constitute the diverse environment are themselves also subject to the "beneficial" breaking down of the limitations of identity? If such a breaking down of the others occurs as well, won't they lose their institutional function as other? For many institutions, this is the announced goal, which leaves them open to the charge that they weren't interested in diversity in the first place, but only in assimilation and acculturation into the dominant culture. Yet to preserve diversity, to keep the other in the position of other, a perhaps more violent exercise of institutional power is necessary.

The most ardent espousal of diversity is thus paradoxically often accompanied by the strongest pressures to fix identities and stabilize differences. The goal of achieving a diverse environment requires concrete measures of difference, but measuring difference habitually emphasizes the lowest *uncommon* denominator. In a renewed form of cultural imperialism, different peoples and cultures are defined from the outside, and by what they are *not*: not white, male, middle-class, or American. From the standpoint of the institution, college education is essentially repetitive, not progressive; a new entering class must be educated every year. In order to ensure and to reproduce the experience of diversity, recognizable distinctions must be maintained.

For example, in hiring a minority faculty member for the purpose of achieving diversity, the institution has a clear investment in preserving this person's otherness, so that he or she can provide the experience of diversity to the majority of students and serve as a role model, as a successful incarnation of a certain identity, for students of the same background. The decision to achieve diversity in terms of identity produces strong pressures on minority faculty to conform to the identity — as defined by others — for which they have been hired. At my institution, minority faculty are constantly expected to play a specific role as a "minority"; at the extreme, they have even been dismissed for not conforming to this role.[10] Academic freedom is severely curtailed when one's opinions must coincide with one's "identity."

The institutional pressures to stabilize differences in order to ensure a diverse environment often also lead to a desire to stabilize meanings in order to produce a diverse curriculum. If the function of a particular text is to add "diversity" to the curriculum, it must be taught in a way that heightens its otherness or difference. A special burden is placed on the text, course, or field of study that is to bring diversity to the curriculum, since diversity does not imply sheer multiplicity.

The goal of diversity proceeds from a recognition of the imbalances around race, class, and gender, and from a recognition of the *asymmetry* between different identities. But any interpretation that does not emphasize the precise imbalances and asymmetries used to define the need for diversity undermines the lesson the text has been chosen to teach; the range of meanings of the noncanonical text is restricted to its function of embodying a specific set of differences.

All noncanonical or Third World texts do not equally fulfill this task of exemplifying the opposition between dominant and subaltern subjects or between dominant and marginalized cultures. Proclamations of academic freedom ring hollow when institutions coerce the faculty to select texts that provide the "proper" Third World challenge to the canon or pressure professors to make the texts they teach fit the prescribed roles or set of cultural identities needed to illustrate the desired lessons of diversity. When it is specified in advance what a student is to hear from these "other" voices, the power of dominant institutions to determine meaning is strengthened, not subverted.

Another aspect of the conflict between the ideals and the practices of diversity is that the call for diversity in the university now often works to reinforce an asymmetrical relation between minority and nonminority professors and between "Third World" and "Eurocentric" texts. It could be argued that this is as it should be: the university is a place that both reflects upon and reflects society, and even if the ideal of diversity presupposes a certain theoretical equality of all individuals, for the present, all voices are not equal and therefore must be treated differently. The *position* from which something is spoken thus becomes one of the most important criteria for determining its meaning and value.

The insistence that identity and position determine meaning is fundamentally in conflict, however, with the vision of the university as a place for the exchange of ideas among free and equal thinkers. Any promise of academic freedom is empty if a student's or a professor's ideas are to be judged in advance as more or less legitimate and significant according to the speaker's position on the grid of race, class, and gender. A common attempt to resolve the tension between these two different views — of the student or professor as a freely thinking individual or as highly determined by his or her "cultural identity" — is to argue that the study of different identities is precisely the means for realizing the goal of a free exchange of ideas. For knowledge, it is often promised, is what frees one from the determining and limiting forces of identity. But when, as often now happens, the basis for knowledge and for participation in the university is defined as a properly sensitive and enlightened understanding of diversity, freedom of thought is reserved only for those who have acceded to the proper knowledge of identities and positions. Everyone else is relegated to the position of not yet being sufficiently "free" and therefore incapable of participating fully in the discourse of the university. In addition, one need not even respect the opinions or academic freedom of those who are not proponents of diversity, since at best they are ignorant or incapable of independent thought, and at worst, racist, sexist, and homophobic. In such a conception of the university (and this conception is widespread), the only real freedom of thought is allotted to those who have the power to define the identities of others.

A widespread embrace of multiculturalism and diversity presents just one example of how the ideals and practices of academic freedom are under pressure from new critical paradigms in the university. By pointing to such conflicts I do not intend to discredit or reject multiculturalism (or conversely, traditional notions of academic freedom); rather, I hope to suggest the need for a new discourse legitimating academic freedom, since it is neither a timeless value nor a custom and ethic of the university that can be called on whenever needed but that otherwise requires no further attention or thought.

Do We Need Truth?

Do philosophical debates about truth have any consequences at all for the traditions and practices that people have in mind when they speak of academic freedom (or scientific integrity or scholarly standards)? And more broadly, does the adoption of postmodern philosophical paradigms, of critical outlooks that reject the ideas about truth and knowledge originally used in formulating policies of academic freedom, have any effect on "the ways in which free universities actually function" (27)? These are the questions that Richard Rorty poses in his essay "Does Academic Freedom Have Philosophical Presuppositions?" Rorty's answer is no — "philosophical debates about the nature of truth" should be, and in fact are, "irrelevant to academic practices" (24). Rorty can thus freely attack customary conceptions about truth,

objectivity, and knowledge, yet still blithely dismiss any critic who suggests that his philosophical arguments might have undesirable effects
on the culture and practices of the university.

Rorty's stance is part of a typical two-step, in which a "conservative" critic (played here by John Searle) first offers the following sort
of argument: that "postmodernists are attempting to challenge certain
traditional assumptions about the nature of truth, objectivity, rationality, reality, and intellectual quality" that make up "the Western
Rationalistic Tradition"; that "our intellectual and educational tradition, especially in the research university, is based on the Western
Rationalistic Tradition"; and that the very existence of the university
is therefore at stake if we do not refute postmodernism.[11] A particular
set of philosophical beliefs is connected here not only to the traditions but to the continued existence of the university. It is easy for
Rorty then to step in and argue that beliefs and practices are not so
tightly bound together and that changing one's belief about the nature
of truth does not constitute "a good reason for altering the practice"
(22) of academic freedom (or scholarly integrity). If anyone supposes
the contrary, that a new set of philosophical beliefs about truth does
provide a reason for altering academic practices, he or she is simply
wrongheaded. These dances yield little, since the conservative need
not grapple with new philosophical arguments, if she dislikes what
she takes to be their consequences, and the postmodernist need not
consider any unwanted institutional or social consequences of his arguments, since when convenient he can always assert that there ought
not to be any consequences at all.

I want to take a position other than the Searlean one, in which
critiques of key aspects of what he calls the "Western Rationalistic Tradition" are necessarily viewed as assaults on everything that
is thoughtful and good in the university, and are therefore to be
forcefully resisted, and the Rortyean one, in which attacks on the
foundational discourses of religious, political, or academic institutions
have little consequence, since social practices do not have philosophical presuppositions. A critique of the foundational discourse of
a liberal institution may be an advance in philosophical understanding, yet nevertheless threaten practices we want to preserve. There is
no reason to suppose that a good critical argument — one that is insightful and persuasive within its context — will necessarily have only
benign consequences in whatever larger sphere it may be taken up.

I agree, for instance, with much of what Rorty glibly characterizes as "my side" in arguments about a correspondence theory of truth (the arguments of Kuhn, Davidson, and Derrida),[12] yet I am nevertheless troubled by changes in academic attitudes and practices that I think follow in the wake of a postmodernist reinterpretation of truth and objectivity. I therefore want to pursue further the ways in which arguments from Rorty's "side" of the philosophical debate about truth may have consequences that he neither envisions nor supports and to explore the strategies by which Rorty disclaims any connection between his philosophy and the future of academic freedom.

Rorty is surely right to argue that adopting Donald Davidson's well-reasoned ideas about truth claims should not result in any great change in academic practices (though one could not make so strong a statement with regard to Rorty's ideas).[13] Yet there is now a widespread suspicion among many academics about making any truth claims at all. A few years ago, I went to a talk by the legal scholar Patricia Williams about the case of "wilding" in which several young men were accused of raping and beating a jogger in Central Park, and a Harvard professor in the audience could not even enunciate the word "truth" — she would only speak of the "T-word" in wondering whether we were even justified in referring to what "actually happened" on that night. Is such suspiciousness simply a result of misreading Rorty and his friends and a failure to properly understand philosophy? And will a rejection of "the free search for truth and its free exposition" as our academic mission have any effect on our practices and on academic freedom? At issue in assessing the consequences of these critiques is what conception of truth one puts in place of "correspondence to reality" and what one takes to be the implications radiating from new theories of truth. "Correspondence to reality" is a powerful and seductive concept because it provides a ground for common understanding, offers a check against wayward beliefs, and holds out an endpoint toward which our ideas can gradually converge. If one puts forth a philosophical idea that "not only ensures that there is a ground level on which speakers share views, but also that what they share is largely a correct picture of the world," as Davidson claims to do,[14] the consequences are very different than if one argues instead that truth is a product of individual experience, is shaped by one's cultural identity, and is determined by where one stands in relation to power. And the ramifications for the academic pursuit and transmission of knowledge

are small if one envisages an improved "grasp of the standards of rationality implicit in all interpretation of thought and action" (Davidson),
but greater if one takes a deflationary and debunking stance, suggests
that truth is now merely a synonym "for whatever we want to believe,"[15] or argues that truth claims are deceptions that cover over the
workings of power.

Rorty is eager to offer new conceptions in place of the old ones
(he proposes we substitute "the widest possible intersubjective agreement" for "correspondence to reality" [23]), and he is not hesitant in
drawing boundaries to delimit the implications of his critique (though
these lines change depending on the audience and on whether he is
speculating "in the short run" or "in the long run"). What I object
to in Rorty's writing is less the basis on which he attempts to redefine our understanding of truth than what he fails or is unwilling to
acknowledge: that how one redefines truth and where one draws the
boundaries around the implications of the critique make a huge difference for academic practices; that others, earnestly proceeding from
philosophical investigations of truth, arrive at conclusions that are indeed damaging "to the good which these universities do, to their role
in keeping government and liberal institutions alive and functioning"
(27); that his own theories, in their departure from and at times dis-
paragement of earlier philosophy, now make necessary a rethinking
and a rejustification of the discourse of academic freedom; and that
you cannot continually attack "truth" and "objectivity" without also
affecting people's notions of the pursuit of truth or objective academic
inquiry.

Rorty, in arguing that his philosophical views about truth have no
importance for academic freedom, draws an analogy with "President
Eisenhower's famous dictum that America is firmly grounded in religious belief, and that it doesn't matter which one" (24). He continues:
"I think that there are a lot of different philosophical beliefs about the
nature of truth and rationality that can be invoked to defend the traditions and practices that we call 'academic freedom,' and that in the
short run, at least, it does not greatly matter which ones we pick."
But philosophical beliefs today are almost as likely to be invoked to
attack as to defend academic freedom. Eisenhower was stressing the
importance of belief in a traditional conception of God, whereas what
we have now is a questioning of the adequacy and sustainability of
every traditional conception of truth. Rorty himself prefers drawing

on instances in which intersubjective agreement replaces belief in a supreme being to make his case that a change in convictions does not alter our practices, and he gives the example of the shift in attitudes toward oaths: taking an oath in a court of law no longer depends on the belief that God will punish those who lie, since "[t]ruthfulness under oath is, by now, a matter of our civic religion, our relation to our fellow Americans rather than to a nonhuman power" (23). Yet some shifts in conviction do affect our practices. If one argues instead for a notion of truth as primarily a product and reflection of (state) power, our "civic religion" would hardly survive.

When others draw different conclusions about what the philosophical views of Kuhn, Derrida, and himself entail, such as the idea that "claims of disinterest, objectivity and universality are not to be trusted," Rorty is simply dismissive and even refers to such people as "the bad guys" (the people who coauthored that sentence are George Levine, Peter Brooks, E. Ann Kaplan, Jonathan Culler, Marjorie Garber, and Catharine Stimpson — Does Rorty really think they are "bad guys"?).[16] He is uninterested in exploring the process of thinking that leads others to different conclusions about what is demonstrated by "the most powerful modern philosophies and theories," and he simply asserts, "I should claim that any philosophy that is dubious about the folkways that we call 'academic freedom' must have something wrong with it" (never mind that the term "folkways" — "the ways of living and acting in a human group, *built up without conscious design* but serving as compelling guides of conduct" — suggests to many only a dubious affirmation of a principle guiding the conduct of professors).[17] Yet even if Rorty is correct that the philosophical views he shares with Kuhn and Derrida do not "entail that the universities have no further use for notions like 'disinterest' and 'objectivity,' " and even if he is correct in thinking that "disinterested, objective inquiry would not only survive the adoption of our philosophical views but might survive in a desirably purified form" (27), it is not hard to see why many use these views to frame their attack on "disinterested, objective inquiry."

In his essay "Solidarity or Objectivity," for instance, Rorty argues that we would be better off if we could set aside "the desire for objectivity altogether," and he disparages those who still seek objectivity rather than solidarity.[18] There is something more than a little disingenuous about constantly attacking objectivity but then complaining, when someone else says "claims of objectivity are not to be trusted," that you were only referring to objectivity in a philosophical sense and not as a folkway, as a compelling guide for academic inquiry. It was Humpty Dumpty who said, "When I use a word...it means just what I choose it to mean — neither more nor less," and "When I make a word do a lot of work like that...I always pay it extra" (and we all know what happened to him).[19]

Rorty can go about deflating and discrediting certain terms in one instance, yet still claim to cherish them in another, only by arguing for a stark separation between philosophical belief and social practice. Rorty's point in making this separation is not to diminish the importance of philosophy but rather to diminish the significance of the questions traditionally explored by philosophers (Rorty typically states, "there is no interesting work to be done in this area")[20] and especially to diminish the significance of adherence to traditional philosophical foundations (God, objectivity, and so on). For Rorty, earlier conceptions of truth and objectivity are merely "rhetorical flourishes" and function only as "optional glosses" for our academic practices (37). They function like training wheels on a bicycle: once we know how to ride, we no longer need their support and can remove them without any ill effect (their removal will only improve our riding).

I think this view of the relation between philosophical ideas and academic practices is deeply flawed. For professors, whose work is often to conceptualize theories for the "practices" that they are studying, their ideas about the nature of knowledge, about what forms of research can best produce knowledge, about the objectivity of researchers, and about the autonomy of institutions definitely affect how they themselves "actually function." When ideas conceptualizing and justifying what it is that we do in universities change, the practices often change as well. With regard to academic freedom, Rorty's claim that we can now dispense with whatever philosophical framework was once used to justify it is even weaker. Academic freedom is not simply a skill or habit that once acquired stays with us forever, and universities are not so committed to protecting freedom of inquiry that we can cast off whatever "optional glosses" about truth guided earlier generations without replacing them. Nor is academic freedom analogous to such ethical virtues as honesty, intellectual fairness, and respect, which every party in a dispute typically claims to cherish and which are usually held apart from whatever notions are in contention. Since academic freedom — the principle that the very peculiar work we do in universities requires a much greater degree of autonomy than is sanctioned for other jobs and professions — often comes into conflict with other values, justifications explaining why our autonomy is essential for knowledge are crucial. It is always important to articulate that the task of the professor is to pursue understanding rather than simply to pass on received dogma. A persuasive rationale is required to defend this unusual autonomy against the external threats of government or trustees (who fear that professors undermine traditional values or needlessly engage in controversy) or the internal threats of administrators and zealous colleagues (who fear that certain professors are disruptive and make waves or lead students in the wrong direction). Arguments connecting professorial autonomy to truth, knowledge, and understanding, rather than merely to the whims, opinions, and self-development of the individual professor, are necessary for preserving the "folkways" of academic freedom and for shaping the habits of each new class or generation. If we are persuaded by theories that challenge the earlier rationale for our autonomy, we then need to build from these ideas a new justification for academic freedom.

Rorty does not make a strong philosophical argument "about a lack of close connection" between academic practices and philosophical debates: "It is simply a *sociological truth* about the lack of interest which most people, intellectuals as well as nonintellectuals, currently have in philosophy" (31, emphasis added). If philosophy is restricted here to the arguments of Donald Davidson, and to the set of philosophers whose work he seeks to modify, perhaps Rorty is correct. But there is no reason to define philosophy so professionally and so narrowly, and it is a "sociological truth" that debates about truth have had a wide effect on the ideals and also the practices of intellectuals.

On the back cover of Barbara Herrnstein Smith's *Belief and Resistance: Dynamics of Contemporary Intellectual Controversy* we read: "*Truth, reason,* and *objectivity* — can we survive without them? What happens to law, science, and the pursuit of social justice when such ideas and ideals are rejected? These questions are at the heart of the controversies between traditionalists and 'postmodernists' that Barbara Herrnstein Smith examines in her wide-ranging new book."[21] Directly below is a blurb from Rorty: "Smith's analyses of recent controversies about objectivity are unusually subtle, and very helpful indeed." When the ideals of truth, reason, and objectivity are rejected, the practice of "disinterested, objective inquiry" changes as well. One does not have to look very hard to find such assertions as "the pretension of professional historians of being objective or neutral is, to my mind, ridiculous."[22] The notion that "academic research should be disinterested and objective" is not, as Rorty implies, largely beyond dispute, nor can it be explained and defended simply "by pointing to the ways in which free universities actually function" (27). One can argue about whether those who distrust "claims of disinterest, objectivity, and universality" have misinterpreted Rorty's writing or completely misunderstood Davidson's ideas (and one need not privilege either Rorty or Davidson as the central voice in a philosophical critique of truth), but postmodernist theorizing has changed the discourse, the ideals, and the practices of professors today.

The Machinery of Academic Freedom

I have no nostalgia for some earlier time in American university life, and again, I do not want to suggest that new paradigms of thought and new critical methodologies pose some heinous threat to universities. My main argument here could itself be described as postmodernist: academic freedom is not a transcendental value or principle in our universities, and those who wish to see it flourish must not ignore the conflicts between traditional rationales for academic freedom and the discourses now prevalent in universities. Rorty and Menand both seek to treat academic freedom as something that is not in play, as something outside the theoretical and ideological fray of contemporary intellectual controversy. Rorty just asserts that philosophy could not possibly have any negative impact on academic freedom, and Menand argues that multiculturalism and postmodernism have "undergone disciplinization" and are simply "what many academics do today, in the same way that they once" practiced other forms of criticism (13), and therefore could not possibly threaten "the machinery of academic freedom" (14).[23] Both treat academic freedom as a machine that functions independently of the philosophical beliefs, methodologies, and critical discourses of professors and administrators.

Kafka's "In der Strafkolonie" begins with the observation, "Es ist ein eigentümlicher Apparat" (It's a wonderful piece of apparatus).[24] The word *eigentümlich* can be translated as "wonderful," but it also

means "belong exclusively (to), proper (to), peculiar (to), characteristic (of)."[25] The story describes the malfunction and breakdown of
this execution machine designed by the Old Commandant, now that
a New Commandant with new attitudes toward punishment has taken
over. The apparatus was "proper to" the old ideology, and there is no
reason to believe that the wonderful "machinery of academic freedom"
will automatically continue to work properly under any new regime
(for anyone who has gone through an academic freedom hearing, the
analogy with Kafka's story is not gratuitous). If one's stance is now
that "claims of autonomy are not to be trusted," for example, why
should one be given (or give others) special autonomy as a professor?
And if truth and objectivity are to be rejected entirely, how is the
principle that professors require adequate and effective protection in
their search for truth to be defended, when a professor is attacked for
voicing unpopular ideas?

Those who wish to keep "democratic and liberal institutions alive
and functioning" (27), yet who also, like Rorty, debunk and discredit
conceptions of truth and objectivity, have the obligation to offer new
supports and justifications to replace the ones they demolish. This
could be done — especially for versions of postmodern thought that
still retain a serviceable notion of truth and knowledge. My larger
concern, however, is to question the assumptions that lead many astute critics to overlook or deny the possibility that new, exciting, and
intellectually respectable developments in academic criticism could
potentially have ill effects on institutional and social practices. Simply
determining whether one finds a theoretical critique to be liberatory,
enlightened, and generous, or on the contrary muddle-headed, mean-
spirited, or nihilistic, does not alone provide a solid guide for judging
whether it will have a beneficial or a destructive impact on our institutions. (How would one judge the work of Marx?) I agree with
Rorty — and disagree with Searle — that one can question philosophical realism, or even the entire field of epistemology, without
necessarily throwing into disarray all the practices of the university.
But for Rorty, "ceasing to concern ourselves with epistemology" will
finally "take away a few more excuses for fanaticism and intolerance"
(38). Assuming that freeing ourselves from the shackles of past beliefs
will automatically make us more pacific and sympathetic is equally un-
justified; dismantling more conventional ways of thinking is just as
likely to provide new excuses for fanaticism and intolerance. Rorty at-

tempts to decouple philosophical belief from social practice, but what we really need to decouple is the expectation that intelligent and illuminating academic criticism will spark, in the short or in the long run, only enlightened, beneficent, and wise reshapings of our institutions and our society. Preserving academic freedom requires more than a receptiveness to new forms of academic discourse; required as well is continued thinking about the discourses that sustain the functions and purposes of the university.

— *Part II* —

Facing the Public

3

FORGING A PUBLIC VOICE
FOR ACADEMIC CRITICS

◆

One of the most compelling issues for academic critics today is the relation of academia to the broader public. At a time when much of the academic criticism in the humanities engages public and social concerns such as race, class, and gender, rather than exclusively scholarly topics of inquiry, the question of what audience the critic reaches is crucial. For criticism that has social change as its horizon, the restriction to a purely professional, academic audience is self-defeating.

The rise of socially oriented academic criticism has not, however, led to a greater public voice for academic critics. Books such as *The Last Intellectuals: American Culture in the Age of Academe* and *Double Agent: The Critic and Society* argue that the gulf between academic critics and general readers continues to widen and suggest that academics bear a large portion of the blame.[1] And when academic criticism does receive wider public attention, it is usually treated as a topic of fashion (a change from deconstruction to multiculturalism is discussed next to an article on what students are wearing when they return to college), eccentricity (how far a new theory departs from what previous generations were taught), or scandal (such as the revelation of Paul de Man's collaborationist writings from more than forty years earlier).

Yet despite the meager impact of academic criticism, many academics also feel that now more than ever they have something to contribute to revitalizing a public sphere of critical dialogue. Can "popularizing" academic criticism — presenting our work in a form that is accessible to those with little or no background in the history and theoretical frameworks of our fields — overcome the barriers between academia and the public? I want to argue, conversely, that "popularization" will do little to broaden the public role of academic criticism or to gain an influential voice for academic critics, as long as there is no space for a public within contemporary criticism. When critics proceed by discrediting the views of most people as necessarily deluded (shaped by the mass media, in subjection to the dominant ideology, and riven by unconscious desires), the translation of their ideas for a nonacademic audience will not "popularize" them. I will conclude that academic critics need to *think publicly* — to think in ways that could sustain, rather than foreclose or discredit, a public discourse — if they hope to expand their audience and their influence.

Popularizing Academic Criticism

The professional vocabulary and style of much academic criticism certainly restricts its appeal, and since academic critics are often writing about important issues, eliminating such obstacles should help to attract a large audience. The popularization of scientific writing seems to offer a good example of what can be achieved. Writers such as Carl Sagan, Stephen Hawking, and Stephen Jay Gould bring some of the most sophisticated insights and problems of contemporary science to an audience that often lacks even basic scientific training. Moreover, these writers have achieved a public voice that enables them to speak influentially on topics beyond the narrowest boundaries of their fields, such as nuclear winter and AIDS. Popularizing academic criticism in the humanities — and when speaking of "academic criticism," I am referring primarily to the writings of humanities professors — would seem to be an easier task, since most people already have a greater familiarity with the topics. Literary criticism provides a good example: there are far more people who read the books discussed by literary critics than there are fossil hunters or amateur astronomers.

Yet whereas writers such as Stephen Jay Gould have quite successfully communicated the interests, discoveries, and consequences of important scientific developments *to* the public, much literary criticism is directed at attacking the basic presuppositions *of* the public, in the hopes of reshaping society; the project of popularization is therefore quite different. Literary theory today is less descriptive than diagnostic and proceeds through methods of demystification, ideology critique, and cultural analysis that challenge the common understanding and the current order of society. Even when popular essays recounting the latest scientific discoveries upset our previous beliefs, they do little to alter our sense of being in the world, much less to renegotiate existing power relations. Contemporary literary criticism, in contrast, seeks to transform society, rather than merely to understand literary works. Feminist criticism, for example, argues, at least implicitly, for a more egalitarian society and for a dramatic change in current gender relations.

I do not want to suggest that if academic criticism is to be "popular" and to have a public voice, it must be noncontroversial or populist. A more apt comparison would be with the popularization of science by T. H. Huxley and others in the nineteenth century, in which the primary conceptions of self and society were challenged. Huxley, known today mostly as the popularizer of Darwin, had a tremendous public impact, while promulgating notions such as an evolutionary rather than a synchronically created world, the descent of man from the apes, and a mechanistic explanation of the mind — ideas that completely overturned received wisdom, religious authority, and popular belief. How does Huxley bridge the gap between a specialized scientific community and a broad public when discussing such controversial topics as evolution?

Huxley spoke to an extremely wide variety of audiences: public lectures at the Royal Institution and at working men's societies, Sunday evening "lay sermons," and "Science Lectures for the People." Some scholars have argued that only later did a "separate, distinct class of people known as 'intellectuals'" emerge in Victorian society, and it might be argued that only in a society that had not yet so rigidly institutionalized the domains of knowledge could such a far-reaching popularization take place.[2] Yet for every era someone always locates a moment in which a freer intercourse between the sage and the people, or the public and the intellectual, has given way to a more stratified and bureaucratized society; institutional changes, though important, do not in themselves tell us enough about the possibilities of popularization. Even if Huxley did address a more homogeneous society, this would explain little about his success as a popularizer.

For popularization is not only always possible — it is always going on. Within literary criticism, for example, Jonathan Culler popularizes Derrida and other writers, and the entire academic publishing enterprise depends on popularizing (that is, appropriating and disseminating) the ideas of others. Every critical discussion of Lacan, for example, or any scholarly usage of the insights of Foucault, is also a popularization of their work, to the extent that it extends the scope of their ideas and brings them to a new audience. Thus an argument that academic criticism should not be popularized since that would constitute a betrayal of the rigors of "reading" (a process that only a few have the training and the time to perform), or some other similar notion about the necessary impenetrability of academic work, only constitutes a radical blindness to the functioning of academic institutions. The real question here is, Why doesn't the audience for academic criticism extend much beyond the boundaries of universities, especially when critics address issues of public concern?

Before proceeding to answer this question, I should remark that my claim that academic criticism in the humanities does not currently have much public impact, and is not already widely "popularized," actually needs to be argued, rather than taken for granted. Many conservative cultural critics assert that academic criticism has unfortunately had a very profound effect, leading, in the wake of Nietzsche and Freud, and Derrida and Foucault, to a widespread "cultural relativism," an erosion of standards, and a loss of faith in established principles and values.[3] It would be difficult, however, to point to many contemporary American academic critics in the humanities who have a prominent public voice. At a time when Lynne Cheney (as head of the National Endowment for the Humanities) was debating Catharine Stimpson (as head of the Modern Language Association) on public television, it was Dan Quayle's attack on the TV character Murphy Brown that received massive attention. The much vaunted "culture wars" have not given a significant public platform to academic critics (even if they have brought attention to critics of academia); the threatening "cultural elite" attacked by Quayle is best personified by the Hollywood director, not the English professor. The views of academics in the humanities enter the public sphere only in highly mediated and filtered forms. A black teenager wearing a T-shirt imprinted with "It's a black thing — you wouldn't understand" may express a popularization of academic thinking on difference and multiculturalism, but not in a form that many academics would embrace as a successful embodiment of their teaching.[4]

Open Thinking

The explanation for the powerful public impact of Huxley's insights, as opposed to the muted impact of contemporary academic criticism, derives less from the sociological changes in the audience than from the writer's conceptualization of the audience. Huxley is brilliant at drawing connections: between the activity of the scientist and that of the artisan; between a piece of chalk, the white cliffs of Dover, and thousands of years of sedimentation of microscopic organisms; between "particular facts" and "the generalisations of which all particular facts are illustrations."[5] Huxley seeks to connect scientific thinking with public understanding, and he presents this process of connection — of moving from the particular to the general, and from the scientist to the public — as the very process of science itself. Thus science is not conceived of as a type of knowledge that radically separates the scientist from the member of the public; rather, Huxley attempts to treat the public "scientifically," as always open to evidence, as persuadable by reasoning and demonstration.

In a famous passage in his essay "On the Method of Zadig," Huxley writes that scientists, like Voltaire's Zadig, "perceive endless minute differences where untrained eyes discern nothing" and that "the unconscious logic of common sense compels them to account for these effects by the causes which they know to be competent to produce them" (166–67). Patrick Brantlinger, among others, has attacked Huxley here for equating scientific thinking with "common sense," and Brantlinger suggests that Huxley achieves his "popularization" by downplaying the many ways in which scientific thinking differs radically from "common sense."[6] I would like to emphasize, in contrast, that the essence of Huxley's project is to *forge* and to educate a "common sense" and that he seeks to do this by offering a common mode of thinking, described here as accounting for effects by looking for the causes that are known "to be competent to produce them." The "common sense" that Huxley appeals to here *compels* people to think and to inquire; it does not describe the passive acceptance of conventional wisdom. Huxley uses the logic of causation as one more link on the chain that connects scientific reasoning to the processes of thought available to and used by the public.

Huxley's persistent attention to the "operation of *natural* causes" — as opposed to other forms of causation such as "the angel of the

Lord" or "wrathful Omnipotence" (as explanations for lightning and for "plague, pestilence, and famine" [111–12]) — offers a new model that displaces earlier forms of "common" knowledge based on tradition, authority, or dogma. Yet Huxley does not regard less-educated people as the unwitting dupes of aristocratic, clerical, or institutional power, insofar as they maintain other ideas or adhere to different models of thought. That is, Huxley does not suggest that those who do not yet embrace his conclusions or his worldview are largely incapable of doing so, since their thinking is systematically constrained by oppressive and unenlightened institutions (such a posture is widespread, however, in contemporary academic criticism). Rather, he treats these people as already on the path to science, and the task of his popular lectures is to move the public farther along this path and to diminish the distance between scientist and citizen. He insists "the mind is so constituted that it does not willingly rest in facts and immediate causes, but seeks always after a knowledge of the remoter links in the chain of causation" (75), and he implies that progress along this chain will also link various audiences and classes through their new, common knowledge.

The significance of Huxley for understanding popularization does not lie in the content of his thought or in his faith in science, individual reason, and progress, but in the ways in which his thinking is open to the public. Huxley does not separate the scientist from the public by declaring that the former, for example, believes in the logic of causation, while the latter does not; if one is not a scientist like Huxley, that does not imply that one adheres to a mode of thinking incompatible with science. Moreover, Huxley's way of thinking is also *opening*; he seeks to bring more people into the orbit of contemporary science, and this extension of science is not limited in advance to a select group. Of course, Huxley is attempting to persuade his audience, and he is also arguing *against* other conceptions; but he does not attempt to disqualify those who do not agree by characterizing them as churchgoers, for example, or as feebleminded women incapable of rational thought. The effort is placed on demonstrating the persuasiveness of the "chain of causation," rather than on attacking those who disagree by demonstrating their incapacity for the processes of thought required to understand biology.

Contemporary academic discourse, in contrast, often functions by excluding the participation of others. And this does not result primarily from employing an arcane vocabulary or style — obstacles that could be overcome by further "translation" — but from critical methods that are based on challenging *any* established consensus. When intellectual validity is defined by an opposition to hegemony, for example, there must necessarily be (at least until the successful revolution) a large populace that is incapable of receiving the fruits of academic wisdom.

At a time when "inclusion" is the motto of universities, it may seem perverse to emphasize that academic discourse is frequently grounded in exclusion, but I will now examine some of the ways in which academic criticism cuts itself off from the public sphere, despite its desires to reach beyond the professional audience and achieve "social change." I especially want to focus on a few representative strategies of inclusion and exclusion that work to position the "public" as always *elsewhere*, always outside the realm of academic discourse. Such strategies present the majority of people as incapable of "critical" thought (and thus unable to participate in a meaningful discussion with the critic), derive the authority of the critic from his or her "marginality" (and thus require a distance between the critic and the large number of people not defined as inhabiting the margins), and defend the academic community as the exclusive space of reasoned discussion (thus negating any external criticism as unreasonable, poisonous, and illegitimate). I will conclude by considering whether the many insights of contemporary criticism are by nature resistant to popularization, insofar as they challenge the foundations of any "common" understanding, or whether such strategies that foreclose public discussion can be excised from their theoretical frameworks.

Ideology and Exclusion

Ideological critiques form a large component of contemporary criticism, and in their attempt to explain the social and intellectual structures that shape every discourse, they would appear to pose no separation between "academic" and "public," or inside and outside. James Kavanagh, for example, in his essay "Ideology" in *Critical Terms for Literary Study* (a volume that serves as a textbook for literary theory), states that "[i]deology is a social process that works on and through every social subject, that, like any other social process, everyone is 'in,' *whether or not they 'know' or understand it.*"[7] This outlook seems to be inherently "inclusive," since it asserts that everyone operates within an ideological framework and that no one has access to transcendental knowledge or a viewpoint free from ideology. The insight that there is no transcendent, neutral, or objective position outside of ideology is central to much recent criticism; it demands an understanding of all the social processes that shape our "construction" of the world, and it fractures the possibility of a truly universal or all-encompassing perspective.[8] In contrast to an earlier, Marxist ideology critique, which juxtaposed ideology (as delusion) to Marxist materialism and science (as truth), this shift to the notion that we are all "in" ideology would appear to place everyone on the same footing for a public debate of the different social and political issues that confront us.

But there is always a twist: the claim that only a few, like-minded critics " 'know' or understand" this, whereas most people remain *unconscious* of "the presence of ideology." This division into the initiated and the unenlightened is not simply a gradient of knowledge (one would expect the critic to be more knowledgeable than the general public), but functions to differentiate between those possessing a greater and a lesser freedom of thought. For despite the claim that there is no vantage point of truth outside ideology, those who are not "sensitized" to the effects of ideology are inevitably described in terms that discount their ability to gain knowledge and think clearly. Two sentences later Kavanagh gives the game away: "The 'nonideological' insistence does not mark one's freedom from ideology, but one's involvement in a specific, quite narrow ideology which has the exact social function of obscuring — even to the individual who inhabits it — the specificity and peculiarity of one's social and political position, and of preventing any knowledge of the real processes that found one's social life."[9] If one does not embrace the new insights about ideology, one is relegated to a "narrow" ideology and prevented from attaining "any knowledge of the real processes." Apparently, some ideologies are more confining than others, and some obscure, while others yield even a knowledge of the real (or at least of "the real processes that found one's social life").

The critique of ideology, which attacks liberalism and the possibility of "freedom from ideology," quickly becomes a tool for debunking one's opponent's ideas — everyone is *not* "in" these social processes in the same way. The claim that even if there is no absolute truth, there is at least a consciousness or an unconsciousness about the presence of ideology is followed by the implication: we are conscious ("sensitized to the effects")[10] of ideology and you are not; therefore we can dismiss your ideas in advance as hopelessly unsophisticated, deluded, and in fact "ideological." Anyone who does not agree is outside the pale of reasonable (that is, academic) argument. Opposing political positions (and competing ideologies) are figured as ignorance and intellectual incompetence, and academia becomes the lone bastion of "knowledge" against all the social forces that work to obscure a genuine understanding of social relations and to maintain the current inequities. There is little room for public dialogue when those who do not share one's viewpoint are known to be prevented from acquiring "any knowledge of the real processes."

There are many ways to explain how a powerful critical method for analyzing the social construction of knowledge, and of our inescapable embeddedness within language, culture, and historical contexts, frequently leads to the self-serving position that the majority of people are incapable of engagement in a meaningful discussion. One could cite the self-interest or the supposedly "radical" politics of academics or discuss how contemporary theory constantly problematizes the distinction between the "analytical" and the "polemical" (between any attempt to distinguish an analysis of ideology from the deployment of this analysis to discredit the ideas of those with whom one disagrees). But here I want to emphasize that academics, trained in procedures of critical division, suspicious of any notion of the universal or the common, have become too comfortable in grounding their critical authority on their separation from any broad "public" and from any commonality that goes beyond ideological divisions.

The strategies of ideology critique, although they come out of Marxist criticism, are hardly limited to Marxists. In Speaking for the Humanities, a document written under the auspices of the American Council for Learned Societies (ACLS) by six of the most eminent humanities professors, one sees a prime example of this logic at work:

> "Objectivity" and "disinterest" are often the means by which the equation of truth and particular ideological positions can be disguised, even from those who unequivocally believe in the possibility of objectivity and disinterest.

One need not make an absolute commitment to the view that no thought can be "uncontaminated" by interests in order to see how intellectually fruitful that view can be. Allowing for the possibility of one's own interests, one can look for irrational elements in otherwise rational arguments, or for disguised ideological assumptions.

...The best contemporary work in the humanities strives to make clear both its critique of the ideologies of previous work, and its own inevitable ideological blindspots. At its best, contemporary humanistic thinking does not peddle ideology, but rather attempts to sensitize us to the presence of ideology in our work, and to its capacity to delude us into promoting as universal values that in fact belong to one nation, one social class, one sect.[11]

The basic premise is clear: ideology is the presentation of the particular as universal or the historical as natural. Questioning appeals to "objectivity," "disinterest," universality, and nature (and the same might go for claims of difference, particularity, and history) may be "intellectually fruitful," but ideological critique here quickly becomes a means for debunking the views of others: any claim to "truth" can now be revealed as merely arising from "a particular ideological position."

Hypocrisy and mushiness of (group) thought are rampant in this passage, and the authors' attempt to produce "a public voice supporting the humanities"[12] — and thereby to write in a tone of moderation and consensus — only makes it easier for them to dismiss the ideas of their attackers. At every stage, the rigor of the critique is weakened in order to trumpet the superiority of "us" (leading academics in the humanities, who are reasonable, sensitive, and self-conscious) over "them" (Lynne Cheney, William Bennett, et al., who are dogmatic, deluded, and deceitfully ideological). If one "need not make an *absolute* commitment to the view that no thought can be 'uncontaminated' by interests" in order to argue against the notion of "disinterest," if one *can* learn to allow "for the possibility of one's own interests," if criticism can even "make clear ... its own inevitable ideological blindspots" (this gives new meaning to the words "inevitable" and "blindspots"), then anyone who remains blind to what these critics call "ideology" must simply be unwilling to put a good faith effort into their "humanistic thinking."[13] Disagreement over ideas is displaced onto a requirement for *confession;* the act of confessing "My discourse is ideo-logical" (and my "truths" come from "particular ideological positions" and "belong to one nation, one social class, one sect") is the criterion that now bestows freedom of the intellect (and the right to participate in discussion).

This wiggling between the position that all thought is "contam-inated" by interests and the idea that humanities professors can to some extent overcome this limitation on thought depends on the use of such words as "disguised," which allows for the meaning of either intentional deceit or inevitable misrecognition. The first step in the ideological critique is to claim that "disguised" assumptions apply to everyone, but the next step distinguishes between three categories: those in power who intentionally deceive, since if they were actually to reveal their interests they would lose their power over others (they "peddle ideology" [rather than the smut or dope peddled by villains of an earlier era], and they have the "capacity to delude us"); the vast majority, who are *unaware* of how ideology works (and who are thereby under the sway of interests *other* than their own); and we en-lightened professors, who want to reveal the mechanisms of disguise to others. Such a distinction relieves us of the obligation of actually listening to what people in these other two groups might have to say. And the definition of what counts as an "interest" or "ideology" of course depends on what "we enlightened professors" hope to change. This is a sort of Ponzi scheme, in which a few professors and students can gain critical leverage, but only so long as there is still a large, un-tapped pool of suckers (people not yet sensitized to the presence of ideology).

I have focused on ideology critique because it involves such a quintessential academic gesture: claiming inclusion (we are all "in" this state), but practicing exclusion (we aren't really in it with *you*).[14] Rather than a means for bridging the gap between academic and nonacademic, we have here the perfection of a method for always dis-missing the views of others. But no meaningful civic discussion can take place if one only attacks the consciousness of one's opponents, rather than the content of their ideas.

The confirmation hearings of Clarence Thomas to the Supreme Court provided an extraordinarily fruitful occasion for academic crit-ics, with its televised drama of race and gender. There is so much to be said — and so much has already been said — about how his nomination, confirmation hearings, and the Anita Hill episode represent a low point for political discourse in this country. But an ideological analysis, which is so tempting in this instance, does little to raise the level of discourse, insofar as it presents Thomas as incapable either of honestly or of intelligently holding the views that he has espoused. Contestation of ideas is displaced by the disqualification of their proponent.

Thomas represents an ideological scandal, since his views seem so radically opposed to his background: black, poor, an affirmative action baby, and a one-time admirer of Malcolm X. Ideology critique depends on a continuity between the individual and the group and delimits a permitted range of ideas. Anything beyond this range is proscribed, as it would challenge the hermeneutical value of the ideological context.

Thomas's dissonance from the accepted view of his background led some to presume that he would alter his views once on the Court and led many others to explain how Thomas had been deluded, co-opted, and even victimized by the dominant ideology.[15] Either Thomas had disguised his ideas to get ahead, or he was overcome by the wiles and disguises of others. In either case, academics could argue that he is incapable of intelligently and freely holding his stated ideas, and thus his disagreeable opinions need not be directly confronted.[16]

Clarence Thomas is an extreme case, but it is totally unclear to me why the average professor of law or literature, who by and large adheres to the academic doxa, has greater powers of thought and independence of mind than this justice of the Supreme Court. Such a strategy of disputing contentious ideas by alleging the diminished capacity of their beholder also cordons off academics from the large number of people for whom these ideas have some resonance. Thomas becomes a trope for the deluded masses. But if academics hope to popularize their ideas, they need to engage rather than discredit the populace.

Fetishizing Resistance

For academic criticism to gain public impact, academics not only must conceive of the public as capable of knowing, but also must not conceive of knowledge as requiring a particular position or viewpoint. That is presumably why courses in African American studies or Marxist criticism are not limited to African American students or avowed Marxists. Yet academic criticism frequently forecloses debate by converting specific positions into a new base of knowledge. A vocabulary of resistance (challenge, transgress, subvert) — with regard to the "dominant culture" at any rate — is now deemed not only ethically but intellectually superior to a vocabulary of legitimation (reaffirm, support, uphold). Persons who go along with rather than resist the current order are cast as "willing subjects and agents of hegemonic authority" — as dupes and collaborators.[17] This posture of resistance, instead of persuading others of their common interests, disqualifies all those who have not yet embraced the latest academic insights from participating in debates about the most public and hotly contested issues. The ideas of "willing subjects and agents of hegemonic authority" on improving economic well-being or achieving better race relations are obviously not worthy of serious attention.

We are rarely told how resistance to hegemonic culture will lead to anything better than will affirmation; this is merely presumed (since it is obviously desirable to resist such products of our culture as racism and poverty) and is almost treated as an article of knowledge. Yet in our society there is much that needs affirming and legitimizing (unless one truly espouses anarchy); the current cynicism toward government is hardly an unmitigated good. For every problem and issue, positions of resistance or legitimation, subversion or affirmation, need to be thought through and debated; every act of legitimation does not imply a passive and unquestioning acceptance of the status quo (and every act of resistance does not imply an active and questioning assault on it — resistance has become sanctioned and institutionalized in much academic criticism).

Any critical reading must in some sense go beyond the present understanding, but an automatic posture of resistance signifies only that the status quo is irredeemably corrupt and that all current systems and institutions are tainted. This is not a strategy for change, so much as one for achieving moral purity. The fetishization of resistance is a means of disengaging from the slow processes of change and of discrediting as contaminated anything less than a revolutionary position. Such a stance may serve as a means of academic legitimation (an argument is accredited if it is properly subversive or "resistant"), but it insulates academics from contending ideas. Framing resistance as essential to knowledge (and affirmation as a product of ignorance) produces a criticism inimical to open discussion and to any broad public involvement.

I do not want to suggest that academics are typically unaware of or insensitive to the divisions between the university and the public — quite the reverse. There is an increasing self-consciousness about the boundaries of academic discourse, and the burgeoning criticism of the "profession" and of the "institution" is a manifestation of an unease with current demarcations. The earnest efforts to question and to rearrange the traditional boundaries of academic knowledge do not automatically lead, however, to more porous and flexible boundaries or to a greater participation in public debates. My main point is that academics frequently *detach* themselves from the broader public, even as they claim greater engagement. This happens both at a theoretical level (fashioning a critical authority that hinges on a separation from what others think) and at the level of professional behavior (the tendency to preach to the converted, to circle the wagons when attacked from outside of academia, and to engage in other forms of insulation and self-protection).

The very provocative questioning of margins and the exploration of structures of exclusion, for instance, have generated a well-meaning desire to detach oneself from tainted practices, beliefs, and institutions that have fostered discrimination. In academia, it has now almost become a professional necessity to claim a position of marginality in order to gain intellectual and moral validation. Marginality is now a sign of authenticity, since if one isn't sufficiently marginal, one's views must be a product of the dominant ideology (and thereby, supposedly, empty of intellectual merit). At the English Institute, even Stanley Fish, who I have always thought of as the consummate professional and insider, remarked that he has always felt like an "outsider" in the profession.[18]

One effect of a professionally governed marginality (Why isn't this an oxymoron?) is to deny the critic's own enforcement of and containment within institutional boundaries; thus any rejection of those with differing views, and every limitation of focus to approved topics, can be repackaged as opposing hegemony and practicing transgression. The pressures in academia are almost always toward preaching to the converted — in this case, toward promoting one's institutional *centrality* by reinforcing one's "oppositional," critical stance. Such prototypical academic gestures as measuring the failure of other critics to achieve an ideal subject position with regard to the categories of race, class, and gender deflect any attempt to "convert" a wider audience into anxiety about ideological purity and intellectual rigor. At the same English Institute, Gerald Graff's talk entitled "Preaching to the Converted" ironically was met with comments primarily about his insufficient attentiveness to issues of class, race, and gender, rather than by suggestions about how best to influence audiences of the "nonconverted." For example, one person objected to his use of the term "Professor Redneck" to characterize traditional attitudes in the profession, arguing that Graff ignored the (lower-) class connotations of this term. Although these and other criticisms were *accurate* — Graff's arguments, like most discourses, could be fruitfully dissected for traces of blindness to dimensions of race, class, and gender in his words — such critiques only reinforce the tendency to preach to the converted or to those who at least share the bulk of one's opinions. The pressure to prove that one is a genuine convert produces a *frisson* of contestation, but it does little to develop the "more public rhetoric" for which Graff persuasively argues.[19]

The equation of marginality with authenticity positions academic institutions in turn as marginal to society. Moreover, such a gesture renders any public space of discourse as elsewhere, as apart from where one speaks; and this distance has to be maintained to preserve the source of one's critical power. Also, a critique that emphasizes everyone else's failure to attain an ideal subject position postpones a "genuine" dialogue to some future time, when people are no longer straitened by various "isms." When criticism itself becomes defined as that which can proceed only through distantiation — from tradition, from the West, from the media, from the hegemonic, from the present — the possibility of dialogue is restricted to the sharing of distance from that which had been represented as universal. The experience of marginality alone is a poor basis on which to reconstruct a public sphere.

The MLA Addresses the Public

If an insistence on marginality deepens the divisions between academia and the public, does the alternative lie in espousing a commitment to rational discussion, willingness to consider another viewpoint, civility, and other such values that promote an exchange of ideas? This is often the stance taken by academics when addressing the public, in an attempt to show that they share a common piety for these values, which are widely associated with the university and which also un-derwrite a public dialogue (a dialogue open potentially to everyone, not dependent on their political view or identity). In a newspaper interview at the height of the controversy around political correct-ness, Catharine Stimpson (a frequent interviewee at the time, as past president of the Modern Language Association [MLA]) concluded: "But the important thing is that our campuses, our colleges and uni-versities, have to really make sure that we are rational and make sure that we are open-minded and make sure that we are democratic so that those words cannot be captured by one point of the polit-ical spectrum. Those words belong to the center, not to one point of the political spectrum."[20] The "center" is apparently an accept-able all-encompassing umbrella term, which somehow is not limited to "one point of the political spectrum," as opposed to the unaccept-able "universal values" espoused by her adversaries, which in contrast can always be shown to "belong to one nation, one social class, one sect" (Stimpson was a coauthor of the ACLS report). But such pledges of allegiance to noncontroversial values do not themselves produce a rational, open-minded, and democratic discourse. Nor do they help to explain or clarify differing ideas; instead they are almost always ac-companied by denunciations of one's opponents outside academia as destroyers of the fragile fabric of democracy.

At a panel sponsored by the executive director of the MLA enti-tled "Answering Back: A Roundtable Discussion on the Future of the Profession,"[21] Stimpson's response to attacks in the press did not re-veal much evidence of open-mindedness, as she stressed the need to tell "our story," "not costermongering"; spoke of a desire for "hon-orable disagreements" instead of the current "dishonorable debate"; and denounced "cultural bombardiers trying to polarize debate" and, "in a vulgar way, trying to politicize debate" (her remarks were filled with war metaphors). This rhetorical strategy of placing one's oppo-nents' views and attitudes outside the circle of acceptable discussion (or in Stimpson's accusation of how others do it, polarizing debate) on the grounds that they are the ones who are "poisoning it"[22] is time-honored and hardly limited to academics, but it is still depressing how comfortable the leading figures of the MLA are with such strategies of denial, dismissal, and containment that avoid the consideration of any merit in opposing ideas and depend on a division between "us" and "them." Despite the espoused goal of entering a public dialogue, the primary professional gesture is to fend off questioning of universities by nonacademics and to *disqualify* hostile critics whose views, whether one likes it or not, have quite widespread support.

And to make sure we do not overlook this division, we (especially the untenured or less eminent academics) are asked to choose our side. Houston Baker, in his first newsletter essay as president of the MLA, writes: "After you have listened [to himself and Aimé Césaire, on the one hand, to an advertisement for *New Criterion*, on the other], I want you — like Milton's Adam and Eve facing a New World future in *Paradise Lost* — to decide which way to choose." He precedes this demand with the remark: "Who speaks and writes here — out of the most humanistic of motives — is a black man who feels that the type of nauseating verbiage that I am soon to quote for you is the last breath of white, male, Western anxiety engaged in a sputtering attempt to put out conflagrations that those of us who call ourselves NEW PEOPLE in no way started."[23] The prose of the *New Criterion* ad is equally overheated, bemoaning the abandonment "of Western thought for the compulsory study of 'third world' propaganda," expressing anxiety about "the politics of 'multiculturalism,'" and hoping to combat the "forces now determined to deconstruct our culture," but the effect of Baker's piece is to suggest that any professor who has misgivings about current trends in modern language studies is on the wrong side, about to be superseded, evil, and a disgrace to the profession. Identifying with the political Right, the male, the white, or the West (and Baker asks us here to choose our identifications, despite Césaire's invocation of "the furious WE" and "US") is apparently now a disqualification for academic employment, at least according to the president of the MLA.[24] Professional identity, Baker's "furious WE," would appear to be restricted to those who share his views. The act of becoming an academic critic is to be *grounded* on a withdrawal from the public, from an arena open to people of all views.

Academic critics, when they wish to be heard by a larger audience, need to reject such exclusionary practices and need to begin to think publicly — to think in ways that do not depend upon a split between the critic and the public. The desire to "popularize" academic criticism in one way or another is growing; one sees this in the turn to autobiography, popular culture, and the use of an informal or personal voice in much recent academic writing, as well as through the many books and articles about the relation of the professor to society. Most of the strategies offered for popularizing criticism suggest forms of *connecting* better with nonacademic audiences: using language that nonacademics can understand and examples with which they are more likely to be familiar; focusing on issues that directly affect large numbers of people, such as the educational programs and funding of community colleges, rather than the humanities debates in the Ivy League; or getting more people interested in and even participating in the debates that excite academic critics.[25] I am arguing, in contrast, that such suggestions will achieve little if the critical stance of the academic so often depends on a *disconnection* from the "public" — from an audience that is not limited in advance by a particular set of political or institutional interests. The hurdle is conceptual, and not simply a by-product of professional practices. Reaching out to selected others can certainly gain greater attention for a few academic critics, but if there is not a space for the public within academic criticism, for those who have not been initiated or do not share the position of the critic, any larger project of rejuvenating public discussion will be unsuccessful. I am not advocating a disinterested or nonpartisan criticism that appeals to a blank, unmarked, nondifferentiated "public," but instead a criticism that invites rather than disqualifies opposing opinions, that is open to the risk of being persuaded by the arguments of others, and that does not demand a *renunciation* of "participation in the present system" before discussion can begin.

Such demands for renunciation, in order to achieve a moral and intellectual purity, are quite common. Michel Foucault, for example, while discussing strategies for defeating "the system," goes so far as to state, "I think that to imagine another system is to extend our participation in the present system."[26] Foucault's desire for this sort of epistemological break helps account for his popularity. It is precisely this wish for a radical break from the ordinary and the present, and for a future not contaminated by or bound up with current institutions, that many academics identify with. But most people do not have the luxury of ending their participation in the present system, and such a stance forecloses any public dialogue until the time at which the "present system" is dismantled.

I have used the example of Huxley to illustrate the highly successful popularization of difficult and disturbing ideas and to emphasize the potential *openness* of his arguments — one need not become a scientist, or join a special "community," in order to learn from and engage with his ideas.[27] I do not want to propose that we "go back" to Huxley's form of criticism, that we embrace a notion of scientific reasoning as the basis for public discussion, or that we reject all of the criticism of the last fifty or one hundred years that challenges ideas of commonality (much less universality) and questions the projects of the Enlightenment. Yet the example of Huxley can still spur us to reconsider our habits, and our tendencies. In the aftermath of a critique of Enlightenment, of liberalism, and of "grand narratives," at a time of poststructuralism, postmodernism, and other forms of criticism that situate us on the other side of an earlier, homogeneous perspective, it has become too easy either to assume that criticism must require an incompatibility between an academic and a public perspective or to deny, in a celebration of difference, heterogeneity, and diversity, that any such divisions take place.

Public Dimensions of Academic Criticism

If my arguments at times sound naive, that is at least in part intentional, as I want to provoke us to think again about our critical assumptions and to question their consequences. A naive stance requires reconsidering what we in fact "know," especially insofar as we seek to communicate with others who do not share this knowledge. I am not suggesting that we reject criticism simply when we dislike what we take to be its consequences; to reject deconstruction, for example, since its "disturbance of a stable cognitive field,"[28] and its attention to indeterminacy, makes any exchange of opinion, any claim of a successful understanding of another's words, problematic. Yet we still need to examine whether our critical practices invite or repel disagreement, allow or foreclose the response of others, and encourage or inhibit further thinking and learning. Academics may very well dismiss the possibility of any meaningful public discussion, but if instead they seek to promote it, they cannot at the same time practice a criticism that negates what others may have to say and denies any common ground on which to forge a public.

Although I have invoked several times a notion of the "public" in

contrast to the "academic" and have insisted on the need to rejuve-
nate the public sphere, I have not provided more than an extremely
minimal conception of the public (potentially open to all the people,
not restricted in advance by institutional ties or political views), nor
have I offered either a theoretical model of public space or an analysis of the current possibilities of public discourse and of the various
"publics" that constitute American society. Such elaborations are all
worthwhile, and much excellent work has been done, particularly in
response to Habermas's writings.[29] But if the forms of thought and
argument of much academic criticism in fact undercut the desired engagement with a broader public (as I have been contending), the work
of academics will do little to contribute to a more vigorous public
sphere. In addition to theories and analyses of the public, we therefore need to scrutinize such "public" dimensions of academic criticism
as its openness to nonacademics, the ways in which the public is figured in academic writing, the extent to which academic criticism can
serve as a model of public space, and the interactions between the
media and academia.

But what is "academic criticism"? This is necessarily a very loose,
but not a meaningless, term. I have been using it both to refer generally to the professional writings of humanities professors (with an
emphasis on literary studies, which is often at the forefront of new
trends) and to characterize the tendencies of much recent criticism.
Although one could find examples of writing by professors that do
not seem to have any of the characteristics that I have described, I
think that it is still a useful designation, since humanities professors
to a large extent belong to the same, or to overlapping, "interpretive
communities" (to employ Stanley Fish's phrase, which he defines as:
"not so much a group of individuals who shared a point of view, but a
point of view or way of organizing experience that shared individuals
in the sense that its assumed distinctions, categories of understanding, and stipulations of relevance and irrelevance were the content
of the consciousness of community members who were therefore no
longer individuals, but, insofar as they were embedded in the community's enterprise, community property").[30] Yet how does one come
to distinguish "a point of view or way of organizing experience" that
defines an "interpretive community"? In this chapter, I have not analyzed any of the major works of the eminent professors that I have
mentioned (Fish, Graff, Stimpson, Baker, Greenblatt), nor have I pro-

vided an analysis of the key intersections of contemporary theory with the idea of the "public" (say, an analysis of the consequences of Foucault's *Discipline and Punish*, with its extreme critique of liberalism, for a reenvisioning of the public sphere), nor even an extended reading of a typical example of academic criticism. Instead, I have discussed pamphlets, prefaces, textbook essays, responses at talks, asides, interviews, newsletters — Can these fairly be said to represent academic criticism?

Yes. I could easily justify such an analysis by using as a model Freud's *Psychopathology of Everyday Life* or even discussing how a work such as Derrida's *Margins of Philosophy*, which analyzes such canonical writers as Plato, Kant, Hegel, and Heidegger, has nevertheless led to a widespread attention to the "margins" of writing ("scraps" like Nietzsche's "I have forgotten my umbrella" for Derrida,[31] all sorts of marginalia for others) rather than to the bold outlines of the major ideas. I could argue that such minor items in turn often reveal more about academic thinking than the polished essay, in which such characteristics as I have been analyzing may be obscured. But I want to suggest that the pamphlet, the preface, the newsletter, the interview, and even the aside are not minor or inconsequential but are in fact central forms for the institutionalization of criticism and for the functioning of an "interpretive community," in that they are a primary means of transmitting and shaping "the content of the consciousness of community members" and of embedding professors "in the community's enterprise."

These "minor" writings have major effects: they provide much of the "glue" of the interpretive community, defining our common interests and expressing the acceptable forms of professional behavior. Moreover, they reflect what is now assumed, understood, and habitual, and it is at this level — at the level of the ordinary — that the critical strategies that I have been analyzing, such as the foreclosure of discussion and the divisions between the academic critic and the public, are important. For although it may be the extraordinary essay, the difficult theory, or the ground-breaking book that offers the most powerful and profound critique of earlier models of thinking and that provokes, for instance, a radical reinterpretation of classic liberal notions of autonomy, the individual, and neutrality, such select writings cannot institutionalize — that is, make routine, accepted without further questioning — the exclusion of the public from academic discourse. Elsewhere I will explore what follows from a critique of liberalism and will discuss on what new basis notions of dialogue, democracy, and a public sphere can be formulated. But in order to address the possibilities of popularizing academic criticism, we need to focus on the disparities between the desires and claims to engage a broader public and the forms of thinking that severely constrain any such engagement.

This disparity is especially clear in the "public face" of academic criticism — in the newspaper interview, the TV appearance, the pamphlet that seeks to achieve a public voice and to reach a larger audience — where the appeals to openness, discussion, and exchange are most pronounced, yet so rarely achieved. Such types of discourse offer a disheartening window on the possibilities of popularizing academic criticism. For such a popularization to occur, aside from all the hurdles of gaining public attention in an age of television and celebrity, the divisions between the critic and the public that are interior to academic criticism will first have to be overcome.

institutional incentives, and professional boundaries that will have to be changed if criticism is again to play its Habermasian role of generating a public sphere, rather than its current function of discrediting the few remaining foundations on which a public dialogue might be established. But first I will discuss some of my own experiences in attempting to speak with a public voice and especially to consider how such a practice runs counter to my own training and formation as an academic critic.

✦

When the administration of Hampshire College (where I still teach) tried to deny me reappointment, I became embroiled in a controversy about academic freedom, political correctness, and the function of literary criticism. For the next year and a half, as my appeal wound its way through labyrinthine hearings to an ultimate victory, my case attracted a widening array of publicity: from the student newspaper, to local, regional, and finally national newspapers; to weekly journals and syndicated columnists; and to cable, local, and national public television. During this time I also gave talks at several universities, spoke at a university forum that was being filmed by the *MacNeil-Lehrer NewsHour*, and was interviewed on local public television.

I therefore had repeated occasions to speak and write to academic and to nonacademic audiences, and in these discussions and conversations I attempted not only (and often, not at all) to present my specific "case," but to convey my ideas about the relation of current controversies to developments in literary studies, critical theory, and academic behavior. To my surprise, I experienced a strong tension between addressing a public and an academic audience, and I felt more successful and more articulate in communicating my ideas to the anonymous lens of the TV camera than to an audience of my peers and colleagues. In contrast to earlier talks that I had given at conferences, in which the topic was one of specifically literary or theoretical interest (such as questioning the notion of "illustration" with regard to Oscar Wilde's *Salome*), here I was speaking about the intellectual and social consequences of certain trends of thought, about the principles that underlie a genuinely critical and educational dialogue, and about the criteria for judging professional competence and academic merit — that is, about the ways in which teaching and academic criticism are connected to the broader concerns of a democratic society. Why, for someone who does not really enjoy public speaking, who gets nervous before unfamiliar audiences, and who can be slow at responding to impromptu questions, was the imagined "public" of a TV audience preferable to the actual audience at a university?

In speaking not only *about* the public dimensions of literary criticism and university policies, but *to* a nonacademic audience, I had to conceive of the public as capable of making critical judgments and of participating in rational discussion. The whole point of addressing a public about academic issues is to invoke judgments about what is reasonable, fair, and in the social interest, and to do this one must speak not simply as a particular sort of literary critic (for example, someone highly versed in deconstruction or a scholar of aestheticism), but also as a citizen and as a member of society whose work as a professor has some significance and impact outside the groves of academe. One might therefore assume that talking to academics would be similar to and good preparation for talking to a general audience — after all, the one thing that academics should be most capable of is critical judgment. Yet the forms of critical judgment that appeal to an academic audience not only differ from those that one calls upon in addressing the public, but in fact cut the ground out from under them.

For example, instead of scrutinizing current practices and discourses as to how well they embody the ideals and traditions of democratic society, an academic critique is much more likely to challenge the worthiness and even the existence of any common ideals and principles or to argue for their subversion. Much of contemporary literary criticism derives its power precisely from challenging the possibility of a critical public and from attacking the philosophical foundations on which such a public could be conceptualized.

The common academic posture is one of suspicion and disbelief toward any widely held views, and the typical academic argument proceeds by challenging the wisdom of the past, discrediting traditional principles, and asserting that the real consequences of actions are the opposite of the stated intentions. Thus prison reform, rather than leading to more humane treatment of prisoners, yields greater discipline and control, and other social institutions, such as schools and families, are revealed in fact to have prison as their underlying model, not their antithesis.[2] But this habit of taking a "critical" stance has now become institutionalized to the point of presuming that the "public" is always under the ideological sway of distorting dominant forces and that whatever is commonly assumed is necessarily wrong. The broader public is therefore characterized not only as misguided, but as incapable even of participating in a genuinely critical discussion.

Only the oppositional voice, either of the academic or of someone outside the so-called dominant culture, is given credence by many academic audiences. The academic critique of institutions, which locates discriminatory attitudes in current social institutions rather than in individuals, implies that everyone is guilty until proven innocent. Only those who have already had their sensitivity raised to the insidiousness of sexism, racism, classism, and homophobia are deemed capable of participating in a free and open critical exchange of views with others. Moreover, the basic concepts of liberalism that ground the notion of a critical exchange of ideas as fundamental to a democratic society, and to the modern university as well, are especially subject to critique. Academic criticism not only bemoans the passing of the bourgeois public sphere, but insists on driving a stake through its faintly beating heart.

It is impossible to ground a public argument on such forms of criticism. Instead of telling people why they are incapable of correctly understanding one's arguments, one has to act as if *whoever* is listening is capable of being persuaded. And persuasion depends upon appealing to common principles and values. In speaking to a TV camera, and imagining a public, I, at any rate, felt that I needed to invoke principles such as toleration, rather than placing them perpetually *en abyme;* to support my arguments by connecting them to earlier texts and to moral and democratic traditions, rather than radically severing myself from a past contaminated by its unenlightened prejudices; and to presume that arguments do not depend irreducibly on the position of the speaker. What I found most frustrating in talking to academic audiences was the pressure always to declare what subject position I was speaking from — either progressive or reactionary, supporting or resisting "power" — so that the auditor could then filter and determine the real meaning of my ideas. Any purposeful public discussion, however, depends on the supposition that the interests and the position of the participants do not fully determine their ideas; otherwise there is nothing to discuss, and the "public" dissolves into an aggregation of private groups.

I am hardly suggesting that the public relations of literary criticism would be improved if academics appeared more often on television.

The popularity of television has obviously not contributed to a revitalization of the public sphere, and the performance of most literary critics on television during the political correctness controversy was disheartening. Nor am I suggesting that academics should act more like politicians and temper their critical views according to what the public might be ready to accept, being guided by surveys of public opinion. And I am certainly not advocating giving up the "critical" enterprise altogether and turning literary criticism into an adjunct of cultural marketing. But speaking to a TV camera can definitely help in formulating a criticism that appeals *for* a public, rather than erodes the foundations on which a public depends.

It is a good exercise to imagine a public and to ask of each critical project whether it can sustain a public discourse. For example, when criticism, as is often the case today, is defined as inherently "oppositional," as deriving its legitimacy from "opposing the social mainstream,"[3] it fails the test and is itself "in opposition" to a public discourse. For the stance of "opposition to the social mainstream" necessarily excludes the majority of the public and instead reinforces the gap between the academic critic and any present or future public. At some level, there are usually specific reasons for "opposition"—the discontent usually has some content to it—but when the actual goals, desires, views, and principles that motivate it are not articulated, they cannot be openly discussed and debated. Academic criticism too often fails to articulate views that invite public discussion and relies instead on pricking the ideological balloons of others.

A negative criticism generated from an epistemological resistance to "the ever-present danger of various sorts of totalizing and or totalitarian thinking," in the words of J. Hillis Miller,[4] or perhaps more simply, from a resistance to the dominant ideology, offers little basis for considering and evaluating different views, other than a united opposition against some internal or external bogeyman. Such a resolutely critical and oppositional stance not only undermines the grounds for a public discourse, but weakens the very frameworks for a just society. All of the cries for "social justice" do not supply the positive foundations upon which any public appeal to justice must rest. Academics, whatever their political or methodological orientation, have become too comfortable with their imagined oppositionality (perhaps as a compensation and a denial of their actual institutional, bureaucratic, and repetitive task of educating succeeding classes of students).

Even when the oppositional target is confined to some particular social evil such as "domination" or "inequality," the question constantly needs to be posed whether the criticism invites the public into a discussion about which forms of domination should be condemned or sanctioned, about the necessity or contingency of inequality in society, and about what role these concepts should play in our judgments; or whether the critical aim is instead to discredit any opposing views by characterizing them as complicit in domination and inequality, to divide the public into those who are on either the right or the wrong side, or to restrict discussion to those who already agree about the nature of the sins of contemporary society. Could any professor, whose institutional function is to certify students, really in good conscience argue unreservedly against complicity and domination? Academic criticism, by casting adherence to a polemical, critical vocabulary as intellectual accreditation, too often forecloses debate on the most contentious contemporary issues.

I am suggesting that the public relations of literary criticism should be based not on an appeal to the public (in an effort to win over the public to "our" side), but on an appeal *for* a public, and that this requires an appeal to commonalities, principles, and, yes, traditions, and not merely their questioning or debunking. The cutting edges of literary criticism (all the forms of negation, subversion, deconstruction, marginalization, difference, and so on, that now constitute an acceptable argument) can be reinterrogated by asking whether they can also give rise to a potentially public discourse. Yet more than a matter of principles or strategies is required if the public relations of literary criticism are really to be improved. For the current problems are not primarily a product of overzealousness, shortsightedness, critical rambunctiousness, or political discontent with the Reagan-Bush years. Institutional incentives create a frequent disjunction between academic and "public" perspectives. In academia, it is almost as if one had stepped through the looking glass with Alice and entered an inverted realm, in which what elsewhere is rejected as leading to failure is here embraced as the key to success.

It would be worthwhile to explore the evolution of criticism from a Habermasian function of grounding a public sphere to its current state in which a theoretical critique, driven by, in Paul de Man's words, a "principle of disbelief,"[5] has been conflated with an oppositional, political analysis to produce an academic criticism antagonistic to the very public it claims to speak for. Here I will only offer a typical example of the gap between academic and public thinking. In an essay solicited by the MLA for its volume entitled *The Transformation of English and American Literary Studies*, Homi Bhabha writes: "In this salutary sense, a range of contemporary critical theories suggest that it is from those who have suffered the sentence of history — subjugation, domination, diaspora, displacement — that we learn our most enduring lessons for living and thinking."[6] This "we" claims to speak with both an academic and a public voice; but the lessons are not the same for each. Although this statement has much in common with pious pronouncements from the Christian tradition, the usual message of education is that we learn from those who have *overcome* suffering, subordination, and displacement. For Bhabha, the lessons are to be learned from those who still speak from a subordinate position and who still suffer the *sentence* of history (Odysseus would here be a better model if he had remained forever with Kalypso). This is morally powerful — How can one deny the legitimacy and truth of a voice that suffers from the privileges that you have been given? — but it does not represent the "lessons for living and thinking" that most people need to get along.

For in the world outside of academia, speaking as one who suffers and is subordinated is emphatically *not* the way to succeed; such "lessons for living and thinking" lead to economic and social failure. It would be more accurate — and less compelling — to teach such lessons as morally correct, but as also entailing sacrifice and a renunciation of worldly gain. In academia, however, these attitudes, these lessons, are precisely the *road to* institutional success. The academic and the nonacademic person must learn very different lessons. We would take a step toward improving the public relations of literary criticism if we were less sanctimonious about the lessons that we have to offer and more willing to interrogate the disparities between academic and public voices.

5

CROSSING OVER:
THE ACADEMIC AS PORN STAR

◆

For anyone who has been away from academia for the last ten or twenty years, the idea that pornography would be a serious and widespread topic for discussion, especially in literary studies, would be shocking. After all, great works of literature reside at the opposite end of the cultural scale from mere pornography, and the entire function of education is involved in moving beyond the most primal instincts. That there would now be a professional interest in pornography — and not simply an attempt to claim that exceptional "pornographic" works by writers such as Sade and Bataille are in fact literary — seems only one more sign of the degeneration of the university and of the abdication of the responsibility (in Matthew Arnold's words) to "propagate the best that is known and thought in the world."[1]

Yet from inside the ivory tower, the rise of an academic discourse on pornography seems unexceptionable and even predictable. For the strongest current in recent literary criticism has been an interest in exploring and crossing boundaries. Terms such as "transgression," "subversion," and "violation" haunt the average academic essay, and the most common critical strategies demand a calling into question of accepted demarcations. If one wants to probe and to "problematize" borders, nothing offers so many possibilities as pornography. As soon as one moves pornography from an excluded topic to an object of study, one puts further pressure on such distinctions as those between disinterested criticism and arousal, the public and the personal, the mind and the body, high and low culture, or theory and practice. Pornography, as an exemplary limit case, forces us to rethink the construction of limits. And the very act of examining the power of pornography already works to redraw boundaries, even, perhaps, against our intentions. The "pornographic" opening of Catharine MacKinnon's *Only Words* may be an appeal to recriminalize pornography, but it also functions to break down the etiquette of Harvard University Press and to legitimize pornography by further incorporating it into the realm of exclusive scholarship.[2] The emerging academic discourse on pornography may still have some shock value, but it is also part of the mainstream of contemporary academic criticism.[3]

If the study of pornography offers an exemplary means of exploring the current border crossings of academia, of performing "transgression," and even of pursuing what is often left implicit, unexamined, or repressed in much academic discourse, one way to write the recent history of literary criticism would be to chart the collapse of a radical and obvious opposition between "literary merit" and "pornography" and to portray this collapse as emblematic of the challenging of so many hierarchical oppositions. One could begin by quoting, for example, from Judge Woolsey's decision, still found at the beginning of the Random House edition of *Ulysses*, which speaks of "Joyce's sincerity and of his honest effort to show exactly how the minds of his characters operate."[4] These phrases do little to offer us a compelling version of what literary merit or artistic value is. Rather, what is curious is that a federal judge's decision serves as the preface to one of the masterpieces of twentieth-century literature (and my editions of Baudelaire's *Les fleurs du mal* and Flaubert's *Madame Bovary* also contain judges' decisions about these works). The founding gesture of the institutionalization of modernism is, "This is not pornography." Why is there a need to proclaim these works' legitimacy? And why is this achieved by reference to pornography, even if only in negation?

At stake are defining and controlling the strategies of reading. Judge Woolsey writes that in *Ulysses* "I do not detect anywhere the leer of the sensualist," find nothing "that I consider to be dirt for dirt's sake," that "nowhere does it tend to be an aphrodisiac," and especially, that the book "did not tend to excite sexual impulses or lustful thoughts." And this is what he must conclude in order to determine that *Ulysses* is not legally obscene: that the work does not tend "to stir the sex impulses or to lead to sexually impure and lustful thoughts." But an entire programmatics of reading is contained here. The normal reader, or *l'homme moyen sensuel* that Woolsey appeals to, *should* not be aroused by this work, *should* maintain a clear separation between his own thoughts and those of the characters, and *should* find "sexual impulses" or "lustful thoughts" sublimated into "a somewhat tragic and very powerful commentary on the inner lives of men and women."

This distinction between the lustful and the literary is already troubled by an author who, in Woolsey's words, "has honestly attempted to tell fully what his characters think about" and who has therefore used "certain words which are generally considered dirty words" and presented "what many think is a too poignant preoccupation with sex in the thoughts of his characters."[5] If an honest portrayal may require a "preoccupation with sex," what is to preclude the stirring of the sexual impulses of the reader, whose thoughts may be equally preoccupied with sex? Judge Woolsey states, "In respect of the recurrent emergence of the theme of sex in the minds of his characters, it must always be remembered that his locale was Celtic and his season Spring," and he adds, Joyce "seeks to draw a true picture of the lower middle class in a European city" (x). The "normal reader" of the American public is further protected from "impure and lustful thoughts" by the divisions of ethnicity, class, and geography.

But what if one were to be aroused while reading *Ulysses?* What if the book did stir one's sex impulses? To undo the defense against pornography is to offer up other possible ways of reading, to question all of the presumptions that go into the construction of the "normal reader," and to erode the division between one's own sensations and those of the characters. Leopold Bloom may get off watching Gerty MacDowell reveal her thighs, but the reader is not supposed to (and Judge Woolsey, through checking his impressions by the "hypothetical reagent" of "a person with average sex instincts" — in this case, "two friends of mine who in my opinion answered to the above stated requirement for my reagent" — concludes that the reader will not be stirred by this masturbatory scene). Yet the distinctions between literature and pornography, sublimation and arousal, self and other, are on shaky ground here, as this episode of *Ulysses* is, among other things, a parody of pornographic writing. Here is the scene of orgasm:

> She would fain have cried to him chokingly, held out her snowy slender arms to him to come, to feel his lips laid on her white brow the cry of a young girl's love, a little strangled cry, wrung from her, that cry that has rung through the ages. And then a rocket sprang and bang shot blind and O! then the Roman candle burst and it was like a sigh of O! and everyone cried O!

O! in raptures and it gushed out of it a stream of rain gold hair
threads and they shed and ah! they were all greeny dewy stars
falling with golden, O so lively! O so soft, sweet, soft! (366–67)

This scene also collapses the internal thoughts and sensations of the
characters with the external description of a scene of fireworks, but
this multiplicity of references cannot define the work as intrinsically
literary.[6] It may have been necessary to establish a firm boundary between pornography and literature in order to allow *Ulysses* to cross
our borders, in order to allow the book to be imported into the United
States, but the dictum "This is not pornography" functions to set strict
limits within which our reading should take place. The legitimation of
modernism patrols the very borders that the work transgresses.

All of the strategies of reading that are now current under the
rubric of "postmodernism" attack these divisions that the law is trying to maintain, these boundaries that separate off the deviant from
the normal, that present *l'homme moyen sensuel* as the figure of universal experience, that distinguish between the idiosyncratic and the
"more objective" reading, and that seek to preclude the body of
the reader from the literary experience. Pornography, as that which
aims to stimulate the body of the beholder, puts especial pressure on
these oppositions that regulate the relation between public discourse
and private experience. Pornography, in fact, often involves precisely
crossing the line between public and private; sexual activity becomes
pornographic when it is made public, when it is presented before
others. I particularly want to explore the crossings of the lines between
private and public, since one of the key features of contemporary academic criticism is the publicization, the performance, and even the
professionalization of the private; there is an odd symmetry between
pornography and current academic discourse. But first I want to consider more generally some of the ways in which the engagement with
pornography functions as the quintessential form of academic border
crossing, and to consider the ramifications of these excursions.

Border Crossing

Pornography immediately puts in question the boundary between the
academic and the nonacademic, between the legitimate and the ille-

gitimate object of inquiry. If pornography, even, can become a "text" for academic analysis, is there anything that still remains excluded? Pornography, as a refusal of the avenues of sublimation, challenges the criteria of value and distinction by which decisions of exclusion and inclusion into the academic domain are made. Pornography is therefore an excellent vehicle for attempting to reach beyond the traditional borders of academia.

Moreover, pornography explicitly raises questions of legitimacy and legality. Certain forms of pornography are still illegal, and any examination of pornography forces a consideration of the primary social mechanisms for drawing and enforcing laws, norms, and codes of behavior. The interrogation of pornography brings into the open the often disguised forces of administration and control. Pornography, then, offers the academic a powerful opportunity to explore — and also to cross — the societal boundaries of the "law" and of the academic institution itself.

A favorite border for the divagations of academic criticism these days is that of gender, and pornography inescapably forces consideration of gender, sexuality, and sexual orientation, for these categories present fault lines across which a common response cannot be assumed or hypothesized. There is not *one* proper, acceptable, or common response to pornography; the subject position in pornography is not universalizable. Porn fractures the mythology of the common, which is built around a possibility of shared discourse, and of an always attainable intersubjectivity. Differences are activated by pornography, whether along the spectrum of male and female, passive and active, homosexual and heterosexual, dominant and subordinated, or inhibited and permissive. Despite the mobility within these categories, there is an irreducibility of difference in the responses to pornography that challenges the Arnoldian — and the academic — ideal of a "right reason" and a general "humanity" that overcomes difference, even to the point of achieving Arnold's goal (and I have been using Matthew Arnold as the convenient whipping boy for contemporary criticism, despite the ways in which this inspector of schools often provides a none-too-plump target for such attacks), the goal of taking the Barbarians, the Philistines, and the Populace "out of their class."[7]

Pornography also puts the subject at risk. For the teacher, there are genuine risks to studying pornography with students, and porn, as a topic of study, generates discomfort.[8] The constant discourse today on sexuality finally attains a safeness and a security that the move to experiencing pornography shatters. Porn performs a type of assault, an invasion. The integrity of the body is fragmented by pornography, and for everyone some variety of porn, whether due to its explicitness, its violence, its sexual orientation, its breaking of taboos, or its choice of orifice, will be received as an attack. Pornography assaults the integrity of the subject.

Pornography crosses the boundaries not only of law and institution, and of subjectivity, but of the critical act itself. Pornography undermines a pretense to critical distance and a stance of aesthetic judgment, insofar as it negates any pure claim of disinterestedness. A purely "disinterested" experiencing of pornography — in which there is no engagement of desire — is finally no experience at all.

I could go on at great length establishing in further detail what I hope by now is an obvious point: pornography engages many of the favorite aspects of academic border crossing and in fact provides an exemplary space for the playing out of theory insofar as it consists of various forms of putting into question the limits and boundaries of interpretative categories. But if I have succeeded in making the case that pornography can be understood as an academic topic par excellence, I have not yet asserted that its academic scrutiny accomplishes much of anything. What does one do to a boundary when one crosses it? Does one change a border merely by demonstrating that it is traversable? What is accomplished by acts of critical transgression, subversion, or violation? Is anything liberated by *overtly* bringing pornography into the groves of academe?

The answer I think, which one might either laud or decry, is: very little. Academic border crossing does not necessarily do much even to redraw the borders of academia. I will briefly consider why the incorporation of porn into academia does little to stimulate academic thought; I will not mount a comprehensive argument for this failure of critical invigoration, but only point out some of the paradoxes of this failure. For I want to explore the much more compelling phenomenon of crossing the academic border in the other direction: the attempt to cross over into more public spheres and to reconfigure social boundaries, which I will argue only achieves the illicit public status of the porn star.

Academic Masochism

The reception of pornography as a legitimate topic of academic inquiry offers the sign that academic thought is not cordoned off by the walls of high culture or bourgeois morality and is in fact open to penetration and violation. The burgeoning interest in sadomasochism even dramatizes the various and ambivalent pleasures of this reception. Yet the ease of the reception of the previously forbidden topic is inversely proportional to the disturbance that it then offers to the teleology, to the aims and endpoints, of the critical argument. Too great an openness results in foreclosing any challenge to the foundations of one's ideas. Fashionable academic criticism may be able to accommodate even the most outrageous object, but the institutional context, in which one now knows what to do with the disturbing text — that is, to use it to offer, say, yet another challenge to male subjectivity or to "perform" yet another "radical" critique of the failure of the text to achieve its revolutionary potential — repositions, resituates, and reconstitutes pornography as just one more analogous object for academic discourse. Pornography becomes just another text. Institutional receptivity, by providing a *sanctioned* space in which certain borders may be, must be, crossed, functions as a prophylactic and can contain any too disturbing consequences with its always available models for theorizing transgression. Academics really do promote "safe sex," but the porousness of the canonical boundaries that now makes it so much easier to bring new objects under academic scrutiny displaces attention away from all the ways in which academic discourses insulate the critic from a broader public and diminishes greatly any impact that a "transgressive" critique may have on others.

I recently read an essay that had as its epigraph: "A hunky blond slave, totally hairless, his mouth hanging open like a dog's, his cock hard for his master."[9] The modern essay begins with Montaigne, who called his writings *essais* for their attempt to try out thoughts, to test ideas, to speculate. He began his essays with epigraphs and excerpts from classical writers, and especially in his early writings, he proceeded by using these fragments from the past as spurs for scrutinizing his ideas (and Montaigne, of course, had a medal engraved with the motto "Que scay-je?" [What do I know?]).[10] Beginning an essay with "his cock hard for his master" offers a parody and a travesty of Montaigne and violates so many of our received notions of propriety. Yet once one does this, what else is to be said? Only that nothing much has happened — one can still go on to write an extremely predictable academic essay. This "hard cock" finally offers no more stimulus for "thinking," for having to consider the world in a different manner, than anything else. In this end-of-the-line version of the essay, we get the reverse of Montaigne: rather than a harvest of classical quotes providing the essential stimulation for original "essays," for trying something out, even the most blatant figures of stimulation cannot rouse one to think very much at all. Academic masochism — the receptivity by which any foreign object can be incorporated — only reflects back the all-too-knowing gaze of the professor. The academicization of pornography yields diminishing returns. Its disruptive potential depends on its shocking a public, but the assimilation of pornography into the mainstream of academic discourse deprives it of both its shock and its "public," encapsulating it in a discourse that is largely inaccessible to those outside the academy.[11]

Pornography functions as the perfect fantasy of border crossing. One goes out into the gritty world of sleaze, semen, and exploitation in order to bring these experiences into the formalized domain of academic writing. But at a moment when cultural studies has already displaced any monumental notion of the literary work, the critical framework need not be disturbed by the introjection of the pornographic text. Freud, in his essay "Die Verneinung" (On negation), states that a psychological origin of the function of intellectual judgment can be found in the decision "to assert or deny that a thing has a particular property," a decision that, "expressed in the language of the oldest, that is, of the oral, instinctual impulses," runs thus: " 'I should like to eat that, or I should like to spit it out'; or, carried a stage further: 'I should like to take this into me and keep that out of me.' That is to say: it is to be either *inside* me or *outside* me."[12] The academic attention to pornography introjects what has been deemed "bad" or "harmful" by proper society and thus assumes to have challenged the foundational categories of social judgment. Yet only another form of denial and displacement is at work here, to the extent that academic writing on pornography fails to challenge the borders that cordon off academic work from the broader arenas of public discussion. The improper may be introjected, but this changes little of the judgmental structures at work in society. Academia is not a simple synecdoche for other institutions, and the *frisson* of transgression at crossing one boundary only masks the recognition of the impotence to affect others.

Whether or not the academic institution can incorporate pornography without difficulty finally makes little difference for changing or enlarging the realm within which academic discourse has any effect at all. The interest in pornography may arise from a reaction against the confines of traditional academic topics and be part of an effort to open things up, to look outward, and to put into question any boundaries that separate "academic" experience from all other types, but the actual purpose is only to change the way people think within academia. Another aspect of academic border crossing, however, is aimed at accomplishing something much more profound, at radically altering all that it touches. The objective of socially oriented criticism has long been to reinvigorate, or even re-create, public spheres of discussion and activity, but in the age of the triumph of the electronic media, any faith that the best thoughts will win out in the marketplace of ideas has wilted.

Performers That Matter

Without a well-functioning, Habermasian public sphere, and in the face of an overwhelmingly hegemonic consumer culture, there is little public place for the voices of literary critics or humanities professors. In order to "go public" and have academic discourse make a difference, one of the main currents has been to rethink and reshape the character of discourse itself. Thus we now continually have a shift from a cognitive to a performative strategy — from the attainment and transmission of knowledge to an insistent playing out of the ways that words "actually do things."[13] A focus on the performative aspect of language draws attention to the ways in which language engages others and accomplishes an action.[14] Under this dual imperative of performance and performativity, the critic's own person often becomes the vehicle for insight, impact, and success.

At first glance, it is not at all clear why socially effective or critical thought should have anything to do with personal exposure. Narcissism provides one of the strongest barriers to insight. Fifteen years ago, in an essay that explores so many forms of academic resistance, Paul de Man still tries to maintain the barrier against the exposure of the personal in academic thought, a barrier that his own "case" finally did a lot to demolish. In the essay "The Resistance to Theory" he writes:

Overfacile opinion notwithstanding, teaching is not primarily an intersubjective relationship between people but a cognitive process in which self and other are only tangentially and contiguously involved. The only teaching worthy of the name is scholarly, not personal; analogies between teaching and various aspects of show business or guidance counseling are more often than not excuses for having abdicated the task.[15]

This assertion that the scholarly is in direct opposition to the personal has been challenged by many forms of contemporary criticism that bring sharp attention to the functioning of the body, of sexuality, of materiality, of desire, and of identity, in discourse and in its analysis. It is almost de rigueur to include autobiographical moments, personal anecdotes, or at least familial stories in one's criticism today, as a means of situating and displacing the critical act away from an earlier, discredited model of objective, neutral, and disinterested scholarship. But the move to foreground the personal is an attempt less to "ground" a cognitive insight in personal truth than to insist that the "cognitive process" always has a performative dimension and that the act of "knowing" can be one not only of deconstruction, but of reconstruction as well. The move to the personal is a means of harnessing the "performative force"[16] of the critical act to disrupt the traditional barriers that frame criticism as completely independent from the conditions of its enunciation. De Man, of course, is one of the figures whose analysis of performatives has taught us a lot about "how to do things with words," and after a "linguistic turn," in which the importance of language and discourse in the construction of reality has been recognized, it is only a short step to arriving at a criticism that valorizes "making a spectacle of oneself."

I can only allude here to the shift that has occurred from analyzing the disruptive potential of performatives in literary texts to the attempts to incorporate the lessons that "words... actually do things"[17] into a critical discourse that now seeks to change the very conditions that it analyzes. It would take a long study to examine the changes in criticism in the last twenty or so years, in which an emphasis on a deconstruction that analyzes the unsynthesizable differences within texts has been incorporated into, or given way to, a critique that focuses on categories of difference in the hope, finally, of making a difference in society. It is not hard to understand the appeal, for example, of hearing that the very critical act that calls "a presupposition into question" can thereby "permit the term to occupy and to serve different political aims" and to initiate "new possibilities."[18] The literary or cultural critic can now hope to have some impact, can hope to reroute political trajectories and open up new possibilities, all through deploying our hard-learned critical lessons. But to have much effect, this performance requires a larger audience: the performance and the exposure of the personal, the making public of one's self, now function as the paradigm for this attempt to cross over from academia into other public spheres.

The supposition is that crossing the boundary between the private and the public offers a model not only for inserting oneself into public categories, but for actually performing in a way that demonstrates the constructedness and fluidity of categories taken for natural and fixed (such as gender). Thus the academic performance holds out the possibility of contagion, of leading many others to speak and act out, and in turn to redirect and recast their performances. But what kind of public effect do these academic border crossings actually have? How shall we review these performances? And does the achievement of notoriety or even celebrity offer a useful criterion for gauging their impact or success?

There has been a lot of "personal exposure" of academics lately. This has been happening both from the directions of biography and autobiography. Biographical exposure primarily takes the form of revealing something previously hidden, such as Paul de Man's collaborationist writings or Michel Foucault's bathhouse exploits and sadomasochism. The revelation of the personal here often works to delegitimate, or at least contextualize, the critical voice in a way that makes it appear idiosyncratic and thereby less authoritative. There is no claim for greater public impact of the critical work through the revelation of the personal, even if very interesting questions about the relation between the thought and the life are raised.[19]

Autobiographical exposure, however, is more a making public of the private than of the hidden and is an attempt to gain legitimacy and authority by making one's own body matter. Eve Sedgwick's autobiographical and poetic anal eroticism, to use an early example, works to establish her authority and does so not only by demonstrating a per-

sonal experience of a field of knowledge, or demonstrating a high level
of insight or self-awareness, but also by performing the gesture, "I am
now a public figure."[20] The assertion in such acts of exposure is not
only that my ideas gain impact through my body, but that my private
life, my sexuality, my body, is of interest — even a source of desire —
to others. What we have then is an assumption of celebrity, an acting
in the mode of the star, about whom there is always a public interest
in the most private details.

This mode of "going public" is grounded on the claim, "I can
cross the line" — the line between personal and public, anonymity
and recognition, propriety and impropriety, taking it in and talking
back. Such a gesture negates the traditional boundaries of academic
professionalism, but what sort of engagement with a "public" does it
achieve?

The notion of the "public" in our postmodern televisual age is no-
toriously problematic, and it is far easier to use as an oppositional
term (public versus private, or public versus academic) than to define in any minimally adequate manner. Moreover, there are always
various "publics," rather than one homogenous or all-encompassing
public. Yet the public sphere that intellectuals ardently yearn for would
require an arena for discussing and contesting issues of broad social interest. When the notion of the "public" is itself framed along
the lines of celebrity, of coming into the view of many (anonymous)
others, however, there is no place for discussion with those who disagree, no possibility to persuade others through conversation, and no
participation in an interchange with those who have widely different
presuppositions or ideas. The appeal here is only for those who want
to cross over in turn.

A model of the "public" that is achieved by transgressing the
boundaries of the "private" is at odds with the critical goal of forging a public through intellectual exchange; these two conceptions of
the "public" have not been reconciled. A public sphere (or even a
"national conversation," as envisioned by President Clinton) cannot
be founded on a continual performance of transgression. A public
dialogue requires a conception of the individual as freely able to formulate his or her opinions; a politics of transgression, in contrast,
presupposes enslaving conventions that must be breached in order to
enter into the arena of the "public." Transgression is not equivalent to
contestation and succeeds more by arousing mimetic desire (you too

can join our select group) than by achieving persuasion (these ideas are more valid than others).[21]

The phenomenon of academic celebrity — of some academics becoming "stars" within academia, for particular nonacademic audiences, and even occasionally becoming the subject of *New York Times Sunday Magazine* profiles (thus becoming officially endowed with a biography that is of interest to others) — provides scant evidence of an important civic sphere of "critical exchange and broad reflection,"[22] in which academics in the humanities could play a leading role. Although Madonna (the subject of so much academic discussion) continually attracts a public through transgression, academic border crossing — which still relies ultimately on some conception of the intellectual, and all of the borders that this role entails, for its claim of authority and effectivity — comes off as a form of parody. Always questioning the legitimacy of other institutional and cultural structures, academic critics only confirm their own relegation to a realm of quasi-legitimacy, and only achieve the celebrity of the porn star.

The analogy of academic and porn star may seem a bit forced, but it actually brings out a lot of similarities. One of the less-talked-about aspects of being a professor is the sheer repetition of what is supposed to be a new and initiatory act of learning: doing it again for the very first time. Moreover, pornography always offers the promise of an ultimate revelation, of attaining an explicitness that will finally expose the mystery of the sexual act. But this promise, like the academic enticement of gaining an ultimate knowledge and mastery, is never fulfilled. Pornography and higher education both always promise more than they can deliver, appealing to the insatiable drives to look and to know (the "Schau- und Wisstrieb," brilliantly analyzed by Freud in his essay on Leonardo). Here, however, I mainly want to suggest the similarity of status between the celebrity critic and the porn star, neither able, with rare exceptions, to cross over into "legitimacy" and into a more-than-marginal public prominence.

The "disrepute" of the academic haunts critical writing these days. Whether in a book like *Secular Vocations: Intellectuals, Professionalism, Culture*, which seeks to defend the contemporary academic against the charges of betraying the role of the intellectual, or a jeremiad like *Dogmatic Wisdom: How the Culture Wars Divert Education and Distract America*,[23] which aims to confirm an impression of how bad the situation really is even as it claims to direct a searing attack on the

right-wing critics of academia, the status of the "academic intellectual" is the source of immense anxiety. The driving concern is around
the ability of the academic intellectual to play a meaningful and consequential role in society, and "disrepute" is figured as a lack of public
currency, as an inability to achieve the public influence commensu-
rate with the vast accumulation of knowledge and intelligence. From
both the Left and the Right, from both those who claim academics
have betrayed their profession and from those who attack a consumer
society that has lost sight of the importance of intellectual pursuits,
there is the suggestion that intellectuals are not fulfilling their public
mission and that academics in the humanities are undergoing a crisis
of legitimation.

The argument that pornography is not a legitimate form of public
expression arises from many fronts and involves more than the notion
that the border between public and private has been violated (that
explicit sexual activity ought to remain strictly private). There is also
the claim that the performance itself is "illegitimate," is not a genuine form of acting, and is only a matter of body parts, rather than
a skillful incarnation of a fully developed persona, with an expressive,
interior consciousness. Pornography thus assaults the cherished conception of the autonomous, unified, and self-controlling individual,
upon which distinctions between public and private rest. The stage
was at one time described as the "legitimate" theater, against the acting in Hollywood in which the camera, rather than a "live" audience,
was the medium for reception, and pornography further shatters this
dream of a present, public audience, which in its ideal form is figured
as the polis that attended the Athenian theater.

The academic faces a similar bind, of only further rupturing the polis that he or she seeks to influence. The challenge is not only to "cross
over" the boundaries that restrict academic discourse — whether to a
tarnished goal of objectivity and disinterestedness, to social inefficacy,
or merely to a small audience — but to envision and establish a domain that can be crossed into as well. Every academic discourse that
seeks the lure of a genuinely public horizon must be tested against
what social possibilities — and not only what forms of critique — it
gives rise to.

Pornography then, despite its entry into the academic mainstream,
is neither a vehicle nor a model for academics seeking to enter the
mainstream. Only if one adopts the perspective of Catharine MacKin-

non and Edwin Meese, in which pornography functions either as the basic model of patriarchal society or as the most prominent threat to social values, only if one adopts this view of porn as either coextensive with the basic institutional structures of society or containing the power utterly to erode them, does pornography offer a promise for an effective academic discourse.[24] Both of these positions require a resolutely antitheatrical understanding of pornography (for Meese and MacKinnon, pornography is less performed than inflicted), since it is the literalness of the act — of degradation, violation, or even only penetration — that is the source of its power. The public penetration of bodies, the crossing of the limits that should properly separate individuals, becomes an instance of the failure to protect either the autonomy of women or the integrity of the uncorrupted. If one accepts this view of pornography, however, the promise is no longer one of performance and border crossing, but only of securing the borders all that much tighter.

~ Part III ~

Failed Encounters: Dialogue or Chatter?

6

CRITICISM AS DISPLACEMENT

◆

The literary critic typically proceeds by applying a framework of interpretation to a literary text. Such a statement, which emphasizes our structures of thought rather than the "primary" work to which we respond, is not terribly controversial in the aftermath of literary theory.[1] For the rise of literary theory has heightened our awareness of the interpretative frameworks that we employ and of the implications of our methodological choices. It is no longer respectable to presume that we could somehow dispense with the entire panoply of frameworks and schools of interpretation and either achieve an unmediated relation to "the text itself" or arrive at the "true" (and thus final) understanding of the work.[2] The ability to generate critical readings by consciously employing such frameworks as deconstruction, new historicism, postmodernism, and queer theory certifies one's professional competence.

The knowledge that we cannot transcend all interpretative frameworks (the set of concerns, the strategies of reading, the assumptions about texts, and the hopes for analysis that structure our criticism) has not led to a greater contentment with the prevailing models. Quite the contrary. Many critics want to break free from their constraint, particularly insofar as they have come to see the forms of interpretation as institutional, professional, and academic — as driven by the logic of the discipline and the university, rather than by the concerns of the larger society. This desire is no longer directed toward gaining an individual experience of the literary work, free from social or institutional mediation, but instead toward situating the "institution" within a societal context, in order to overcome all that insulates the literature professor from the world beyond the university. Rather than attempts to get "outside" any framework, we now see efforts to incorporate the concerns and the problems of the "outside" world into

115

our modes of interpretation. The aim is to reorient (not deny) our interpretative frameworks and to move beyond a preoccupation with issues that are "internal" to literary study in order to address matters of public concern.

Edward Said has been instrumental in this shift from "pure" literary theory to socially oriented criticism. Although his book *Beginnings* and his essays that helped introduce Foucault to an American audience established Said early on as a central figure in literary theory, he has long attacked theory, and he has advocated in contrast the role of the public (and the "organic") intellectual.[3] One instance of this appeal for a less insular criticism is Said's attack, in his recent *Culture and Imperialism*, on the transformation of theory into an academic subspeciality. He deplores the current emphasis on theory:

Cults like post-modernism, discourse analysis, New Historicism, deconstruction, new-pragmatism transport them [intellectuals in the American university] into the country of the blue; an astonishing sense of weightlessness with regard to the gravity of history and individual responsibility fritters away attention to public matters, and to public discourse. The result is a kind of floundering about that is most dispiriting to witness, even as the society as a whole drifts without direction or coherence. Racism, poverty, ecological ravages, disease, and an appallingly widespread ignorance: these are left to the media and the odd political candidate during an election campaign.[4]

It is striking that Said published these remarks in 1993; they seem more apposite for 1983. He speaks as if the substantial changes in literary criticism of recent years had not taken place; as if race, class, and gender were not the most discussed topics of the day. The new critical orientation is almost entirely in the direction of "social justice" and embraces the leftish political concerns sketched by Said (the call is not one for individual liberty or greater freedom from government). He suggests that a more socially oriented and coherent literary criticism can fulfill an important public function, one that is being poorly served by the media and by politicians: that of an educator and a conscience for the public. It is no longer sufficient, however, to discuss a criticism directed toward "public matters" in purely prospective terms.

For Said, the major barrier to a more socially significant literary criticism is the professional and theoretical self-absorption of the academic critic. He asserts that we now have

> a steadily more powerful cult of expertise, whose main ideological burden stipulates that social, political, and class-based commitments should be subsumed under the professional disciplines, so that if you are a professional scholar of literature or a critic of culture, all your *affiliations* with the real world are subordinate to your professing in those fields. Similarly, you are *responsible* not so much to an audience in your community or society, as to and for your corporate guild of fellow experts, your department of specialization, your discipline. (321; emphasis added)[5]

The issue here is that of the critic's *connections:* to the community, society, and the "real world"; or to the cult, the guild, and the profession. Said condemns interpretative frameworks based primarily on a theoretical and technical mastery insofar as they lead to a "cult of expertise" and to placing one's allegiance to the profession above all else.

Such arguments about the need for a more socially and politically engaged criticism have been well heeded; but what has been the result? Does the acknowledgment of social commitments by academic critics in any way "deprofessionalize" criticism or yield work that is not "subsumed under the professional disciplines"? Stanley Fish has repeatedly argued the contrary and asserted that "anti-professionalism" is in fact the quintessential professional gesture of academic literary criticism.[6] And Bruce Robbins, a critic very sympathetic to Said, straddles the positions of Fish and Said as he attempts to articulate "how oppositional work is conceivable within a professional framework."[7] What would it mean for such a subsumption "under the professional disciplines" not to take place? What would such a criticism look like?

I ask these questions because we now have in the universities a literary criticism that claims a strong responsibility to "community or society," even though it is still highly professional, academic, and addressed largely to "a corporate guild of fellow experts." I want to consider whether shifting the concerns of literary criticism — away from the "technical," professional interests of the discipline toward much broader cultural and social issues — will provide us with a more significant criticism, and one that is of interest also to those who are not professional critics. If literary critics are to do more than engage in "a powerful cult of expertise," not only must social concerns be brought into the critical arena, but the discussion must extend out-ward as well; otherwise we will have a politics just for literary criticism. Can literary criticism help begin a critical dialogue that confronts the concerns of those outside academia — of the inequalities between people, not just the formal relations of literary language — and encour-age people other than professors (and their students) to participate in this much needed discussion?

Said argues that literary critics need to reestablish connections, and not just between the university and the "community or society," but also between the dominant cultural tradition and all that it has ex-cluded, repressed, or ignored. One of Said's major aims is to get us to read texts such as Austen's *Mansfield Park* and Dickens's *Great Ex-pectations* — texts that do not directly thematize imperialism as does Conrad's *Heart of Darkness* — with an awareness of all that connects culture to "the imperial process of which they were manifestly and un-concealedly a part" (xiv). He now often gets his wish. In his wake, readers now rarely look for a catachresis, an aporia, or a moment of undecidability with which to deconstruct a text, but instead resolutely seek out all the traces of imperialism in a novel in order to make their arguments.

I do not see how postcolonial studies (at least in American univer-sities) or other new specialties such as queer theory or Chicano studies are less cultish or guildlike than ones that do not overtly stress a so-cial connection. Postcolonial or gay studies is not simply an "area" — a group of texts that have something to do with imperialism or homo-sexuality — but an academically trained way of reading (and Said, of course, is not calling for a rejection of academic training in order to read more like the man in the street, but only for a redirection of critical interests). Both a new-pragmatist and a postcolonial reading ask a set of questions and employ a set of techniques that have been defined and validated largely by previous scholars. A shift in interpre-tative frameworks does not bring about a criticism that is less oriented toward or less shaped by one's academic colleagues. A queer theorist can be very involved in ACT-UP or in gay community work and still write essays that deploy "a powerful cult of expertise" inaccessible to those beyond the university and that rely on political and social as-sumptions whose validity is apparent mainly to other academics. At a time when the profession now embraces an ethos of social concern, displaying community allegiances can even be the right step to take for professional advancement.

Said, by downplaying the extent to which literary criticism has moved in the directions he advocates, avoids the heavy burden of either demonstrating that the new criticisms are in fact leading toward "the improvement and non-coercive enhancement of life in a community" — Said's goal for criticism — or explaining why they are not. He also avoids acknowledging how much recent socially oriented criticism (including his own) has borrowed from "theory." Many of the lessons and practices of deconstruction (attention to margins, strategies for disrupting the logic of binary oppositions and for "decentering," and so on) have been appropriated in critiques that now stress cultural "difference" rather than *différance*. Even many of the people who used to practice the types of criticism denounced by Said as "cultish" now produce more socially concerned analyses.

I do not think we can wait, therefore, until there is sufficient evidence that literary criticism has become intimately connected again to the vital forces of society, before exploring whether the attempt to address public matters through literary studies is succeeding. I have been placing an emphasis on interpretative frameworks to help highlight the political ideas, social aims, and philosophical theories that animate recent criticism. Despite the seeming proliferation of new theories, and the conflicts about which texts should be taught and even about whether "literature" is still a meaningful term, academic criticism is by no means in a state of anarchy. Such new approaches as ethnic, feminist, gay, post-Marxist, cultural, and postcolonial criticism largely share a common paradigm. They focus above all on analyzing forms of inequality and domination, and they aim to envision and help bring about a more equal world, or in Said's words, "a community or culture . . . that is not based on coercion or domination" (335). Can the adoption of this paradigm generate a criticism that is socially engaged, politically effective, democratic, and liberatory?

My contention is that so far it has not and that literary analysis now offers a poor vehicle for debating political issues. The usual response by writers who seek a more socially significant criticism is that academics need to address a "public" audience and forgo their jargon, their merely technical interests, and their professional habits. I will argue instead that although the new interpretative frameworks are directly motivated by concerns that are at the center of social debate,

the readings that flow from these frameworks do not stimulate a productive discussion of the ideas, suppositions, and desires behind the
frameworks — the areas precisely where there is the most significant
disagreement. Literary criticism actually displaces debate away from
the issues that most require it.

The new criticisms hope to bring about social change by exposing
the many forms in which our culture has condoned, sanctioned, and
legitimated inequality. More specifically, they attack forms of inequality — around race, sex, gender, class, and so forth — in precisely those
areas where there now is no social consensus. There is great confusion
and disagreement about what the legal, political, civic, and cultural relations between different groups (men and women, whites and blacks,
the U.S. and the Third World) and different individuals ought to be.
When there is not already widespread agreement about the nature
and basis of equality, it is essential to try to convince others about
what constitutes domination, why it is wrong, and how it might be
avoided or overcome; simply pointing out one's own favorite instances
of domination or oppression will achieve little. This attempt at persuasion presupposes a dialogue with those who do not (yet) share one's
viewpoint, since a commitment to equality (much less to academia)
entails that others may, in fact, have compelling, even better, ideas. A
new political criticism, if it seeks to remedy inequality, needs to create
a political and philosophical dialogue that can begin to do the work of
formulating a viable foundation in a post–Cold War world for a "community or culture . . . that is not based on coercion or domination" and
that can actively engage diverse perspectives and participants, so as to
move beyond the historical polarizations of dominant and dominated
(West and non-West, male and female). Above all, this requires an
open dialogue about the possibilities of equality, a subject that is debatable at its core; there is no philosophical or political definition that
can adequately respond to all the questions and decisions about equality that we face. The dialogues we have now, despite all the attention
to conflict, hardly fulfill this need.[8]

Literary criticism, instead of promoting such a discussion of equality, often employs the new frameworks to sniff out previously overlooked signs of domination and inequality in whatever the critic
examines. The presuppositions of the critic are thereby confirmed
more than interrogated. The work of the typical essay is to demonstrate, for instance, that the lens of postcolonialism can produce a

new and vibrant interpretation of a much discussed novel. But a rich reading of a literary text does little to validate the theoretical underpinnings of the framework that shapes the reading. The new socially oriented interpretative frameworks are not simply critical strategies, but always also contain, whether implicitly or explicitly, a historical understanding, a social theory, a set of moral judgments, and an agenda for political change. It is these positions — not the actual interpretations of literary texts — that are most controversial, and it is around these topics that dialogue would be most beneficial.

Literary criticism rarely lays forth or persuasively argues for its social theory, its moral judgments, its political agendas. The literary analysis only demonstrates how important certain forms of inequality are for understanding culture; it does not confirm the social critique, the desirability and viability of whatever changes are envisioned. The new forms of literary criticism displace discussion away from the key areas of social, philosophical, and political disagreement and confine productive discussion to a few questions about the interpretation of literary texts. Competing readings of a literary text offer a meager terrain for fighting out the highly debatable nonliterary issues that are at stake in these interpretations. The question of whether a particular theory of economic exploitation does or does not illuminate the complexities of Wordsworth's "Michael" has little to do with whether the vision of economic equality that motivates the analysis would in fact help to ameliorate the inequities of our contemporary world. Nor are the conflicting visions of "public matters" brought into the open by the literary debate. The critic enjoys a charge from touching on political issues, even as the political and public spheres are left largely undisturbed.

✦

I want to explore quickly why reading literature with an eye for unequal power relations has energized so many critics, even if, as I will be arguing, it does not generate the dialogues that would help to bring about the desired political changes, and if, in contrast to most earlier models of literary criticism, such readings do not even serve to demonstrate the validity of their theoretical suppositions. These new ways of reading appeal to the skills and training of critics and also to the hope of making the "literary," in Terry Eagleton's words, again "the medium of vital concerns deeply rooted in the general intellectual, cultural and political life of [our] epoch."[9] Adopting the stance that inequities of power are to be remarked and criticized is in itself a means of opening a new political horizon of more egalitarian relations; the critique depends on imagining that things might be different. Gender, race, class, imperialism, and sexual orientation today provide the best axes with which to offer alternative and opposing perspectives, since they help us to see, instead of a seemingly "universal" point of view, female and/against male, black and/against white, non-Western and/against Western. The *asymmetry* of these paired terms generates their critical force, as they put into relief relations of domination and subordination whose logic (for example, men are superior to women) is no longer accepted. The critic, to help raise the status of the historically subordinate group, now attempts to give voice to what previously had been ignored or suppressed. The project of reconfiguring our cultural traditions has been tremendously productive, both in recovering works neglected by the dominant history and in rereading texts from a "marginal" perspective in order to reveal how they resist or subvert the structures that maintain inequality.

Critics who focus on inequality not only gain a wonderful tool for coming up with something new about the text under discussion; they also receive an extremely powerful instrument for judging all previous literature and literary criticism. For the critic, in addition to demonstrating that a particular group has been overlooked and treated unequally, can also challenge any text for its complicity in a system of domination. A framework that attacks what had been until recently the prevailing attitude, such as the cultural superiority of the West or the unacceptability and abnormality of homosexuals, provides the critic with the grand opportunity to explore new areas and offer radically new accounts of the old ones, all the while battling against social injustice. After Marx, Nietzsche, and Freud, the realms of the previously repressed, suppressed, and oppressed have become particularly rich for intellectual investigation. Not only must one reexamine the poorly charted domains of the proletariat and the unconscious, but one must reconceptualize the bourgeoisie and the conscious as well, since they are now revealed to be highly unstable concepts.

The intellectual appeal of mapping a new, vital terrain is always joined with an expectation for social change. The attempt to show, for example, that race is a constitutive element for the nineteenth-century American novel is aimed not only at improving our historical understanding, but at changing our current attitudes and policies. The supposition is not that the civil rights movement of the 1960s has brought on a time when racial difference no longer matters, so that we can finally see how much it mattered before. Rather, the starting point is always that race continues to be a crucial determinant of social injustice, and the hope is that by bringing to light the complicity in discrimination of otherwise admired texts, we will question our own practices. The critical analysis might depend on a shift of the locus of discrimination from individual bigots to social institutions, and the unspoken agenda might be to promote demands for institutional remedies to what are perceived as ongoing racial inequities. The point I wish to make is that whatever social changes are envisioned, the discussion around the literary work neither addresses the current sources of disagreement that stand in the way of such changes, nor lays out a theory that would explain why new policies would help bring about a better society. The shift in the concerns of the critic is not enough to make literary criticism again a vital medium of social dialogue. The new frameworks of interpretation meet many of the demands and expectations of academic criticism, but they accomplish few of the social goals for regenerating a critical public sphere.

To begin to clarify the forms of displacement in contemporary literary criticism, I want to look at how the typical critical essay proceeds. A favorite strategy is to bring to light traces of inequality that previous commentators, in their inattentiveness to and complicity in systems of domination, have not noticed. Several things are at play here: a contemporary perspective that allows us to see what before could not be clearly perceived or articulated (for example, how deeply racial inequality structured the world of the text); the continued relevance of what is analyzed historically to our own society ("race" provides a powerful critical lens solely to the extent that one can argue that unacknowledged and institutional racism still structure our world); and the conviction that there is now clearly a right and a wrong view (racism is indefensible). Yet the act of reading is always meant to be more than just an illumination, a bringing to light of the forgotten or overlooked; there is the claim that the new interpretation is also a political act, an "intervention" into current problems, that both proceeds from a political position (it is not "disinterested" nor seeking transcendental knowledge) and attacks opposing positions. Finding instances of inequality in old texts is a means to make arguments about what should happen today.

The critic may locate, for example, the three times, in the nine hundred pages of *Our Mutual Friend*, that "Dickens invokes racial difference" and then attempt to show that although these instances are "textually marginal," they are nevertheless "ideologically central."[10] This strategy, popularized by deconstruction, is so common because it provides the critic with tremendous leverage; just a very few words in a text can be used to disrupt and subvert the manifest ideology. Racial difference has here, according to the critic, an "increasingly foundational status" and underlies and underwrites the entire conceptual scheme of identities, valuations, and differences in the text; it also "holds the key to his [Dickens's] ability to recuperate the moralized image of woman." The critic then demonstrates that the moral elevation of the heroine depends on her differentiation from, and the displacement of her negative qualities onto, a black man. There is always the need for multiple registers of difference/inequality: race provides a further turn of the screw to the insights of gender criticism.[11] More extensively, the understanding of "home," "nation," and "order," and the operation of economic as well as ideological structures, are shown to require the differentiation, denigration, and suppression of an "other."

One might then draw the conclusion that despite Dickens's concern for the poor, and his pleas for reforms in education, sanitation, and prisons, his texts "perform ideological work" and uphold and confirm a social order that rests on domination and oppression.[12] From our current vantage point, it is always easy to trump Dickens's social criticism with a more profound critique of Dickens's complicity in the ills of his society. Or alternatively, one might argue a bit differently that the text under analysis fails "to stabilize the cultural system" and instead reveals "its susceptibility to destabilization and change." It is the task of the critic to perform "such readings" that "can display the inherent instability of and emergent challenges to what appear to be homogenous, unassailable ideological formations."[13] In either case, the sensitivity of the contemporary critic to racial difference and inequality provides the lever for exposing and attacking earlier "ideological formations," by revealing that "difference" is not grounded in nature, nor even fixed in culture. The reader can then recognize the "constitutive instability," systemic inequality, and assailability of our own cultural systems and ideological formations.

I do not want to suggest that such analyses of Dickens are ridiculous or fallacious. "Race," indeed, is shown to be "ideologically central" (it would certainly be a surprise if the favored critical category, although "textually marginal," was ever to be deemed ideologically marginal as well) and an effective critical category; a possibility of more enlightened racial attitudes is held forth as a beacon by which to illuminate and judge the past. The guiding presuppositions of this analysis, however, are mostly unarticulated and insulated from debate. This procedure — illuminating ideological formations and inequities — might be adequate if consciousness-raising were sufficient to bring about social and political change. If the main obstacles to greater social equity were merely that people have not yet come to realize how their ordinary attitudes are in fact discriminatory — that the values of suburbia exclude and repress the disadvantaged — a cultural criticism that centers on bringing the repressed (Dickens's "racist" views and their implications for his novels) to the surface might be effective.

But unenlightenment is not the only obstacle to greater equality. The disagreements today are about what constitutes the "proper" consciousness, about what forms of equality are desirable and attainable, and about what policies might work to achieve these ends. The cultural critic assumes that reading a text in light of racial inequity not only will provide a better understanding of the text, but will also help us to avoid complicity in oppression; cultural analysis will help us to improve our own society by making us less blind to its ills.

This critical stance presupposes that we know what a good, nondominant culture would be. One idea of a nondominant culture, or a noncoercive relation between cultures, however, will probably be someone else's idea of totalitarianism, or anarchy. These different views of social relations need to be debated, but the analysis of race in literary texts usually presents our current conflicts as essentially between forms of blindness and insight (or between a knowledge and an ignorance of "history"; but a scholarly appeal to history will not settle disputes about affirmative action, for example, as the disagreements between Jews and blacks on this issue demonstrate).[14] Literary criticism rarely gets at the heart of the issues that divide people on the question of race.

An interpretative framework that focuses on race always also con-tains an attack on the status quo and on the "dominant ideology" that perpetuates racial inequality, even if the critic makes no direct claims to a political agenda. Literary critics hardly ever state what pos-sible changes are presumed, desired, or envisioned in their criticism; it is implied that we already know what should change (and we must therefore raise people's consciousness to the existence of the prob-lem), so that there really is no subject here for political debate (thus critics can stick to demonstrating social problems through construing "cultural texts," rather than setting forth their theory of equality). The supposed work of destabilizing and assailing "ideological formations" is achieved by refusing to put one's own "formations" or framework into play and shielding them from examination and contestation by those whose consciousness has not yet been properly elevated.

I am not suggesting that literary critics ought to make explicitly "political" arguments. But when the analyses are motivated by a desire to be more socially significant and politically effective, they will add little to any debate if the sources of disagreement with others — the political premises — are hidden and not subject to scrutiny. A partic-ular problem is that the political premises are not exposed to people other than fellow literature professors. Thus you will find many lit-erary critics employing similar notions of "class" for cultural analysis, but they would have a hard time defending these notions to political theorists, economists, and sociologists, much less businessmen, factory workers, and computer programmers.

Race is meant to be the tool for performing a critique, for argu-ing for social change, for providing the leverage to attack "ideological formations" — but what is to go in the place of the discredited "formations"? What alternative vision is offered? What policies are advocated? What vision of equality is being promoted? How might it be implemented? What views are to be contested by this privileging of race? All these questions remain largely unaddressed. Now, when "race" has less clear-cut significance than during the civil rights strug-gles of the 1950s and 1960s, when racial discrimination is no longer legally sanctioned, critical readings must repeatedly demonstrate the analytic power of race. Instead of laying forth a theory of equality or a vision of social change, discussions of race in literary criticism aim at maximizing the efficacy of race as an analytic category and at refining a technique for challenging competing interpretations.

In contrast to earlier forms of literary criticism, where the "reading" worked to illustrate or "prove," or in the case of deconstruction to complicate, the theoretical framework, the readings that focus on forms of inequality, and the debates that ensue, do little to prove or disprove the suppositions of the interpretative framework. Agreement or disagreement over "the significance of the black men" in *Our Mutual Friend* neither confirms nor contests the important positions on race and inequality that lie behind the privileging of race for interpretation. Despite the claim of a shift from aesthetics to politics in recent criticism, we have an almost aesthetic justification of political positions. The problem for literary and cultural criticism is not that they have strayed too far away from "literature" — into politics and into "lesser" cultural forms such as comic books, television, and advertising — but that they still hold on to the "text" as the privileged vehicle for analysis. Literary critics have spent too long acquiring the skills of reading to give up their accredited techniques. The critical essay becomes a means to show how one's favorite theories can produce an elaborate new reading of a text, rather than a step towards opening a public dialogue.

Academia offers a privileged space for dialogue. The academic commitment to the scrutiny and contestation of ideas is highly unusual in American society; most other forms of employment provide a much narrower arena for dialogue. At the current time, there is obviously a need for better forms of expressing, disseminating, considering, and contesting ideas in almost all civic and political arenas. The goal of recent critiques of inequality is to improve the content of academic discussion, making it significant for "an audience in your community or society" instead of only for academics, and to improve the form as well, making it accessible to others outside the universities. Increased participation in political, civic, and cultural life, especially by those who have previously been excluded, is one index of equality, and in a democratic system, dialogue, with its possibilities of noncoercive persuasion, is a prime motor for bringing about social change. The issues that underlie contemporary literary criticism — concerning the possibilities of equality and the relations between individuals, groups, and societies — are fundamentally dialogical and require open and sustained discussion.[15]

Yet the discussions that ensue from the literary critique of inequality mainly distract us from addressing these issues, despite critics' claims to make the "literary" "the medium of vital concerns deeply rooted in the...life of [our] epoch." When an interpretative framework is applied to a text, the questioning of the highly debatable presuppositions of the framework is largely foreclosed. Even when there is a heated discussion about the interpretative framework, as in the case of arguments over "essentialism" with regard to race and gender, the animating impulse is still how to arrive at the most effective notion for "criticism." That is, the criterion for judgment is still literary and academic (the success of a framework for challenging or subverting the dominant ideology through textual analysis), rather than philosophical or political (the persuasiveness or viability of the outlook). Such a discussion is only important for those who already see the wisdom of subverting the dominant ideology. Whether one adopts an essentialist or an antiessentialist view, there is little attempt to consider the viewpoints or persuade those who do not share goals of the race or gender critique. The discussion remains insular, to the extent that the views of one's political and ideological opponents are rarely treated as principled arguments worthy of deliberation. The lack of a more productive dialogue, one that engages others in thinking through commonalities and differences, possible alternatives and next steps, is covered over by the necessarily conflictual nature of literary interpretation. The continual disagreements over textual interpretations, and now over even what texts to teach, supply only an appearance of meaningful political debate.

◆

Amid the overwhelming thicket of academic publication, which multiply by performing only minor mutations to what has just preceded, it would be easy, now that political concerns are so prominent in literary criticism, to find example after example of political critiques of cultural texts in which there is hardly an acknowledgment of, much less an argument for, the political positions that are implicitly embraced. The institutionalization of socially or politically "aware" forms of reading necessarily dulls such "awareness," as disciplinary and formal concerns regulate the spread and the appropriation of new ideas. It would therefore be surprising if one could not show that academic criticism often displaces debate away from the significant issues that underlie the critical orientation. And it would be easy to insert such an argument within Said's attack on professionalism, describing this displacement as yet a further effect of professional criticism, in which even the attempt to engage social concerns still yields a criticism that is not sufficiently alert and open to the interests and ideas of those outside academia.

I want to make a much stronger argument, however: that contemporary literary criticism, even as the companion to an explicit political agenda, does not provide the vehicle for a dialogue on the "vital concerns" of the "intellectual, cultural, and political life" of our epoch. For this reason, I will turn to Said's own criticism. He would seem to be the last person one might accuse of "displacing" political debate. He has written several books of political criticism, has articulated specific goals for Middle East policy, and has appeared on *Nightline*. Moreover, Said's criticism is hardly epigonal; he cannot be accused of writing "political" literary criticism because it is fashionable or of not considering or articulating his political vision. His literary criticism is central to the new "interpretative frameworks" I have been describing, and it lays the groundwork not only for postcolonial criticism, but for much of the engagement with the (foreign) other. Said would appear to set the example for literary discussion that might revitalize a critical public sphere, and many people will certainly continue to follow his lead in offering their own anti-imperial readings.

In *Culture and Imperialism*, Said argues that imperialism is the major, in fact the "determining, political horizon of modern Western culture" (60). His project is to restore this political horizon to cultural analysis and to attack what he feels are the unwarranted claims for the autonomy of the aesthetic sphere. Said states:

> Instead we have on the one hand an isolated cultural sphere, believed to be freely and unconditionally available to weightless theoretical speculation and investigation, and, on the other, a debased political sphere, where the real struggle between interests is supposed to occur. To the professional student of culture — the humanist, the critic, the scholar — only one sphere is relevant, and, more to the point, it is accepted that the two spheres are separated, whereas the two are not only connected but ultimately the same.
>
> A radical falsification has become established in this separation. (57)

Said focuses particularly on the novel, since he believes that "[w]ithout empire, I would go so far as saying, there is no European novel as we know it" (69), and even more poignantly, "that the novel, as a cultural artefact of bourgeois society, and imperialism are unthinkable *without each other*" (70–71; emphasis added). If the European novel is so important for imperialism, a critical analysis of the novel can itself be a major step toward understanding and combating imperialism. Said hopes to show how novels make imperialism "thinkable."

Said has four major aims here: to support his claims for the strong interrelation between modern Western culture and imperialism; to provide model interpretations that demonstrate what is revealed by analyzing key texts with regard to imperialism; to question what is at stake in our being able to see only now how important imperialism is for understanding culture; and finally, but not least in importance, to argue for an end to the "imperial ideology" that still permeates our society. The assertion that the cultural and political spheres "are not only connected but ultimately the same" gives great importance to the work of the cultural critic, since the culture that fostered and still continues to foster imperialism must be radically critiqued if the desired social and political changes are to occur.

A similar description, with substitutions of only a few key words, could be supplied for many other influential works of contemporary criticism, such as Eve Kosofsky Sedgwick's *Between Men: English Literature and Male Homosocial Desire* (and her *Epistemology of the Closet* as well),[16] which shares the same aims of connection, reinterpretation, cultural critique, and political change, but with respect to (male) homosexuality. One could also use a modified version of the following statement as a rallying cry for much current work: "What I should like to note is that these colonial and imperial [or substitute chosen terms] realities are overlooked in criticism that has otherwise been extraordinarily thorough and resourceful in finding themes to discuss" (64). In considering an example of Said's criticism, I want to keep these similarities in mind, in order to raise the broader question of the political impact of academic literary criticism. Said relies very heavily on his exceptionalism, on his great difference from "the professional student of culture." What might it mean if the critical stance that grounds its insights on a resistance to the dominant ideology, and on giving critical weight to voices that have been largely ignored or suppressed (of Third World writers and of women, and somewhat differently, of people from the working class and of homosexuals), is no longer "marginal" in academia, but is in fact sanctioned, promoted, and rewarded? Have we thereby succeeded in regrounding and reenergizing the spheres of culture and politics, or in disrupting imperial ideology? I want to examine Said's reading of Jane Austen's *Mansfield Park* in order to question — with regard to a project that openly avows its political aims and employs "the perspective provided by anti-imperialist resistance" (66) — whether such literary criticism still displaces debate away from the issues that most require it.[17] Or to use Said's terms, whether he achieves the following: "opposing and alleviating coercive domination, transforming the present by trying rationally and analytically to lift some of its burdens, situating the works of various literatures with reference to one another and to their historical modes of being" (319). That is, does the literary critical task of "situating" provide an effective means for "opposing" coercive domination and "transforming" the present?

Said argues that Austen's novel is "more implicated in the rationale for imperialist expansion" (84) than has previously been thought. His contention is that the estate in Antigua (owned by Sir Thomas Bertram, the proprietor of Mansfield Park), which receives only glancing attention by the novelist (or as Said puts it, Austen "sublimates the agonies of Caribbean existence to a mere half dozen passing references to Antigua" [59]), is not merely a plot device by which to get the head of the household off the scene for the first half of the novel, or simply a source of wealth for this particular baronet; rather, it is intimately and inextricably connected to the world of Mansfield Park. Said hopes to demonstrate that the attitudes and values scrutinized and finally esteemed in the domain of Mansfield Park are also crucial to this off-scene world of Antigua, but with very different, unpraiseworthy consequences. He writes:

> More clearly than elsewhere in her fiction, Austen here synchronizes domestic with international authority, making it plain that the values associated with such higher things as ordination, law, and propriety must be grounded firmly in actual rule over and possession of territory. She sees clearly that to hold and rule Mansfield Park is to hold and rule an imperial estate in close, not to say inevitable association with it. What assures the domestic tranquility and attractive harmony of one is the productivity and regulated discipline of the other. (87)

Domestic tranquility and attractive harmony (ends whose desirability is hard to question) are thus not only dependent on the profits from an oppressive colonial enterprise, but in fact require the same authority as that used to ensure "productivity and regulated discipline" overseas, that is, an authority that does not balk at sordid cruelty and slavery (to nonwhite peoples, beyond the domestic gaze, outside of England).

Said, with great care and sophistication, goes on to connect the major drama of the plot, the importation of the lowly cousin Fanny Price and her elevation into the guiding moral conscious of Mansfield Park, with the importation of the wealth derived from the Caribbean colony. Here, as elsewhere in *Culture and Imperialism*, his emphasis is *geographical* (Said highlights the "'out there' that frames the ... action *here*" [93], thus giving voice to the "resistance to empire" [xiii]), in contrast to the usual emphasis on temporality in the novel).[18] He argues that the geographical process, "approved" by the novelist for its wholesome results of bringing Fanny from a distant though still English world into the domain of Mansfield Park, is not only analogous to, but interdependent with, the other, imperial process. Said states: "What was wanting *within* was in fact supplied by the wealth derived from a West Indian plantation and a poor provincial relative, both brought in to Mansfield Park and set to work. Yet on their own, neither the one nor the other could have sufficed; *they require each other*" (92; emphasis added). Said can therefore conclude that "Austen affirms and repeats the geographical process of invoking trade, production, and consumption that predates, underlies, and guarantees the morality" (93). Austen's complicity in imperialism is being established. Even if colonialism receives little direct attention in the novel and its morality is barely touched on, this very absence is significant. When Fanny asks about the slave trade, she is met by "such a dead silence!" which, for Said, is "to suggest that one world could not be connected with the other since there simply is no common language for both" (96). The task of criticism is now to reveal these connections and break the silence.[19]

One of the traditional occupations for critics is to reveal connections by situating the literary work within a larger context. Critics have discussed *Mansfield Park* within the aesthetic context of the genre of the novel or have sought to enrich their interpretations by providing connections to the incidents of Austen's life. Said, in arguing that the political sphere has been falsely separated from the cultural one, seeks to connect "remarkable works of art" with "the imperial process of which they were manifestly and unconcealedly a part" (xiv).

The restoration of a political dimension to culture, of a foreign dimension to the domestic picture, and even of the "sublimated" cruelty that enables (and provides the money for) the gentility, opens up a range of issues neglected by most earlier critics. In the world described by Austen, where the matter of income is of such importance to so many characters, not only the quantity, but the sources of Sir Thomas Bertram's income, and all that produced it, are certainly important. Scrutinizing Sir Thomas's role as father and proprietor, in light of his role as imperialist, poses significant questions: How does his management in one area relate to and help account for the success or failure of his management in the other? Or one might consider how, or if, his ownership of an Antiguan estate differentiates Sir Thomas from the other landholders in Austen's novels, such as Darcy in *Pride and Prejudice* or Mr. Knightly in *Emma*, and explore the role of colonial wealth among the landed gentry, who faced great changes in the early nineteenth century. More broadly, one might juxtapose the moral vision in Austen's writing to the debates about slavery already going on in England at the time (slavery was eliminated for the British colonies in 1834),[20] in order to probe further both the significance of Fanny's question and the silence with which it was met. A focus on Sir Thomas's Antiguan estates also can help us to question what moral equivocations, and what views of non-European and nonwhite peoples, were required in order to sustain early British imperialism.

The critical act of "situating" the literary work, and of connecting it to a "complex history" that not only the characters in the novel, but "Austen herself would not, could not recognize" (93), raises a wide array of questions. Questions, when the answer is not already known or determined in advance, provide a new horizon for inquiry and discussion. A question can also provoke a self-conscious and self-critical look at the grounds for our responses and can bring out and help us to confront different viewpoints. Yet the "connections" that Said establishes by situating the literary work in its imperial context do not provide the basis for an open discussion of the political, philosophical, economic, and cultural questions broached by the analysis of the literary text. I will address four of the ways in which the analysis of the literary text here works against the realization of such a dialogue: the answers to any new questions are for the most part already determined by the interpretative framework and its assumptions about imperialism and culture; any responses are further governed by the need to maintain an oppositional stance and not be complicit in turn in imperialism; the literary text, as an example of a broader "imperial culture," only serves to explain the failures of culture and does not give us any ground for debating new alternatives; and the possibility of dialogue is itself undermined by the requirement to "go elsewhere," outside the domain of Western culture, for any genuine critical response.

When reading with imperialism in mind, the critic must condemn the novel or at least the broader culture of which it is a part. The only roles for the novel are aiding and abetting imperialism or, much more tenuously, providing a critique of, or even resistance to, imperialism.[21] In contrast to Said's interpretation, one might argue that colonial proprietorship does not underwrite the "attractive harmony" and "domestic tranquility" of Mansfield Park but is in fact responsible for the discord, rebellion, and poor transmission of values that results in a crippled heir, a disgraced, adulterous daughter who must seek refuge with her aunt, and another daughter who has eloped and is estranged from her father. The qualities that stand him in good stead as a colonial proprietor — imperial distance and otherness from those beneath him, firm authority and a strong sense of decorum — only teach most of his children to rebel against his example and to flee (or transform, by making their home a theater, with the father's *sanctum sanctorum* now the theater's green room) the paternal hearth. One could suggest that the ways in which the colonial management of landed estates differs from the traditional domestic version (slavery and the employment of subjects, not citizens; absentee management and supervision through foreign overseers; and all the other aspects of colonial alienation) are embodied in the failings of the younger generation of the Bertram family; only the son who chooses his career in the church is unaffected. From here, one might even argue that Mansfield Park offers an implicit critique, rather than an affirmation, of imperialism.

Once one begins to interpret Mansfield Park through the framework of imperialism, there are a whole range of possible readings. But the differences between these interpretations finally do not much matter, since all the readings largely share the same objective: locating and denouncing traces of imperialism and critiquing the culture that enables and supports it. Answers to questions such as how the United States should now interact with the "developing" world, or under what

circumstances the United States should use military force, are neither obvious nor agreed upon by the citizens of this country (much
less by the rest of the world). Yet the guiding assumption of cultural
criticism is that there is an alternative and an antidote to imperialist ideology that is so historically and morally obvious that one need
not even articulate or defend it. The significance of any discussion is
greatly curtailed when the answers to the most important questions
are largely foreordained.

Said is less interested in supplying predictable answers, however,
than in using cultural analysis as a tool for opposition and transformation. If the connection "Jane Austen and empire" is to bear any
fruit for the ongoing struggles against imperialism, the critique must
demystify the powers of domination and resist the allures of culture.
The reading of Mansfield Park is therefore only successful to the extent that it provides leverage for denouncing and distancing ourselves
from imperial culture. At issue here is a process not simply of connection, but of linking something distasteful to something of the highest
taste; that is, imperialism and a cultural masterpiece.

To increase this leverage, the linking of "culture" and "imperialism"
must yield a picture of Western culture as complicit in imperialism and
offer a possibility of positioning ourselves differently and of breaking
from this cultural tradition — this is most easily accomplished by invoking an "elsewhere," a Third World, an " 'out there' that frames the
genuinely important action here" (93). The aim is to make sure that
one can no longer look at Mansfield Park without also seeing the suf-
ferings of others; and more importantly, without also realizing that the
failure to see connections between imperialism and culture is itself an
act of complicity and even an authorization and an affirmation of "domestic imperial culture." The cultural critique performs the function
of certifying that one is not complicit in processes of domination; criticism is now often akin to a rite of purification. No matter how the
individual text is interpreted, we get a reading for evil, in which the
critic always finds and condemns inequality.

Said first establishes the "connection" of Mansfield Park to imperialism by arguing that the proprietorship of an estate in Antigua cannot
be disconnected from the novel. The act of connection here impels
us to ask different questions than the ones that occupy the characters and requires that we consider history and politics in framing
these questions. He then goes on to sketch an ever-widening series

of "connections" in an effort to portray *Mansfield Park* as complicit in imperialism and all its consequences. Said writes: "[W]e must see 'Antigua' held in a precise place in Austen's moral geography, and in her prose, by historical changes that her novel rides like a vessel on a mighty sea. The Bertrams could not have been possible without the slave trade, sugar, and the colonial planter class" (94). Said hopes to make explicit "what is hidden or allusive in Austen." What he finds "hidden," though, is not merely the cruelty of the slave trade, alluded to only by the "dead silence" that meets Fanny's question, but the entire aftermath of colonial slavery as well. Said remarks that in recent scholarship "slavery and empire are shown to have *fostered* the rise and consolidation of capitalism well beyond the old plantation monopolies, as well as to have been a powerful ideological system whose original connections to specific economic interests may have gone, but whose *effects* continued for decades" (94; emphasis added). The implication is that capitalism continues the exploitative practices of slavery and imperialism and that Austen's prose has contributed to a "consolidation of capitalism" whose ill effects still linger today.

Almost any fictional work could be condemned for contributing to "a powerful ideological system . . . whose [ill] effects continued for decades." One might similarly link Austen to militaristic culture, through Captain Wentworth in *Persuasion* or even through William Price, Fanny's brother, in *Mansfield Park*, since none of the brutality of military conflict is mentioned. Such "connections" only demonstrate that culture is entangled with power, something we already know (How could it not be?); the precise texture of this entanglement is what is always at issue. Yet Said sweepingly concludes that reading "*Mansfield Park* as part of the structure of an expanding imperialist venture" helps us to see how "the novel steadily, if unobtrusively, opens up a broad expanse of domestic imperial culture without which Britain's subsequent acquisition of territory would not have been possible" (95).

Said's conclusions may indeed be correct, but the only question then for the novel is *how* it opens this broad expanse of imperial culture (that is, a "broad expanse" that forecloses the desires and rights of others). Said's "connections" always reveal the larger, sordid story of imperialism that engulfs the literary work. He states that understanding such connections requires "working through the novel" and "reading it in full," "reading it carefully," but only so as "to understand the strength of the way it was activated and maintained in literature"

(95). Such a reading will inform us of the failings of our culture, which countenances imperialism; it will not offer any arena for imagining equality. Placing the work in the historical trajectory of imperialism alone does not put forth the alternative social vision on which this analysis rests. Envisioning new political structures and social ideals, anchoring this vision within the horizon of what may now be possible, and persuading others of the validity and justice of this outlook are much greater tasks. There is a disjunction between the effects of the critical act and the wider aims of the interpretative framework that guide it. Arguing against "imperial culture" by demonstrating "connections" between cultural texts and the systemic ills of our society is not equivalent to presenting arguments for any alternatives; both the work and the critique are reduced to the contours of the "powerful ideological system" of capitalism. Moreover, attacking the complicity of others in imperial culture hardly confirms the truth or justice of our own arguments.

Said concludes his analysis of *Mansfield Park* by pointing out "a paradox here in reading Jane Austen which I have been impressed by but can in no way resolve": the paradox between "holding slaves on a West Indian sugar plantation" and the fact that "everything we know about Austen and her values is at odds with the cruelty of slavery" (96). This paradox does not, however, cause confusion or raise genuine questions for further discussion. Paradox is what the critic *must* find. If Austen's values were not "at odds with the cruelty of slavery," if we could not see *Mansfield Park* "in the main as resisting or avoiding that other setting" (96), but instead as either wholeheartedly endorsing or condemning brutality in Antigua, there would be no need for a sophisticated critique that brings to light what has been avoided and resisted by generations of readers. Nor would there be any opening for the critic's revaluation.

Reading for evil always uncovers a paradox, for the function of criticism is to disrupt ongoing complicity in systems of domination. The critic must argue that "great literary masterpieces" (a category to which *Mansfield Park* "most certainly belongs," according to Said) sanction attitudes and practices that are incompatible with the ideals of our culture (and with the ideals that these works help articulate); hence the utility of paradox. But the critic must also establish the difficulties, the obstacles, and the resistances to achieving this insight (all the benefits and habits that promote complicity) in order to explain why the perspective of "that other setting" of the Third World (or of an oppressed domestic minority) is required. If the apparent paradox were due to hypocrisy, and if the new insights could be supplied fully from within the discourse of the dominant ideology, there would be no need to turn elsewhere and no ground for a radical critique of the dominant culture. Some variant of liberalism and of the notion that "Western" culture can reform, critique, and improve itself would be sufficient. Contemporary cultural critics, like earlier deconstructive and even earlier "new" critics, thrive on paradox.

Said describes his method as reading *contrapuntally*, reading "with a simultaneous awareness both of the metropolitan history that is narrated and of those other histories against which (and together with which) the dominating discourse acts" (51).[22] Said explicitly rejects a "rhetoric of blame" that attacks Austen "and others like her, retrospectively, for being white, privileged, insensitive, complicit," and states that instead we must "take seriously our intellectual and interpretative vocation to make connections, to deal with as much of the evidence as possible, fully and actually, to read what is there or not there, above all, to see complementarity and interdependence instead of isolated, venerated, or formalized experience that excludes and forbids the hybridizing intrusions of human history" (96). Said's counterpoint itself alternates, however, between arguing for the interdependence, interaction, and overlapping of these histories and trying to locate the "imperial dynamic" so as to demonstrate which history should be resisted and attacked and which should be elevated and valued. At one moment Said writes:

> So vast and yet so detailed is imperialism as an experience with crucial critical dimensions, that we must speak of overlapping territories, intertwined histories common to men and women, whites and non-whites, dwellers in the metropolis and on the peripheries, past as well as present and future; these territories and histories can only be seen from the perspective of the whole of secular human history. (61)

Yet elsewhere Said suggests that this "perspective of the whole" can be grasped only by moving beyond "the universalizing discourses of modern Europe and the United States" and looking "at the domination of the non-European world from the perspective of a resisting, gradually more and more challenging alternative" (50). Said switches between calling for us to listen to all voices, consider all perspectives, and suggesting that for a genuine critique we now must turn only to those "unstinted in [their] hatred of implanted colonialism or the imperialism that kept it going" (18).

In his analysis of *Mansfield Park,* the "hybridizing intrusions of human history" are brought to bear only insofar as they cast a gruesome shadow on Western culture. The work of making connections, and of seeing complementarity and interdependence, always achieves the result of linking Austen, however weakly, to all that we now consider exploitative, if not evil. Against the "broad expanse of domestic imperial culture," especially insofar as it lingers today, the only possible stance is to condemn the relations of culture to power. If "resistance" is the only legitimate critical position, the conclusions of the reading are, in a large sense, predetermined. Any discussion of the essential questions posed by the topic of imperialism — what can and what ought to be, the relations between nations of unequal power and between different cultures — is constrained by the need to prove that one is not taken in by "imperial culture." And for those who disagree entirely with this view of imperialism, the most likely response is to strike the opposing attitude, demand proper reverence for the great works of culture, and insist that Austen's works not be sullied by the sins of others. No discussion of the widely divergent ideas concerning the proper uses of power — of the differences that underlie the opposing readings and approaches to Austen — will take place when the literary work is primarily a vehicle for upholding or resisting the dominant culture.[23]

To what extent does Said's analysis oppose and alleviate coercive domination and transform "the present by trying rationally and analytically to lift some of its burdens"? The real accomplishment is one of de-legitimation. The political task of Said's work is to argue that we must now attend to other voices, must now listen to the voices neglected and suppressed by imperial culture, and must turn elsewhere for our intellectual wisdom and political vision. The insistence on the connection between Western culture and inequality, and on the perpetuation of imperialism through "American ascendancy," implies that to achieve "Freedom from Domination in the Future" (a chapter heading) we must look outside the West for possible models and solutions. Said, in contrast to most literary critics, has specific ideas for shifts in political power and alignments. The cultural analysis, however, only demonstrates that there has been blindness in regard to imperialism; it does not persuade us what to do, now that we see better. The only political force of this literary criticism is to critique, and finally to discredit, Western culture as complicit in domination.

One goal of looking elsewhere, and of reading contrapuntally, is to encourage the "tremendously energetic efforts to engage with the metropolitan world in equal debate," efforts that "testify to the diversity and differences of the non-European world and to its own agendas, priorities, and history" (30). Polyphony, "a crossing over in discussion, borrowing back and forth, debate" are praised. Yet if literary criticism discredits in advance any position other than "resistance" to those forms of "domination" that it seeks to dispel, there is little possibility of an open dialogue in which competing ideas can be scrutinized and contested. Despite the frequent calls for debate, critical exchange, and conversation, and despite the exhortations to listen to other voices, literary criticism now undermines more than it fosters the possible grounds on which such interchanges might take place.

Efforts to make literary criticism responsive to the needs of our communities and our society have not yet produced debates that have much significance beyond the domain of the participants. Literary critics may have learned to incorporate social concerns into their critical practices, but they have not achieved an effective social criticism. Locating "evil" is *not* the same as actually resisting it. Reading for evil is, however, eminently teachable, and students who miss all the subtleties and problematics of literary analysis — all the knowledge of language and literature that produces a framework for interpretation, rather than just a simplistic criterion for judgment — easily come away with a powerful critical syllogism: colonialism is a horrendous evil; imperialism is the acceptance of other people's inequality and still permeates our culture; I am therefore fighting against imperialism (or any other "ism") by showing that it operates in literary texts. In this approach, literature is reduced to a frozen portrait of the thoughts of another era. Any ethical complexity is transformed into a Manichean division between abetting and resisting inequality, and the contemporary reader assumes a thoroughly unwarranted moral superiority.[24] Said, in his masterly and often brilliant book, does not indulge in such trite forms of reading.

Yet he helps to construct its fundamental logic. I do not look forward to the effects that *Culture and Imperialism* will have on literary studies.

If many of the current approaches to literary study displace dialogue away from the fundamentally debatable political and philosophical issues that permeate our public sphere, would an attempt to foreground the differences in our approaches provide a remedy? This is the path Gerald Graff takes in proposing that we ought to "teach the [our] conflicts."[25] The basic idea is very appealing, especially insofar as it encourages us to question our interpretative frameworks (or stimulate a "reflective, second-order discourse about practices" [819]); to cross the boundaries of the classroom, the specialty, and even the discipline (to overcome the unwarranted partitions of a "disjunctive curriculum"); and to have open discussions about our disagreements. The examples that Graff offers, such as a debate about Matthew Arnold's "Dover Beach," are disappointing and bring into relief the shortcomings of what he characterizes as "the crucial debate over the politics of literature" (833). His sample debate presents us with a series of conflicting positions:

one of the great masterpieces of the Western tradition	vs.	the arch example of phallocentric discourse
a work of art	vs.	a piece of political propaganda
universal structures of language	vs.	local and transitory problems
universal human experience	vs.	male experience presented as if it were universal (818)

These categorizations, which arise from the attempt to reflect on the politics of literary studies, are not very helpful either for literary understanding or for political debate. Instead, we enter a twilight zone of bad literary criticism (whether or not the poem exemplifies such hollow concepts as "great masterpiece" or "universal human experience" — Does anyone teach by saying, "Class, our task today is to see why this poem is a great masterpiece, an example of universal human experience"?) and barren political analysis (whether the phallocentric discourse of the poem oppresses women).

It is not Graff's imagination that is at fault here. Such bland terms result from the attempt to provide simple categories that capture both the political and literary positions of opposing critics. The "debate over the politics of literature" (or more precisely, the politics of academic literary studies) is not a substitute for important political debate. Staging a feminist or a Marxist reading of "Dover Beach" against whatever may be put forth as a "traditional" interpretation in no way stands in for a dialogue on how we conceive equality between men and women or about whether an immediate redistribution of wealth and ownership would create a better society or, on the contrary, would only produce greater impoverishment and loss of freedom. The effort to portray the conflicts over literary interpretation as paradigmatic for public debate elevates the importance of literature professors, but it does not strengthen the connections between literary criticism and political discourse. Graff's project is admirable for attempting to initiate students into the intellectual questions and conflicts that animate much professorial research and writing, and it is also admirable for attempting to break down some of the barriers that keep professors with conflicting ideas in different rooms, sterilely separated from the contending ideas next door. But debates between critics who represent widely divergent ideological positions tend to reinforce rather than to question a (lowest) common denominator for literary and political criticism.[26]

I am certainly not advocating that readers of literature should ignore or condone manifestations of inequality. What I am really objecting to is less the "political" reading of literature than the political model that underlies it. For this model is one that is tailored for academic analysis: it postulates complicity, bad consciousness, and subjection as the norm and then declares a mode of *reading* as the path to political and intellectual authenticity. Said expresses "surprise" that "the quotidian processes of hegemony . . . yield surprisingly well to analysis and elucidation" (109). Of course they do! The conceit is always that hegemony triumphs over poorly trained readers and that teaching students to analyze "the quotidian processes of hegemony" will radically challenge the prevailing consciousness. The resulting dialogue, about good and bad forms of reading, deflects attention away from debating the merits of the political theses that are in play. And although I have been using the vocabulary of the Left ("hegemony," and so on), the same strategies of highlighting the cultural forces that mislead and misrepresent others are employed by the Right, with "cultural elites" filling the objectionable role. A cultural critique that requires the blindness of others for its own insights only perpetuates a system that discounts most people's ideas and brings us no closer to the discussions needed for making inequality any less intractable.

7

THE POVERTY OF CONVERSATION

$\blacklozenge$

*Intellectual debate if it were in the right spirit
would be wonderful.*

— JANE TOMPKINS

One frequently encounters pleas for a meaningful dialogue, for a genuine exchange of ideas, or for a new conversation in cultural criticism
today. What ideas about criticism, about the formation and development of ideas, and about academia are at play in these calls for
dialogue? Does a demand for dialogue only arise at moments of addressing certain controversial social or political topics, such as race,
and when the critic is expressing a position not likely to be held by
the majority of the public? Or is dialogue intimately linked to criticism
and particularly suited for the pedagogical and critical tasks of philosophical and literary studies? Appeals for dialogue in academia often
arise in response to issues that have reached the attention of the public. Is dialogue merely a public face for criticism, a platitude that one
trots out to defend practices and remarks that to many appear outrageous or ridiculous? Or do actual dialogues play an integral role in the
learning and thinking that take place in universities?

Calls for better dialogue are hardly limited to academia. One constantly finds them in newspapers and even on television. Bill and
Hillary Clinton, their appointee Sheldon Hackney, and their failed appointee Lani Guinier have all asked for a national conversation. They
claim that conversation is essential for democracy and that a new conversation would respond to "the need for genuine participation for
all." Does some ideal of dialogue still serve a broad political and public function, or is it invoked mainly to advance a particular political
agenda? And does the role of dialogue in the university bear much relation to its place in the public sphere? If dialogue is the quintessential

form of communication and interaction for academia, can academic attempts to theorize and improve dialogue provide a model for revitalizing our democracy? Such a supposition seems to be at work in Hackney's attempts to get a "national conversation" underway by starting with planning groups that consist largely of academics.[1]

It is easy to describe the attractiveness of some notion of dialogue for professors in the humanities. The Socratic dialogues are the beginning of the academic enterprise, and discussion is still pivotal to teaching and scholarship in the humanities. Literary criticism only offers competing interpretations; there is no recourse to an observable world of natural phenomena. The literary critic tests an argument by trying to persuade other readers, not by performing experiments. In contrast to science, the point of reference — the literary "text" — provides only a weak level of verifiability.

A widespread belief in the importance of dialogue arises from its seeming obviousness (How could we conceive of the humanities without any dialogue?) and from a series of educational reforms (tying learning and citizenship to participation). Yet in addressing these questions about dialogue, criticism, and the public sphere, I want to consider this traditional stance (which is integral to the ideology of the modern university and to concepts such as "academic freedom") against two more recent trends: the postmodernist emphasis on the cross-, the multi-, the hetero-, and the inter- that, while arising from a radical questioning of the traditional foundations of humanist inquiry, puts forth a demand for contact with an "other," and thus a new horizon for dialogue; and all the tendencies in recent criticism that suggest that dialogue, at least in the form of public debate or parliamentary discussion, is not intimately connected at all with thinking. Recent critiques of the subject, of institutions, of language — all of which attack the idea of an autonomous, free-thinking, self-conscious, and independent individual — suspend any appeal to dialogue as the obvious mission of philosophy or cultural criticism. Dialogue, rather than being the cornerstone of academia, instead exemplifies all the tensions about the purposes and possibilities of criticism.

Before considering some examples of how the appeals for dialogue function, I want to look a little more closely at some of these recent pressure points. In contrast to fifteen years ago, when critics tried to master "theory," they now strive to be "public intellectuals." There has been a dramatic shift toward engaging social issues and even toward seeking an audience beyond academia in reaction to the conservative political climate since 1980, to an increasing feeling of the insignificance of most academic criticism, and to the attacks on university practices (for example, political correctness) and funding. A notion of critical exchange or meaningful dialogue stakes a claim for the right of intellectuals to participate in public affairs and takes a step toward actually engaging others.

The most popular terms in literary criticism — border crossing, hybridity, counterpoint, transgression, contact zones — all attack insularity and promote contact with others (other cultures, other values, other disciplines). If these contacts are to be more than tourism, more than a happy addition of local color, exchanges that go beyond artifacts and books must take place. Dialogue offers a possible model for interaction. Dialogue also supplies a pedagogical model for postmodern theories that emphasize alterity and "dissensus" rather than similarity and consensus; a dialogue can perform the conflict of ideas.

Yet these different tendencies are not cumulative or even compatible; very different ideas of exchange and contact underlie the criticism of the new "public" intellectual and the non-American postcolonial critic, and there is no common conception of thinking or of criticism that connects the varied practices. What we have then are a variety of desires toward dialogue, even as these very critiques often undermine the basis on which a dialogue would be constructed. The most common topics of critical scrutiny — the autonomy of the subject, the transparency of language, the premises of liberalism — have habitually been the foundation for theories of dialogue. Such different writers as Wittgenstein and Derrida, Adorno and Foucault, have attacked the philosophical and ideological presuppositions behind the idea that "meaningful discussion" or an "exchange of ideas" has any special importance for critical thinking. The point I want to make here is not that most appeals for dialogue are internally inconsistent or contradictory (though that is often the case, and these inconsistencies need to be pursued), but that they are usually complex, putting a mix of insights, desires, and touchstones into play, straddling the divisions of personal and public, present and future, negating and affirming. I want to use this mix to analyze and to shatter the complacency behind most pleas for "a genuine debate," as if everyone knew what that would be and knew that it would solve a problem.

In my own writing, I often find myself caught between these different impulses. I use an ideal of "dialogue" as a yardstick to measure the shortcomings of critics who claim a new and profound engagement with the public or with the vital social and political issues of our time, even as I am suspicious toward any claim that dialogue is meaningful or desirable in itself. And I look to some future horizon of dialogue that might justify the "farce called criticism,"[2] the endless quantity of self-consuming words that we churn out, even as I spend my time dissecting the foreclosures, displacements, and evasions of dialogue that structure academic criticism.

We need to flesh out some of the presuppositions, complications, and problems of even the most simple invocations of dialogue. I am interested in the very large questions hovering about the topic of dialogue: Is a dialogical process, a testing of one person's ideas against another, essential to critical thinking, or is it something that happens only later, or on the side? And what is the place of persuasion, of the exchange of ideas, and of participation by all in a liberal democratic society, and in the age of mass media? But I do not want to begin by laying out a theory of dialogue, as this would presuppose that we already know everything that is at issue, nor by differentiating between conversation (intimacy, talking between people who already know each other), dialogue (differing, conflicting opinions), and debate (an audience, someone else to be persuaded), as this would shift attention to questions of form. I will start much more modestly, by looking at some almost trivial invocations to "genuine debate" and to "arguing together" in an op-ed piece and on a book jacket; in such routine references, we can see the expectations and assumptions that are at play.

A Rich Debate

Frank Rich, the ex-theater critic and now op-ed writer for the *New York Times*, in one of his attacks on Lynne Cheney's attempts to end funding for the National Endowment for the Humanities (NEH) (which she chaired during the Bush administration), concludes with a call "for a genuine debate":

> And that's the greatest hypocrisy of all. By calling for an end to standards in schools, rather than for a genuine debate as to how

such standards might be improved without reducing history to a pablum of names and dates, Mrs. Cheney is only contributing to the national dumbing down. Should she succeed in maiming the N.E.H., she'll knock off programs at the high end of the educational system too. It says everything about how far our broader cultural standards have fallen that Mrs. Cheney's rant has so far dominated the debate while quieter voices like David McCullough's are only now beginning to be heard.[3]

I don't want to go into the details of the "debate" around the national history standards, which Cheney funded and now condemns, nor do I want to analyze all the ways in which Rich's own writing hardly upholds the distinctions between intellectual honesty and political self-promotion on which his argument rests. Instead, I want to question the matter-of-factness of the call for genuine debate — as if we thought it could easily happen and would resolve the controversy — amid the description of how poorly we are now debating.

The appeal for *genuine* debate always points to some future time. From this prospect, whatever discussion is now taking place is inadequate, dominated by "rant" and "ubiquitous misinformation," by illicit means of persuasion. Invoking the possibility of true debate, regulated instead by such honored criteria as rationality, honesty, evidence, consideration of others, openness, or a search for truth, does not necessarily lead us toward meaningful discussion, but it does provide strong leverage for discrediting one set of opinions and even for ruling them outside the sphere of proper debate. This future horizon of genuine debate is always out of reach, however, since at any point it is possible to demonstrate that the legitimate forms of argument are already contaminated by illegitimate ones. And for anyone who is losing, a debate can never be "genuine" enough.

Yet the appeal to a future debate is not simply a tactic for altering or delegitimating a current conflict. The belief that there can be a genuine debate, beyond our immediate shortcomings, legitimates our political and educational institutions. Condemning a political feud from this standpoint reinforces the idea that the essence of our political process is hearing and considering different opinions. The possibility of genuine debate is a necessary horizon: it affirms that there can be a productive engagement of differences and that there is a *public* to be addressed, a group of people conceived as open to persuasion rather than bounded purely by personal interest. Without the assurance of this horizon, the possible abject failure of our political system would have to be contemplated.

The unexceptionable call for debate (Who would argue against it?) does not point to a simple alternative; it hovers between debunking and affirming, an unacceptable present and an unreachable future. And what is to be debated? Not the actual interpretation of historical events, but the national standards for teaching American history. This is the usual site for invoking debate: where intellectual content spills over into public policy. The teaching of American history in the public schools could hardly be free from politics; conceptions of the nation, and of its purpose and role in the world, are central to any historical understanding. The differences of opinion over what should be taught depend deeply on the politics, the positions, and the philosophies of the participants and cannot be resolved by any agreement about the details of historical events. Debate offers the attraction of an intellectual standard of adjudication and an outcome that cannot be strictly determined by political outlook; it incorporates rather than dismisses these differences of outlook. Debate is a figure for mediation between the intellectual and the political. Even if Rich has no interest in the intellectual content of what is taught and seeks only to defend the NEH and the NEA (National Endowment for the Arts) and to disparage "right-wing vigilantes," he still turns toward an intellectual realm, here composed of "quieter voices."

Yet if "debate" suggests a mediation between the political and the intellectual, the word "genuine" calls for their disengagement: in this case, a clear separation between Cheney, who is tainted by political ambition ("whose major concern is to find a Limbaughesque political vehicle to ride to the next G.O.P. Administration"), and McCullough, the professional historian. "Genuine" points to an elsewhere, a purer domain, restricted here to those who already support national standards and composed largely of history professors. Academia is a typical location for this ivory tower, and the ideology of the modern university rests on a commitment to "genuine debate." But why would anyone suppose that academic historians are more capable of genuine debate than politicians? Academic debates are not a free space, where each participant, fully willing to be persuaded by the ideas of others, checks ambition, institutional habits of thought, and political orientation at the door. Certainly most academic discussions do not meet an ideal of genuine debate in contrast to the polemics of congressional hearings, and one ex-academic in Congress, Dick Armey, has claimed that disputes in academia are less collegial, more partisan, and less "genuine" than those in Congress. The call for genuine debate arises where a boundary is being tested, yet it invokes an elsewhere, a place where the political can be perfectly subsumed by the intellectual.

Frank Rich does little to bring about a better discussion, but I still find something compelling in his gesture calling for genuine debate, precisely because I am so discontented with most debates now taking place. The much vaunted "culture wars" engage the central issues for the humanities — the relation of culture to society — but these disputes have not produced an informative dialogue, with anyone learning much from one another. It is more like a game of dodge ball, where opposing players take turns aiming at designated targets. Intelligent people talking together ought to be able to achieve more than this. But what motivates or supports such a belief?

Bringing Us Together

The front cover of Gerald Graff's *Beyond the Culture Wars: How Teaching the Conflicts Can Revitalize American Education* contains a blurb by Henry Louis Gates Jr.: "Graff offers a highly readable and down-to-earth perspective on some of the most ballyhooed issues in higher education today.... By encouraging us to argue together, he may yet help us to reason together."[4] The word "together" does a lot of work here. Any public pronouncement about the usefulness of debate rests on the belief that something is always achieved by arguing "together," no matter the outcome. Forging a "together" transcends the resolution of any particular disputed point. An insistence on "arguing together," rather than just arguing (the title of the book is "*Beyond* the Culture Wars"), assumes that something will happen from the contact with opposing positions, that something more than a clarification of differences will take place. An attempt to understand opposing arguments may broaden into a recognition of common methods, even shared goals. Implicit is the idea that some voices are not being heard and that their expression will change the course of argument, or that the current state (and stalemate) depends partly on misunderstanding and misrepresentation and that the terms of argument can be improved, distortions overcome. Thus the path of reasoning itself will be changed.

In the age of "difference," the repeated use of "together" may seem quaint, but almost all analyses that focus on difference have as their horizon the elimination or the reduction of barriers that keep people apart and the hope of a more vital, open public sphere. In the meantime, an aim of criticism is inclusion, participation in a common enterprise. The prospect of arguing together, and of a public dialogue, also holds out validation and inclusion for humanities professors who, despite their métier of argument, have often been left on the periphery of social conflicts.

All these benefits and justifications for arguing, all these hopes for "together," finally hinge on a shift to reasoning: "He may yet help us to reason together." Without the hope of new thinking, all the divisions and stratifications will reemerge. In Gates's phrasing, "encouraging us to argue together" seems to portend helping "us to reason together." But what is the link? Does the reasoning in argument, dialogue, and debate at some moment cross over into reasoning *together*? Which arguments, which topics of controversy, are actually subject to such a process? The appeal of dialogue is its promise that we can reason together, but this promise is precisely what must be questioned, in each instance. Gates, a master at offering up phrases that appeal to his audience, invokes the hope that we may "reason together" as an obvious teleology, an unquestionably desirable end point for Graff's book, for the academic enterprise, and for our society. I certainly do not want to reject the possibility of reasoning together; I would love to see it happen more often. But an entire ideology is contained in the notion of "reasoning together," and why should we accept this as the obvious goal when it so rarely happens? Most disputes do not end in reasoning together, particularly the literary conflicts that underlie Graff's book, and Gates's own *Loose Canons: Notes on the Culture Wars*.

Again, as with the catchword of "genuine debate," I want to call attention to the touchstones that orient attitudes toward dialogue. As a touchstone, as an unquestioned good, "to reason together" acts as a perpetual horizon for argument, as that which may happen. But in keeping this ideal in place, at a distance, we abdicate a certain responsibility for achieving it. In both Graff's and Gates's books, there is little acknowledgment of any merit in the ideas of those with whom they disagree. Reasoning together is apparently beyond the ken of their antagonists. Gates writes, "Allan Bloom is right to ask about the effect of higher education on our kids' moral development, even though that's probably the only thing he is right about."[5] If one can so easily dismiss the writings of the person who brought the issue of "the effect of higher education on our kids' moral development" to the forefront, what could possibly be gained by reasoning *with* Bloom? Reasoning together, as a future end point, gets everyone off the hook; it offers both a legitimation (everything we do is leading toward it) and an excuse (I don't have to do it yet).

So often, I wish I could get people with clashing opinions in a room and force them, issue by issue, to *understand* exactly what the other person is arguing, to give up their baggage, and actually try to "reason together."[6] In reading "interventions" from across the spectrum of the culture wars, even from such antagonists as Roger Kimball and Houston Baker, I usually find some arguments with which I can agree.[7] With myself functioning as a middle term, as a place of "reason" between these opponents, I can imagine getting them to see certain merits in each other's viewpoints and find common grounds for "reasoning together" and for jointly developing ideas that would improve the state of literary studies and higher education. But of course this is just a fantasy. Any of the staged confrontations between "Right" and "Left" (terms becoming increasing meaningless as "radical" and "revolutionary" are now more frequently coupled with "Right") only produces a defense of the position being represented, not an openness to persuasion or any effort to look for merit in and learn from the other person's ideas.

I can't even pull off such a discussion among my friends — a "reasoning together" that would bring out and bridge deep ideological differences — especially when there is something on the line, such as disagreement over the proper role of affirmative action in hiring decisions. There is usually a whole range of issues that can be discussed, but also a few topics that are too sensitive, too connected to people's fundamental assumptions, to be fully brought into the open and made subjects on which we can reason together. Dialogue rarely enables us to actually bridge perspectives; the most that can be hoped for are cracks or jarrings from contact with others, shocks that produce small openings, or new sympathies. Reasoning together across ideological/polemical boundaries will not happen just by setting up some forum in which we argue together. For what are the ends of argument? Not reason itself, but always a more specific outcome. The most divisive issues either go unstated or become a fulcrum for differentiating oneself from "opponents," not a platform on which to reason together.

What issues, what topics, offer good opportunities for reasoning together? And what circumstances, and what expectations, are necessary to generate a useful dialogue? The occasions on which people with widely divergent views actually reason together and achieve new intellectual insights or political understandings are quite rare. The appeal of "together" is to cross a divide, but reasoning *together* requires sympathy, analogy, common patterns, or overlapping goals: strong attractions, not just shared divisions. The faith that we can reason together papers over the gap between our current disputes and our image of what academic or democratic life ought to be. Hovering around all appeals for dialogue is the fear that our words are only chatter and provide no adequate response to the problems they seek to address.

Conflict in the Classroom

So far, I have been considering dialogue as a *response*, as something one appeals to in order to resolve a controversy or improve an unsatisfactory situation. The beginning point is a problem — educational standards, how to teach history, disagreements about the canon, culture wars, the breakdown of the public sphere, the withering of democracy, an inadequate sense of community — and genuine debate or reasoning together is a proposed solution. The process of dialogue is conceived either as offering the best path for resolving conflict or as itself the embodiment of democracy and rational thought in action.

Gerald Graff, famous for advocating "teaching the conflicts," might at first glance seem to propose a similar conception: there are bitter disagreements over the teaching and the purpose of the humanities, so let's foreground these disputes, let's bring debate to the center of our pedagogy and turn our "courses into conversations."[8] Graff writes, "As I see it, the challenge is to turn these very conflicts to positive account, by transforming a scene of hatred and anger into one of educationally productive debate" (4). Yet for Graff, dialogue, conversation, and debate are not simply possible responses to specific conflicts, but instead are always already occurring and in fact supply the context for any understanding of these conflicts: conversation and critical debate are what produce meaning and even truth.

Graff, in a striking confession for a literature professor, speaks of having no "original passion for literature," no inspired primary experience of "literature itself" that preceded a subsequent acquisition of "the secondary, derivative skills of critical discussion" (69). He tells instead a story of overcoming his boredom and helplessness in the face of literature and of finally experiencing "a personal reaction to it" and "getting into immediate contact with the text" only after being introduced to critical controversies and entering into "a conversation of other readers" (70).[9] For Graff, "genuine debate" is not some future horizon toward which we aspire, but rather something we are always already immersed in, something without which any literary criticism would be impossible. He argues that one cannot make sense of critical interpretations without an awareness of the ongoing dialogue with other views.[10] Graff insists repeatedly "that culture itself is a debate, not a monologue" (8), and even that "when truth is disputed, we can seek it only by entering the debate" (15).

Yet if Graff at times suggests the radical stance of equating conflict and debate (rather than offering debate as the means for resolving conflict), and if he pronounces conflict the basis for understanding, why is there a projected "beyond" (*Beyond the Culture Wars*); why so very many appeals for dialogue, interaction, debate, discussion, and conversation that are not now occurring; and why so much talk of "turning" and "transforming" ("turning conflict into community," "turning courses into conversations," "transforming a scene of hatred and anger into one of educationally productive debate")? What does Graff want from debate that he does not see us getting from our current conflicts? Throughout the book, Graff draws attention to three main inadequacies: conflict at a distance (the ideas and the approaches of different professors are in conflict, but they rarely have to confront each other directly, so little actual debate takes place), conflict hidden from students (when debates do take place, it is not in the classroom, where students might participate), and conflict degenerating into hostility, anger, and misunderstanding (confrontations that serve little educational purpose). To resolve this tension between his view that cultural debate underlies any understanding or interpretation and his critique of the shortcomings of the current culture wars, Graff shifts the focus onto students. He can therefore defend the cultural and especially the professional legitimacy of our debates, while censuring them for not yet being meaningful to *students*. By drawing attention to the students ("teaching the conflicts"), he also hopes to bring professors with opposing views into greater contact with each other and to make these confrontations, in the special space of the classroom, pedagogically productive. Academic debate will be legitimized and reinvigorated by engaging the students — a comforting message at a time when the mission of the university is under attack.

There are problems with this displacement of the validation for debate to the classroom. The attempt to open academic debates to students presupposes the significance and vitality of these conflicts. Russell Jacoby skewers Graff on this supposition. Jacoby writes: *"Beyond the Culture Wars* is . . . permeated by an ethos that it shares with much critical thought, academic boosterism. Graff shows himself less a critic than a cheerleader of professional life. . . . He confuses networking with teaching, back-scratching with scholarship, jargon with thinking."[11] All the strategies one can think of for getting students to participate in academic debates will be worthless if the arguments themselves are of little value. Graff is fundamentally ambivalent about the state of academic debate in the humanities. He frequently defends "today's academic disputes," saying they "mirror broader social conflicts," and he claims that even "the quarrels sparked by esoteric literary theories . . . echo debates . . . in the larger society" (9) (he even goes so far as to lump together "the dynamics of modern academic professionalism and American democracy" [195] — this is what Jacoby finds shallow). Yet much of his book reads like a familiar indictment of the insularity, the divisions, and the "disjunctions" that characterize the modern university, and we are presented with urgent pleas for reform. I do not think that changing some courses and a few aspects of the curriculum will substantially alter academic life and give new meaning to our disputes. Bringing together in one classroom or even one curriculum conflicting views that are not already intellectually substantive, deeply reflective, and productively engaged with the fundamental issues of the discipline will not produce a better education. The topics of greatest controversy rarely draw forth the most intellectually rewarding responses; the volumes of polemic by literature professors on the culture wars offer little insight into the key problems of literary analysis.

A second problem with Graff's account is that too much is invested in the classroom as a unique space for unifying, transforming, and learning from our conflicts. The classroom operates here as a fantasmatic space of possibility for all that cannot be achieved elsewhere. The usual forms of professional activity fall short of the idealized debate, in which there is an openness, an earnest engagement with authors' ideas, and real progress beyond the initial presuppositions. Most academic arguments about the social and political issues that interest Graff are insipid — a form either of preaching to the converted or of denouncing the infidels.[12] The classroom, with its not fully formed students, functions both as an arena for making professors expose and defend their positions to others (staging their conflict) and as a place for *entering* debate (testing out ideas, but not yet having a stake, not yet occupying a determined place in the conflict). At this liminal point, where students cross the boundary from audience to participant, one may imagine an "educationally productive debate," that is, a series of critical exchanges in which each participant gains greater understanding: new insights about the thoughts they began with and about different, conflicting ideas held by others; and also, if all goes well, new thinking, the development of ideas that greatly exceed the starting propositions. Professors, too far advanced in their professional life, are less fluid and rarely learn much from these confrontations, from such clashes of their ideas against those of their unsympathetic colleagues. A group of students (a captive body, defined as in a state of transition, of learning) is needed on which to project a dream of conjunction and transformation, of alchemizing conflict into the gold of learning and community rather than the dross of boredom or culture war. Through an act of transference, the expectations for debate are displaced onto the students, yet too often the real hope is that they will mirror back to us our own cherished opinions, after having scrutinized opposing views through this process of debate.

Despite his insistence on the structuring role of conflict for our understanding, Graff still appeals to a horizon of debate not yet taking place to redeem the entire academic enterprise. Participants in the "conflicts" that Graff emphasizes — conflicts that are less about differences in interpreting the meaning of a passage in a literary work (a traditional site of disagreement for literary criticism) than about the political and epistemological significance of "cultural texts" (the term "literature" itself is now in dispute) — may sharpen or clarify their ideas by striking them against the dull armor of their opponents, but there is rarely any real thinking across the differences that separate the antagonists. In reading through the numerous collections of essays on political correctness or fights about the canon, one would be hard-pressed to find instances in which those who attack, say, "the Killer B's" (Allan Bloom, William Bennett, and Saul Bellow) had actually learned anything from the ideas of these writers, whom they condemn, or even had any hope for changing their antagonists' thinking (and the same is certainly true in the opposite direction). Whatever may be "educationally productive" — inspiring new ideas, not producing new manuscripts (and yes, there is a difference) — does not occur *within* the debate. The scenes of conflict — whether a conference with one's friends or a public encounter with one's enemies — are seldom the desired space of educational vitality.

Models of Debate

In emphasizing the gap between the discussions now taking place ("disputes" or "conflicts") and the ones that Rich, Gates, and Graff would like to see (genuine debate, reasoning together), my aim is not to dismiss the distance between these good and bad versions by debunking the ideal of dialogue or by deconstructing the differences between "rant" and "serious debate." I want instead to clarify the possibilities for moving from one pole to the other; but to do this, we first need to examine the goals of dialogue and debate. What is it that is hoped for from this contact with the ideas of others? What is it that the writer feels cannot be achieved by his or her own words, thus propelling the call for dialogue? Why does Cornel West, to take another example, call for a "crucial debate" over questions of race when he seems so manifestly capable of supplying answers to the questions he highlights?[13]

A basic response is that debate offers a means for changing *other* people's thoughts. The person who holds a position embraced by only a minority, who feels that his or her voice is not being heard, is often the one who appeals for debate. The hope is more to persuade others than to stimulate one's own thinking. There are usually other desires as well, ranging from the hope of building community to a longing for intellectually exciting interactions: desires that require a dynamic dialogue, a back and forth encounter, a mutual transformation, and not just getting people to agree with one's own opinions.

In most appeals to dialogue, there is a mixture of democratic-multicultural and of rational-intellectual goals. There is the hope that participating in dialogue together will lead people from different backgrounds to a greater understanding of other perspectives and a new respect for cultural difference, and also the expectation that dialogue will offer an arena for testing and contesting ideas and for producing or at least validating knowledge. Dialogue offers political legitimacy (different opinions are heard), but also opens the way for movement beyond our current impasses (new thinking may be spurred by the critical exchange of opinion).

Most calls for dialogue or debate assume that these goals are mutually supportive: that a more representative process and better understanding of cultural "others" will sharpen and strengthen the critical debate over which ideas are most true or just. More pointedly, it is often claimed that our current policies and concepts are flawed because a diverse enough range of people was not included in their formulation. But these two sets of goals depend on very different — and in some ways incompatible — guiding assumptions. Contemporary notions of "truth" as perspectival, constructed, and grounded in cultural differences lie behind the recent demands for a more multicultural and democratic dialogue, yet these notions are direct attacks against earlier ideas about rationality, objectivity, and human understanding that support the conception of dialogue as a contest of ideas from which truth will emerge. The emphasis on a multiplicity of perspectives puts into question any shared assumptions or common ground that would regulate the dialogue and supply the pressure and the criteria for moving beyond a mere swapping of opinion. The calls for dialogue today do not offer a solution, a readily available means for mediating between conflicting views and interests, but rather point to a problem and pose a challenge: How can we turn a dialogical encounter into productive engagement of differences and an occasion for better thinking?

The model of rational, critical debate as the means for overcoming error and correcting and testing ideas stems from Enlightenment notions about the free exercise of reason. Central here is the freeing of reason from dogma and authority and the dispelling of ignorance and prejudice. The premise is that dialogue will occur between autonomous, free-thinking individuals (not between representatives of particular "identities" as we often hear today) who, through common inquiry, can arrive together at a better understanding of whatever ideas or issues are in dispute. In such a dialogue, reason supplies the critical power for modifying one's initial views and transcending one's personal interests, and it also supplies a critical framework for evaluating opinions.

The social function of rational-critical debate has received its fullest exposition in Jürgen Habermas's *The Structural Transformation of the Public Sphere: An Inquiry into a Category of Bourgeois Society*, and many recent social theorists use Habermas's descriptions as a starting point for their own hopes of what a reinvigorated public sphere might be like. But Habermas does not suggest that all we need to do is embrace again the values and the forms of rational-critical debate. Habermas presents this public sphere of early bourgeois society as having undergone a "structural transformation"; it no longer provides the model for resisting domination and coercion in civil society. A vital public sphere of rational-critical debate cannot be willed back into being through a set of principles for guiding discussion.

It helps to read Habermas in tandem with Carl Schmitt's earlier *Crisis of Parliamentary Democracy*, in which Schmitt charts, in the political sphere, the crack-up of the liberal, parliamentarian belief in the importance of *openness* and *discussion* on the shoals of modern mass democracy. Schmitt writes: "Discussion means an exchange of opinion that is governed by the purpose of persuading one's opponent through argument of the truth or justice of something, or allowing oneself to be persuaded of something as true and just.... To discussion belong shared convictions as premises, the willingness to be persuaded, independence of party ties, freedom from selfish interests."[14] But Schmitt goes on to say, "The situation of parliamentarism is critical today [1926] because the development of modern mass democracy has made argumentative public discussion an empty formality" (6). Schmitt explains that in twentieth-century democracies the important decisions "are no longer the outcome of parliamentary debate" (49), and he contrasts "conduct that is...concerned with discovering what is rationally correct" against that which is concerned "with calculating particular interests and the chances of winning and with carrying these through according to one's own interests" (5–6). In the latter case, which Schmitt applies to modern mass democracy and to business negotiations, "these are not discussions in the specific sense" (as defined above). The crisis "in parliamentarism, in government by discussion" (8), is structural — a product of modern, mass society — and cannot be overcome simply by advocating anew the liberal virtues of openness and discussion; the pressures of mass democracy have brought out "the inescapable contradiction of liberal individualism and democratic homogeneity" (17).[15] In our age of mass media, and with the feedback loops of continuous polling, any notion of "government by discussion" (with discussion defined as persuasion "through argument of the truth or justice of something" and as "freedom from selfish interests") sounds quaint. Whenever any political event now appears to approach this ideal of discussion, with the participants appearing to open themselves to persuasion by their opponents, it is quickly dismissed as an anomaly and as a facade masking other purposes, rather than treated as a fruitful beginning for better discussions.[16]

I do not want to argue that the model of "rational-critical debate" has been completely superseded and is no longer available for resolving any of our current conflicts, now that Habermas and Schmitt have shown that the institutional structures that at one time supported such debate have been greatly transformed. Many scientific, academic, and political discussions are still guided (successfully) by this model of dialogue. Such debates cannot flourish, however, without a supportive institutional framework. A call for genuine debate is hollow when the institutional structures — political or academic — promote other means for mediating disagreement. In academia, it is often assumed that some model of rational-critical debate still underpins the enterprise; it is far from clear that any such assumption is justified.[17]

The concept of rational-critical debate as the means for resolving political and intellectual conflict has also been severely challenged on philosophical grounds. The picture that Schmitt paints of the supersession of discussion has many analogies in recent theory. Twentieth-century thinkers have attacked the conceptions of autonomy, reason, the individual, and truth that are central to envisioning discussion as the means for "discovering what is rationally correct" (5). If one employs a postmodern notion of truth as socially constructed and dependent on perspective (as opposed to considering "perspective" as something that has to be overcome in order to reach the truth), then it is no longer possible to view "critical public debate" as "a noncoercive inquiry into what was at the same time correct and right," as Habermas puts it,[18] or in Schmitt's terms, as a discussion of what is "true and just." What is "correct" or "just" will now depend on the cultural contexts and subject positions of the speakers. Dialogue may help bring about greater understanding of and respect for these differences, but it cannot arbitrate between them.

I will not rehearse here the post-Nietzschean and post-Freudian questionings of truth, consciousness, and subjectivity. Any attempt to put forth a new *theory* of dialogue would require a sustained engagement with all these challenges to communication, interpretability, and intersubjectivity;[19] I will only consider their impact on expectations for dialogue. In recent years, such critiques have been widely disseminated and assimilated, so that difference, otherness, and a relativity of cultures and values are now the presumptions on which arguments are built. This new critical paradigm has spawned an impetus toward cross-cultural dialogue; acknowledging cultural difference, the impossibility of any "disinterested" discourse, and the social construction of knowledge requires a new conversation to cross the divisions between us. Recognition and understanding of the differences of the other, rather than the resolution of difference through a common search for truth, become the goals for dialogue. Yet it is still expected that a successful dialogue will adjudicate between conflicting views or at least offer a shared framework for critiquing each other's ideas, notwithstanding the challenge to the foundations of rational-critical debate. Otherwise little would be gained by getting opposing parties to examine together their conflict. But what is to provide a common ground for discussion? Most appeals for dialogue cover over the incompatibilities between these models of rational-critical debate and cross-cultural conversation, and "dialogue" in itself can provide no overarching framework when the very foundations of dialogue are in dispute. Dialogue is being invoked to heal the very rifts that put into question whether any "successful" dialogue or a "genuine" debate can span these ideological divides.

A National Conversation

I want to consider briefly an example of a project for conversation that adopts much of this new critical paradigm, in order to bring out some of the problems of ignoring the shift away from earlier models of dialogue, to emphasize that any call for dialogue today is highly problematic rather than obviously just the right prescription, and especially, to suggest that the process of conversation is not sufficient for revitalizing democracy. The National Endowment of the Humanities program entitled "A National Conversation on American Pluralism and Identity" is a predictable response at a time when many say that the fundamental problems of social disharmony stem from a failure to recognize, respect, and appreciate cultural difference. The introduction makes a typical contrast between "signs of fragmentation" ("debates over school and university curricula, disputes over immigration, ethnic rivalries in our cities, the increasing use of violence to resolve conflicts" — all representing "bad" forms of dialogue) and "an expressed longing for community," which a good conversation (one where "Americans of all backgrounds... study, learn, and speak face-to-face about our differences") will help to fulfill.[20] The emphasis throughout is on discussing our differences, and the first goal is to "[e]ncourage discussion among and between different ethnic, racial, and cultural groups about American pluralism and identity" (7). Conversation is put forth as the mechanism for overcoming fragmentation and for transforming destructive conflict into a unifying, educational experience.

In response to the question "Why a conversation?" we are told: "The key elements are exchange and reciprocity, rather than competition or imposition of one's views on another. During a genuine conversation, participants expand their own horizons through greater understanding of perspectives different from their own. In response, they are challenged to think more clearly about their own assumptions" (8).[21] The emphasis on exchange and reciprocity, and an expansion of horizons (as opposed to the Gadamerian *fusion* of horizons),[22] puts the primary focus on acknowledging and respecting difference, in sharp contrast to Schmitt's description of discussion as "persuading one's opponent through argument of the truth or justice of something." The goal is more to get someone from a different cultural group to acknowledge one's own view of "the truth or justice of something" than to get them to agree with it. Cultural, racial, and ethnic differences, as the primary dividing points and the bases on which one speaks, require an adherence to rather than an abandonment of one's differential perspective. The individual is conceived here as representing a group (that he or she was born into and did not choose), rather than as someone who aspires toward reason.

There are many things to question about this project to fund actual series of conversations "on American pluralism and identity": the belief that an inadequate "understanding of perspectives different from [the participants'] own" is central to the breakdown of community; the assumption that there exists some common "American identity" that can bridge the chasm between different perspectives, even as the sponsors retreat from any Jeffersonian enunciation of principles of American identity in the fear of imposing "one's views on another"; the expectation that mutual understanding will resolve conflict (as if the problems underlying class conflict result from an inadequate understanding of the feelings and outlooks of those in the other group); and above all, faith that the correct *process* of conversation — with conversation starters, conversation leaders and partners, and other planning elements gleaned from an education-school textbook — will achieve the desired result.

I want to emphasize that this model of conversation is extremely weak; we get only very pale versions of understanding and criticism, feeble notions of difference and of the public sphere. Understanding is reduced to the mere awareness of what someone else thinks or feels. Dialogue as a forum for arguing about differences, sharpening ideas, and resolving disagreement is replaced by the tepid goals of bringing "diverse groups of Americans together" (6) in order "to study, learn, and speak face-to-face about our differences" (5) and to achieve a greater understanding "of different perspectives" (7). The process of conversation is treated as an end, as itself an affirmation of our democracy. Getting people to talk to each other does not, however, produce a functioning democracy. A conversation about "who we are" is no substitute for discussing the economic, political, and social problems that are the evidence of how far we still are from the ideals of democracy. There is little substance to this project and surprisingly little content concerning the "questions that are at the heart of our democratic society" (7). Any fuller articulation of the problems of "our democracy" would shatter the pretense that understanding someone else's perspective offers an adequate means for addressing these questions.

The challenge for any dialogue is to move beyond an exchange of opinion (or a trading of insults) to a critical engagement with other ideas. This is why Cornel West, when appealing for dialogue, always appends an adjective such as "critical," "candid," "honest," or "frank";

the hope is to bring out a self-consciousness and truthfulness that will begin to change our own opinions as well. For Habermas, the noteworthy aspect of public debate in the late eighteenth and early nineteenth centuries was that it was a realm for *critical* thinking — for challenging dogma and inherited forms of authority. In the NEH project, the only prospect for criticism is the inclusion of groups that have not been sufficiently represented or listened to in the past. The critical component of dialogue is expected to take care of itself, arising from exposure to others (this is a timid brand of multiculturalism; there is no mention of subordination or oppression as a basis for critical thought). It is still hoped that conversation will bring all the fruits of philosophical dialogue and of public, rational-critical debate, while muffling the contestatory power of any ideas that might interfere with the quest to ensure that no one's self-esteem is ever damaged.

Even the notion of difference is fudged in this project (as it is in so much recent criticism). Everything is so painless here; learning about others requires no challenge to cultural identity, and there is no need to give up any of one's own interests. On the one hand, if the differences that are to generate the conversation are essential, if they really matter, then the existence of an "American identity" that is to provide the common ground is in doubt, and the possibility that conversation can bridge these differences between "ethnic, racial, and cultural groups" must be questioned, not assumed. On the other hand, if these differences are finally not consequential, and if social fragmentation along these lines is only the result of misunderstanding, then the overwhelming attention to difference is misplaced. The NEH model of conversation can only mediate conflicts that stem from ignorance. This squishy liberalism does not have the courage to take "difference" seriously; differences are merely noted (in the language of one successful proposal, "The goal is to determine what values are shared and which are contested amid Arizona's diverse society"), not engaged, critiqued, and debated.

The project also makes gestures toward revivifying the public sphere; one of the goals is to "[e]stablish public spaces, opportunities for Americans to engage in civil conversations about questions that are at the heart of our democratic society" (7). Yet it provides neither the conceptual nor the structural framework for a public sphere. Conversations whose "key elements are exchange and reciprocity" offer no basis for a "public" beyond some possible identification with America. For Habermas, the notion of the *public* is so important because it is transformative. The act of speaking publicly is not simply the expression of one's own views to others; it also requires envisioning a public, tailoring one's ideas according to common criteria, and making arguments that potentially apply to everyone. Notions such as reason, truth, and justice support an emerging public sphere, whereas earlier criteria for judgment such as lineage, revelation, and authority created unbridgeable distinctions between people. Today, in contrast, the public sphere is often recast as the public expression of one's true self or private identity, a form of confession and coming out that is validated by the Oprah Winfrey–Bill Clinton empathic response of "I feel your pain." The NEH project dreams of a new public and of new forms of community forged by discussion, but it offers no foundation on which to rebuild the communal bonds of society.

The poverty of conversation is a *symptom* of the breakdown of communal structures and of the breakdown of ideas that uphold communal bonds. Federally sponsored "conversations" can hardly be expected to repair the dislocations of capitalism or to replicate the informal neighborhood places, extolled by Christopher Lasch, "in which people meet as equals" and "that promote general conversations across class lines."[23] Lasch argues that organized and supervised activities have replaced the "involuntary and therefore somewhat haphazard, promiscuous, and unpredictable types of informal association" (126); the NEH projects only accentuate this tendency.[24] An effort to fund a few conversations about "our American identity" will do little to repair a "fragmented" society; at best it might project unity against common threats, against those who somehow, in our televisual world, remain un-American.

The NEH project, by assuming that there is a model of "genuine conversation" ready at hand, which we can employ for addressing our conflicts of opinion, ignores the crisis of dialogue it hopes to confront. There is little consensus among the imagined participants of "genuine" or "productive" debate about the suppositions that would guide it (How does one even interpret the words of another? as self-conscious, clear expressions of an idea? or as shaped by unconscious drives and imbricated in layers of ideology?) or about the possibilities and proper forms of communication. In our age of mass media, when every reasoned argument is transformed by retransmission, repetition, decontextualization, and reduction into a mediatic pronouncement,

the prospects for any type of successful conversation are slim.[25] To reduce the wide disparity between what we hope for and what we get
from these dialogical interactions with others, every appeal for dialogue needs also to elaborate how it will produce whatever results are
envisioned. There are more sophisticated conceptions of dialogue that
emphasize cultural difference than the NEH project, but it is not just
a question of choosing the theory of dialogue we find most suitable for
our tastes (upholding standards, encouraging toleration, and so on).
An expressed longing for rational-critical debate among all the participants in an argument will do little to overcome the institutional
pressures or the ideological disagreements that undercut such a framework. Conversation is not a value that transcends whatever values are
in dispute. The challenge is always twofold: to explain why conversation can be an adequate response to the conflicts and the problems at
hand and to explain how an effective conversation can be built up and
sustained, in the face of inadequate structures for dialogue (an anemic
public sphere, a decline of civility, an age of sound bites).

Sparring Partners

We do not lack theories of dialogue. Postulating persuasive theories —
either ones that more accurately correspond to our current episte-
mologies or ones that lay out guiding propositions to which all the
disputants would give consent — will not bring about the desired conversations. In many instances, the participants all invoke a similar
ideal of dialogue, yet their encounter in no way embodies the ideal
they claim to embrace. Instead, recourse to a higher ground of dialogue is a favorite tactic for delegitimating the ideas of the opponent:
she should not be listened to because she refuses to be guided by the
norms of genuine discussion and instead engages in distortion, mere
rhetoric, or rant. Or in the words of Stanley Fish (from his "debates"
with Dinesh D'Souza):

> This is perhaps why the story they tell of an educational pro-
> cess corrupted by strange theories and ideological motives that
> have only recently polluted the pristine world of the academy
> will not be shaken by something so paltry as *evidence*. Evidence,
> after all, is derived from history, and it acquires its force from his-

torical contexts. Consequently, it weighs as nothing against the conviction of someone so self-righteous that he will immediately hear challenges to his present opinions as either tainted in their source or irrelevant to what he already knows to be the case. An ideologue of this type regards assertions made by his opponents not as arguments to be considered but as debating points to be dismissed; and since he isn't taking the back and forth of argument seriously, but as an occasion for forensic display — an occasion not for persuading an audience but diverting it (in two senses of the word) — he is no more invested in what *he* says than he is in what is said by those on the other side. In a sense, then, he doesn't mean anything by his words — he doesn't stand by them — for he regards them as merely instrumental to the promotion of a truth he is in possession of before any discussion begins.[26]

This is the ultimate strategy for dismissing the ideas of your opponent: "He doesn't mean anything by his words." Fish, by defining D'Souza's arguments as "forensic display" and therefore outside the realm of productive discussion, performs the sin of which he is accusing D'Souza: he declares that we need not seriously consider his opponent's ideas. Yet he portrays himself as the one who upholds the standards of dialogue against all threats: he favors "taking the back and forth of argument seriously" rather than practicing "forensic display"; regarding the opponent's assertions as "arguments to be considered" rather than "as debating points to be dismissed"; "persuading" rather than "diverting" the audience; and standing by his words, in contrast to D'Souza, who "regards them as merely instrumental to the promotion of a truth he is in possession of before any discussion begins." D'Souza, no doubt, would also claim that he is on the side of serious argument, weighing evidence, persuasion, and standing — meaning something — by one's words. The goals of discussion are not in dispute here; only who best represents them.

For anyone familiar with Fish's writing, this passage is hilarious. Fish's means of argument — describing and denouncing "an ideologue of this type" — undermine all the boundaries of discussion he is claiming to uphold, and he in turn neither provides a detailed analysis of historical "evidence" to support his position (defending affirmative action), nor demonstrates any willingness to take seriously D'Souza's arguments. Fish has made a nice living deconstructing the difference between the Serious and the Rhetorical, arguing that any attempt to cordon off a proper use of language, uncontaminated by rhetoric, bias, or partisanship, is doomed to failure.[27] Now when he is on the defensive (defending academia, literary studies, affirmative action, and speech codes against widespread attacks by conservatives and others), he leans on such oft-attacked (by him) distinctions as "serious argument" versus "forensic display" and "persuasion" versus "diversion" that he thinks will still be persuasive for his new audience containing few English professors or literature majors. As Fish has amply demonstrated before, it is much easier to invoke such distinctions than to abide by them.

If, as I claim, Fish and D'Souza could agree on the proper model for dialogue, why can't they hold a discussion where evidence is weighed, the back and forth of argument is taken seriously, and they learn from each other? It would be easy to supply a cynical answer: they make too much money with their popular road show to change the style, and such denunciatory tactics are actually more persuasive for the audience. Yet I don't want to accuse Fish (or D'Souza) of cynically claiming the high ground of serious, intellectual dialogue while in fact slinging mud at the other. It would be nice to say: Why don't you each take the ideas of the other seriously, assume that they are the product of good faith and intelligence, and address their strengths rather than attack their weaknesses or just debunk them? Such a question assumes that Fish chooses not to appeal to D'Souza's understanding and attempts instead to avoid "genuine debate" by discrediting him. Fish's attacks on D'Souza, however, cannot be separated from his larger arguments for affirmative action, speech codes, and other forms of sensitivity to racial or sexual background, since these arguments hinge on the bad faith of those who espouse the contrary position and hence their impenetrability to argument.

The passage cited above comes from an essay entitled "Speaking in Code," in which Fish argues that conservatives use "coded" language to express racism (or sexism or hatred of gays) that is no longer socially acceptable in more overt forms. Fish writes, "My point is that the practices of those who have declared themselves against curricular reform, multiculturalism, affirmative action, deconstruction, feminism, gay and lesbian studies, etc., are informed by a massive bad faith" (92). The proper response for Fish is to decode these declarations and reveal the bad faith: *exposing* an attack on multiculturalism as "racist" is sufficient rebuttal. One need not engage the actual terms of the argument, since they only serve as the disguise for a bigoted meaning. Affirmative action would be unnecessary if there were not a group of self-righteous ideologues — epitomized by D'Souza, former editor of the *Dartmouth Review* — who speak in code and still discriminate against blacks, women, and gays, and if there were not a much larger group susceptible to their influence. To consider D'Souza's ideas seriously, according to Fish's analysis, would be tragically to *misinterpret* them.

Fish and D'Souza may agree on what a good discussion would be like and may even agree that dialogue is the best means for adjudicating the social and intellectual conflict around such issues as multiculturalism, affirmative action, or (pace Rich) national standards for teaching history. But dialogue cannot bridge such a wide ideological divide, when what is at issue is the suitability of each party for participating in dialogue and for making a genuine contribution to "our" understanding. Again, I would want to say: give up this hostile view of those with whom you disagree; give up forms of criticism that delegitimate the other and that hinder the very dialogue you advocate; the public is highly divided and confused on these issues, and if you want to diminish the racial fissures in our society, your own "debate" ought to be an example for overcoming these divisions. Yet perhaps Fish's criticism is appropriate in this case; perhaps D'Souza is an ideologue whose arguments should be decoded and then dismissed, not treated as good faith efforts to achieve fairness and justice; and perhaps such disqualifications apply to all those who espouse similar views.[28] I do not agree; I do not think that all attacks on curricular reform, multiculturalism, and so on are "nothing more than a smoke screen behind which there lies a familiar set of prejudices rooted in personal interest" (92). Fish's plea for discussion while avoiding it by portraying his opponent as beyond the pale only solidifies the current stalemates. The fact that Fish's arguments do not actually promote dialogue, however, does not render them invalid. His judgments about D'Souza, and about opposition to recent academic trends, need to be evaluated for their validity, and not simply for their consequences (closing off dialogue with conservative critics of academia). Criticism and dialogue may be at odds with each other.

It is a lot easier to lay out certain conditions necessary for a productive dialogue (such as seriously considering rather than delegitimating or not listening to each other's ideas) than to achieve one, or even to explain how to go about doing so. The obstacle is not that Fish or D'Souza, by virtue of being a literary theorist or a far-right conservative, is constitutionally incapable of reasoned discussion. Both of them are certainly capable of taking seriously "the back and forth of argument" among their colleagues.[29] With few exceptions, the current critical methodologies and political outlooks are not closed to all other arguments; bringing widely disparate perspectives into a productive dialogue with each other, with hopes of mutual edification, is another matter. The strategies of a deconstructive interpretation, with its destabilization of difference, conflict greatly with those of an Afro-centric interpretation; simply setting up a dialogue about difference between adherents of these practices is unlikely to prove illuminating. Only rarely can "dialogue" bridge ideological chasms. A large amount of preliminary agreements, common goals, and good will must first be established. A dialogue between the "black" Cornel West and the "Jew" Michael Lerner only works (to the extent that it does) because they share so many leftist/socialist ideas about the best directions for society.[30]

My aims in this chapter seem contradictory: to push for better dialogues, yet to challenge the presumptions and the arguments of those who appeal for a productive dialogue, and even to question whether, or in what circumstances, such a discussion is possible. I want to hold on to some notion of dialogue and to some hope for substantive engagement across boundaries of interest, familiarity, and ideology, especially in the university and in the political sphere. To give up on dialogue would be intellectually and institutionally stultifying. It would allow participation to be restricted to the like-minded; this may be fine for a club, but not for a university or a democracy. Yet I do not want to erect "amenability to dialogue" as the criterion for judging ideas. Much of the most profound thinking attacks the habitual foundations of dialogue, such as the possibility of clear communication between one person and another. By such a standard, it would be easy to dismiss Freud's theories of the unconscious insofar as every utterance is potentially a slip of the tongue and overdetermined; even the "subject" itself is exploded into conflicting parts. The psychoanalytic process is so lengthy because the patient is incapable of grasping insights that the therapist might offer early on; dialogue here cannot provide understanding. The possibility of whatever form of dialogue is envisioned needs to be defended, not assumed.

Paradoxically, I think it is in these areas of contestation pointed to by Rich, Gates, Graff, West, Fish, et al. — where dialogue appears to have broken down yet there is still the hope that improved understanding will produce a better society — that dialogue has the most potential. The aims of social criticism (and by "social criticism" I mean all the arguments and analyses that aim at changing society, whether new formulations for public policy or esoteric cultural critiques of literary texts) require the persuasion of those who now hold different beliefs. Social criticism that ignores the views of those it hopes to persuade will be parochial and ineffective; reconsidering ideas in light of others' opinions is crucial. Here, the critical task of rethinking the prevailing wisdom cannot be separated from the dialogical project of acknowledging and accommodating the thoughts of others.[31]

This is not true for all forms of thinking; Gilles Deleuze and Félix Guattari make a strong argument against the utility of discussion for philosophy. They assert that discussing differences of opinion has nothing to do with the real philosophical task of creating concepts and that in discussion "we fall back into the most abject conditions": "a reduction of the concept to propositions like simple opinions; false perceptions and bad feelings (illusions of transcendence or of universals) engulfing the plane of immanence; the model of a form of knowledge that constitutes only a supposedly higher opinion, *Urdoxa*; a replacement of conceptual personae by teachers or leaders of schools."[32] They argue that discussion displaces, reduces, and simplifies philosophical thinking and leads to honoring the wrong criteria for judgment. The prescription for advancing philosophy would not be to bring the leading philosophers together for lengthy discussions.

They also write:

> Philosophy has a horror of discussions. It always has something else to do. Debate is unbearable to it. . . . In fact, Socrates constantly made all discussion impossible, both in the short form of the contest of questions and answers and in the long form of a rivalry between discourses. He turned the friend into the friend of the single concept, and the concept into the pitiless monologue that eliminates the rivals one by one. (29)

Socrates does not value giving everyone a chance to express their views, in order to ensure a representative range of opinion or to promote democracy (Cornel West has described dialogue as "the en-actment of democratic practices"). Dialogue for Plato functions as a means to test ideas, to see how well they hold up to questioning; not as the means for sustaining the heterogeneous voices of the *agora*, or a marketplace of ideas. Gerald Graff may assert that "when truth is disputed, we can seek it only by entering the debate — as Socrates knew when he taught the conflicts two millennia ago," but Socrates did not try to "teach the conflicts";[33] he hoped to defeat competing conceptions of courage, love, language, or the best form of govern-ment and to eliminate "rivals one by one." Plato's dialogues undercut more than they endorse the ethos of discussion behind appeals for "genuine debate" or a "new conversation."[34]

I bring up Deleuze and Guattari to bring pressure against the ex-pectation that "the back and forth of argument" is the natural and necessary mode of intellectual inquiry, even as I want to press those who call for dialogue to make it happen, to make their own appeals ef-fective. Arguing with an opponent can be a distraction from thinking. Fish invokes a paradigm of discussion in order to beat down his oppo-nent, but he ignores the ways in which his own criticism is hostile to this paradigm. The appeal to dialogue is often yet another symptom of a crisis in criticism: the critic needs an illusion of community to justify the entire enterprise, even as the force of criticism is directed against the bulwarks (myths) of consensus, communication, and shared under-standing that create community. Almost always unchallenged is the reassuring fiction that "critical thinking" is in harmony with whatever hopes one has for political progress.

Bite Size Discussions

If (place your favorite adjective here — genuine, honest, frank, criti-cal) dialogue is a promised land, which we cannot yet hope to enter, perhaps it is best to proclaim it as our goal, but not to be constricted by its limitations. This is the tack taken by Michael Bérubé, who in a remarkable and confused conclusion to his essay entitled "Bite Size Theory: Popularizing Academic Criticism" wants to defend "discursive models of social contestation" while finding a more effective means for struggling against "our" enemies:

The lesson here is clear...: most people in national media just don't *want* to understand, no matter what language we speak or how nicely we speak it, even if we're addressing them directly in words they're familiar with....

...[T]here's a broader principle at stake, I think. Too often, when academics deal with political disputes, they imagine such disputes as variants on the model of *conversation*. Whether you're looking at the work of Richard Rorty, Seyla Benhabib, Wayne Booth, Stanley Fish, Barbara Herrnstein Smith or Gerald Graff, you'll find that we tend to place extraordinary and often unwarranted emphasis on discursive rationality, rhetorical persuasion, communicative ethics or teaching the conflicts. What are these, I wonder, if not academic models of political dispute, where procedural and practical advantages accrue to the most articulate, or to those with the greatest capacity for metacommentary and narrative self-justification? I don't mean, in asking such a question, to dismiss such models; on the contrary, I aspire to the ideal of operating according to them....Still, it's crucial for us to remember that most of our interlocutors in the PC wars have no commitment to what intellectuals recognize as legitimate and rational exchange. As Ellen Messer-Davidow's painstaking and splendid research reminds us once again, the opponents of the cultural left are not going about their business by engaging our arguments; they seek to delegitimize higher education....Indeed, lurking behind cultural conservatives' chronic complaints about the decline of academic standards is the sorry (and unpublicized) fact that conservatives have, by and large, failed to meet the precipitously *rising* standards for the production of cultural criticism....

...As cultural critics, we cannot place our faith solely in models of cultural contestation based on the ideals of rational discursive exchange; but neither can we simply abandon discursive models of social contestation in favor of more "tangible" forms of politics. The future of our ability to produce new knowledges for and about ordinary people — and the availability of higher education *to* ordinary people — may well depend on how effectively we can expose the right's well-financed disinformation campaigns. Our success in that endeavor may in turn depend on our ability to make our work intelligible *to* nonacademics —

who then, we hope, will be able to recognize far-right rant about academe for what it is.... But we won't accomplish that goal if we concentrate our energies only on conversing in ever more scrupulous and egalitarian ways with interlocutors whose chief objective is to silence us.[35]

Bérubé, like most people who write about the relations between academics and the public, comes out in favor of "the ideals of rational discursive exchange." Yet he recognizes that academic "discursive models" do not govern public opinion and political decisions, and he chides academics for putting their energy into "conversing in ever more scrupulous and egalitarian ways" rather than into winning public support in whatever manner is most effective. His own criticism, unfortunately, does not offer a better model either for engaging the public or for furthering dialogue. Bérubé's condescension draped in populism is one of the more distasteful features of the academic Left. Even when we speak in simple words, the national media just won't be convinced by our arguments! Others fail to be guided by our wisdom because they "have no commitment to what intellectuals recognize as legitimate or rational exchange." In a stirring defense of credentialed yuppiedom, only intellectuals are deemed capable of recognizing the legitimacy of any exchange of opinion, now that the mission of the university is "to produce new knowledges for and about ordinary people." God forbid that any of these "ordinary people" should presume to claim any knowledge about us extraordinary ones (in the leftist vocabulary, knowledge is always "produced"; the hope of sharing some of the righteousness of authentic labor mixes with the academic version of creationism, where everything must be made, not found). The linkage of "for and about" is symptomatic of our narcissistic age of identity politics; "ordinary people," those of limited imagination, need to be taught about themselves. Bérubé seeks to gain popular support by discrediting "far-right rant about academe," but every piece of his argument rests on the superior insight of like-minded cultural critics and only reinforces the cleavage between academic leftists and the "ordinary people" he hopes to cultivate.

Bérubé offers what I take to be a damning description of academic conversation, "where procedural and practical advantage accrue to the most articulate, or to those with the greatest capacity for metacommentary and narrative self-justification." But he continues, "I don't mean...to dismiss such models; on the contrary, I aspire to the ideal of operating according to them." It is difficult to see how these criteria for advancement could offer "ideals of rational discursive exchange" for "social contestation." A "capacity for metacommentary" may come in handy for TV commentators and for academics who get paid to generate ever more articles perpetuating the current discourse; it offers little basis for better public debate. The merits and the consequences of any position are here less important than the ability to talk knowingly about the entire process of discussion. "Narrative self-justification" accrues advantage to those trained in telling stories that promote their interests; it hardly substitutes for logic, analytic power, integrity, or historical knowledge.

This version of academic conversation does not offer a model for political dispute and could only be taken for one by those who have mastered these skills in attaining professional advancement and thereby concluded that similar criteria should operate in all of society. Bérubé reduces political theory to academic parody, and in place of scrupulous conversation he gives us only attempts to "delegitimize" in turn the arguments of his opponents (they "have thus far displayed no reluctance to spread lies" and have "well-financed disinformation campaigns"). He even stoops to claiming that those he disagrees with just aren't smart enough to make it in the contemporary academic world; "conservatives have, by and large, failed to meet the precipitously *rising* standards." The belief that conservatives are less intelligent is widely held in the humanities; thus we need to "expose" them, rather than consider their ideas.

It is much easier to demonstrate how Bérubé fails to adhere to the "ideals of rational discursive exchange" and fails to achieve his popularizing/populist goals, than to dismiss the important questions he raises: Does adherence to an ideal of conversation limit the efficacy of cultural criticism? How are we to "engage" those who do not want to enter our sort of dialogue? And what does it mean to "engage" the arguments of others? Bérubé's conclusions about the academic "model of conversation" appear after his retelling of a spat (or at least an attempt at one) with John Leo, of *U.S. News and World Report*, who in a column had briefly referred to a talk by Bérubé at an MLA convention.[36] It does not take the "painstaking and splendid research" of Ellen Messer-Davidow to demonstrate that neither Leo's column, Bérubé's letter to Leo, Leo's response to his editor, nor Bérubé's comments in his published essay "engage" the ideas of the opponent in any substantive way or do much to further the "honest intellectual exchange" that Bérubé calls for in his letter to Leo.

Could there be an "honest intellectual exchange" between Bérubé and Leo (or between people expressing similar views), and would it serve any purpose? The points of contention between Bérubé and Leo—teaching music videos versus teaching canonical literary works, the effects of "leftist politics" on literary studies — could lead to an excellent discussion about the nature of the (cultural, literary, and pedagogical) "text" and the purposes of education. Is the role of undergraduate education primarily to generate "serious reflection" (and Bérubé rightly states that the analysis of video can serve this end), or is it to study the most profound work of earlier writers? What are the differences in analyzing a George Michael music video and a Wordsworth poem?[37]

I can imagine, somewhere, an excellent discussion taking place about the issues touched on by Bérubé and Leo, but I cannot conceive it happening between the two of them. For Leo, it is too easy to score points against liberals to bother finding out what actually happens in classrooms or to reflect seriously on either romantic poetry or music videos; for Bérubé, the only point in "engaging" Leo's ideas is to refute them, since he could not possibly have anything to learn from a conservative journalist (except, perhaps, strategies for winning over public sentiment). Any "debate" between Bérubé and Leo would only alternate between crude attack and smug defense, with each claiming that only he values "honest intellectual exchange." If Leo were to attend some classes at the university where Bérubé teaches,[38] and if they were to have a weekly dinner for a semester, they might begin to reassess their ideas under the critical eye of the other, to acknowledge and partially accommodate opposing perspectives, to find some overlap in their goals and understanding, and even to generate together some new ideas about the role and the possibilities of literary studies in higher education. Simply calling for "dialogue" between Leo and Bérubé or between leftist academics and cultural conservatives, however, will not produce anything much more than their misdirected exchange, in which Leo writes to his editor and Bérubé writes for the audience that reads the *Village Voice* and books published by Verso.

For Bérubé, it is easy to turn away from conversation since what he wants from this "rational discursive exchange" is success: to beat out Leo and his ilk in the sphere of public opinion. Once the poor showing of adherents to this model is recognized, he happily looks for a new conception of "struggle." "Exchange" and "engage" are still such treasured words since they imply a recognition of the other and a possibility of community: they point toward public values. Yet operating in Bérubé's descriptions of conversation is a market notion of exchange. If the "discursive rational exchange" were functioning optimally, the best arguments according "to what intellectuals recognize as legitimate" would triumph. This model of conversation is a mechanism for deciding the value of arguments, for winnowing the academic wheat from the bombastic chaff, and Bérubé wants academics to control the market. To "engage" the arguments of another means only employing "rational discursive" criteria to dispute their value. Thus Bérubé can "engage" Leo's mockery of literature professors who teach music videos by equating the dismissal of video with the dismissal of "the novels of hack writers like Charles Dickens or Daniel Defoe"; this scholarly riposte is meant to put to rest any qualms about the value of teaching popular culture, without entailing any need to persuade Leo or to explore his concerns. All this follows from the view of cultural criticism as "social contestation." Bérubé's populist sympathies cannot cover over the fault lines within the conception of "exchange" as a market for ideas yet also a basis for enlarged thought, and of "engage" as an effective means for fending off and also for entering into someone else's ideas.[39]

The "marketplace of ideas" is embraced by academics who despise market capitalism in the hopes that here, on the home turf of "ideas," they will be triumphant. Yet when they enter the markets outside academia, they no longer have control of the game and find themselves at a disadvantage when faced with others who ignore academic rules of engagement. Thus Bérubé proposes better marketing as the appropriate response, even if this means betraying that which it is hoped will triumph — academic models of criticism and conversation. Academics typically want better dialogue with others, but only if they can have it on their own critical grounds. The ethos of Bérubé's cultural criticism — the academic Left as the producer of knowledge for (and of course "about") others — is at odds with the social claims for conversation, that "ordinary people" do have something to contribute. Academic models of conversation *are* inadequate for political disputes, but the major problem is not that professors are too fair-minded and naive and overlook the power of less intellectual forms of persuasion. Academics, especially when addressing their "criticism" toward political disputes and the public sphere, ought to ensure that their own practices can offer an adequate model for public conversation.

Troubling the Horizon

I could go on glossing many further examples of how dialogue is invoked; once one starts looking for the words "dialogue," "debate," "conversation," and "discussion," they turn up with amazing frequency. In each instance, I might show that the writer assumes a prospect of dialogue — a talking through of an issue or question, a meaningful exchange of ideas — that is not justified by the writer's own analyses, practices, or proposals, or I could explain further the ways in which every appeal to dialogue has become problematic. This would be a useful exercise to continue: each additional example would provide another version of a desire for dialogue that goes unfulfilled. I have been focusing on these places where dialogue is invoked, rather then analyzing in depth the trajectory of specific debates or offering yet another model of "public dialogue," since these examples display the *horizon*, the expectations for dialogue, that are projected from our critical vantage points. Even the harshest assessments of current conflicts usually set forth a future of genuine debate or meaningful discussion. Throughout this chapter, I have been exploring the ways in which this horizon is disconnected from our actual practices. The diagnoses of what ails our forms of discussion do not lead us down a path to whatever healthy notion of dialogue is envisioned. I am not aiming to discredit these ideals of communication and mediation, so much as to draw attention to the disjunctions between the aspirations and the functions of criticism.

A typical approach is to lay out a revised understanding of how dialogue ought to work and then to argue that each contribution should now conform to this model. These models often respond to whatever is now seen as our most serious shortcomings, such as inadequate respect for gender or ethnic differences or insufficient adherence to principles of rationality. I will not propose my own model, since I am not convinced that criticism, philosophy, or rigorous thinking are necessarily compatible with a model of dialogue. Even in the political sphere,

where the claims for any theory have more to do with social consequences than attaining insight, I would want to see justifications for
the plausibility of any imagined dialogue and explanations of how the
projected horizon would in fact be reached, in place of the assumption
that it might easily happen.

Moreover, I have been arguing that our current disputes point to
a crisis in the notion of dialogue itself; there is no functioning and
accessible model of dialogue that can be called in to mediate or resolve
these conflicts. Better dialogue cannot be imposed, and I will not offer
a new set of rules or methods for conducting discussions. My aim here
is to begin analyzing the horizon of dialogue, explicit or implicit, in
each critical sally and to ask how it is connected to or is reachable
from the analysis of where we are now. Too frequently, dialogue is
invoked as something that *must* be possible and therefore exists (like
an old philosophical proof for the existence of God). Each request for
"a rational, intelligent debate"[40] might at least include references to
some previous occasion in which this standard was met. A horizon of
possible dialogue provides an insulating reassurance for every critic's
work: your work has the potential to affect everyone, no matter how
narrowly you tailor your writing.

Academic criticism, more than ever, requires a horizon of public
dialogue. In literary studies and related disciplines, there has been a
shift to forms of criticism that challenge the "dominant culture" by
employing a different perspective (feminist, queer, African American)
and by implicating each text within broader hegemonic practices. For
this challenge to be effective, not only must the "text" be reinter-
preted, but the consumers and producers of culture must be reached
as well. Most academic cultural criticism does not address a public
audience, yet it presumes that its critique is compatible with some
broader public (that is, it is not inherently restricted to an elite group
of initiates) and is in fact allied with the "public interest" or at least
with the interests of those who are not part of the dominant class.
Some version of noncoercive persuasion (in contrast to the hegemony being contested) is usually set forth as the means for reaching
outward and influencing others. Academic writing, no matter how
"leftist," now almost always invokes a democratic rubric; the subti-
tle of Ernesto Laclau and Chantal Mouffe's oft-cited work, *Hegemony
and Socialist Strategy: Towards a Radical Democratic Politics*, is emblematic.[41] A horizon of dialogue — a possibility of engaging the public in

a free and open discussion — is necessary to ground the entire critical project.

Criticism can go placidly on its way, challenging the appropriate targets, in the approved modes, so long as its mission seems attainable. With a secure horizon, there is no need to question how each critical interjection can actually lead us toward the dialogue it envisions or requires. By troubling the horizon, I want to force this questioning. Instead of appealing to some external, supposedly transcendent criteria — the idea of an education, the values of a civilized society, intelligence, and scholarship — that are themselves being fought over, I am pushing for a more *internal* critique. One path to better dialogue is to overcome some of the contradictions between the aims and the actual practices of criticism. The typical stance of claiming that any problems are the responsibility of the other party (we are fair-minded, clear-thinking, and public-spirited, but you are not) gets us nowhere.

The legitimating function of dialogue is even more apparent in politics and in the media, and appeals to the value of debate and discussion are accordingly numerous. They span the entire political spectrum and, contrary to my initial expectation, are not found only in predictable places (among those seeking access to the mainstream or among liberals who have always had great faith in the power of their arguments). *Wall Street Journal* editorialists, Heritage Foundation fellows, and columnists for the *Nation* frequently write of the need for debate, and all politicians declare their belief that a substantive political dialogue can take place, no matter what evidence C-Span provides to the contrary. What would happen if these speakers were confined, in a scenario from Sartre's *No Exit,* to the actual boundaries of their own interchanges, without the justifying horizons of some vast public dialogue? The horizons conjured by politicians are largely hallucinatory. The institutional position of the speaker is especially important; most pronouncements by politicians and editorialists ignore their own complicity in the deficiencies that they deplore and their own control of the terms of the dialogue. President Clinton deigns to acknowledge commoners, but the ensuing "conversation" is hardly conducted on equal ground; members of the "public" exist only as long as they are in the president's or the media's gaze. Nor will much be accomplished simply by pushing for political debates that come closer to the standard of Lincoln-Douglas (even Nixon-Kennedy looks surprisingly good in retrospect). The magnitude of the appeals for conversation and debate points to a breakdown in other forms of community, citizenship, and public involvement. Dialogue is being proffered as the new social glue, delivered to us through the pronouncements of politicians and media spokesmen, the "representatives" of the people. It is more difficult — and more essential — to confront the holes in the social fabric that dialogue cannot repair.

I too, along with Jane Tompkins, long for an "intellectual debate in the right spirit."[42] And I also wish that academic debates could one day serve as a model for rejuvenating the public sphere. Right now, the call for better dialogue strikes me as a gesture similar to opening the door at Passover, singing to Elijah. It declares a stance of openness (against the pressures to restrict discussion to those already around the table), yet still leaves us awaiting the ideal interlocutor. Any wonderful "intellectual debate" depends on some other, who will never arrive (and if he does, all we get is John Leo, listening haphazardly at the doorway of Hilton conference rooms).[43] Maybe it's time to learn a new song.

Afterword

FELLOW TRAVELING WITH THE RIGHT

◆

> Could we understand ourselves, so as to de-
> bate about the responsibility proper to the
> university?...I am asking myself beforehand
> if we could say "we" and debate together, in
> a common language, about the general forms
> of responsibility in this area. Of this I am not
> sure, and herein lies a being-ill doubtless more
> grave than a malady or a crisis.
>
> — JACQUES DERRIDA,
> "Mochlos; or The Conflict of the Faculties"

I have been analyzing some of the ways in which academic critics
fail to realize their underlying social and institutional goals, but I do
not want anyone to draw the conclusion that we should therefore
renounce any ambitions for criticism that extend beyond a narrow,
disciplinary sphere. Nor would I want to suggest that literary critics
should write exclusively for each other or only address strictly "literary" concerns. Yet in drawing attention to contradictions between the
aims and the practices of criticism, I have said little about the imagined other party in these transactions. Would it make any difference
at all if everyone took everything I said to heart and worked earnestly
to get beyond all the strategies that enhance the critic at the expense
of the envisioned transformation? Is there really much possibility for
dynamic interaction with any other parties? Is there any openness to
persuasion among, for instance, political conservatives, civic groups,
or the media?

Anyone reading through the analyses and jeremiads of cultural
critics might be tempted to answer "no" to all of the questions. I
have argued that the intellectual project of much recent criticism is

incoherent to the extent that it simultaneously both demands and undermines the prospects for dialogue. But does the incoherence lie in
invoking dialogue at all (Should we seek instead, perhaps, a "community of dissensus"?)[1] or rather in employing critical strategies that
foreclose the imagined dialogue? In an age of clashing philosophical
paradigms about the nature of truth and communication, does the
possibility of a productive interaction with those who hold very different views already presume a preliminary agreement — which does
not exist — about the role or the nature of dialogue? Does the "otherness" of potential other parties represent an insurmountable obstacle
to dialogue? (Or conversely, does a framework of dialogue repress the
very "otherness" it claims to engage?)

We all, I assume, participate in discussions that we find illuminating and productive, at least within limited circles. Hardly anyone
wants to give up entirely on dialogue, and I do not think that any of
the philosophical or political obstacles to widening these circles are
insurmountable. I hope to provide some basis for this optimism by
considering briefly the paradox of whether meaningful dialogue now
requires a prior consensus that cannot be presumed and by making
some observations about the forms of argument that I witnessed at a
bastion of conservative political thinking, the Heritage Foundation.

✦

We do not have any overriding mechanism for resolving academic
controversies (and that is a good thing). There is no Supreme Court
to appeal to, and none of the governing associations play such a
judicial role. Any appeal for dialogue, or even for "teaching the conflicts," does not envision a mechanism for putting an end to conflict
or disagreement. Yet Bill Readings, among others, argues that the
act of institutionalizing conflict in the manner that Gerald Graff
proposes draws on a "second-order consensus" that does not exist
and illegitimately enshrines the values of consensus.[2] Readings argues
further:

> Paradoxically, an agreement that founds the possibility of free
> and fair communication is presumed to have been made freely
> and fairly, despite the absence of the agreement.
>
> Such a metalepsis can only be permitted if it is assumed that
> the language in which differences are sorted out is not itself

prey to the action of those differences. We can only agree to disagree if we can establish agreement concerning what it is that we are disagreeing about, and we can only establish communication if we can ascertain that we are in communication without first communicating that fact. Hence all problems of communication, any differences of idiom, must be presumed to be merely secondary to, or parasitical upon, a fundamental clarity of communication.[3]

Readings uses these arguments to challenge the "horizon of consensus that guides the modern thought of community." Does every presumption of the possibility of dialogue also depend on an unjustifiable belief in "a fundamental clarity of communication"?[4]

Literary critics have brilliantly analyzed the lack of any fundamental clarity or transparency of communication, and theorists in many fields have challenged any universal or noncontingent foundation for communication and understanding. But what are the consequences of no longer assuming "a fundamental clarity of communication"? Do the academic horizons of dialogue that I have been analyzing — the desire to engage others, the elevation of notions of persuasion, the hopes for a public sphere — depend on the assumption "that communicative transparency is possible"?[5]

Another way to phrase the question would be to ask whether these horizons of dialogue rest "on a potential agreement with others." Hannah Arendt, taking off from Kant, argues that "a potential agreement with others" is the ground for judgments that "have validity in the public realm."[6] Arendt calls attention to Kant's discussion of "the idea of a *public* sense" in *The Critique of Judgment*. For Kant, this "public sense" is "a critical faculty which in its reflective act takes account (*a priori*) of the mode of representation of everyone else, in order, *as it were*, to weigh its judgment with the collective reason of mankind. . . . This is accomplished by weighing the judgment, not so much with actual, as rather with the merely possible, judgments of others, and by putting ourselves in the position of everyone else."[7] Arendt is enamored of this public quality of judgment, and she argues that aesthetic judgments share with political opinions the quality of noncoercive persuasion that can only " 'woo the consent of everyone else' [Kant] in the hopes of coming to an agreement with him eventually."[8] For Arendt, the possibility of wooing the consent of others depends on "an anticipated communication with others with whom I know I *must finally come to some agreement*."[9] At issue is what happens when we no longer know that we "must finally come to some agreement." Does a critique of universality lead only to a prospect of heterogeneity or even dissensus? Many critics now reject the Kantian operation of "putting ourselves in the position of everyone else" and opt instead for listening (more intently) to the voice of the other, and many also question the Arendtian assertion that judgment derives its specific validity from "a potential agreement with others." Do the frameworks for dialogue collapse without the imperative or even the hope for an eventual agreement?

A critique of transparent communication or anticipated agreement would only have dire consequences for the possibility of dialogue if it implied that communication and agreement were impossible. What these critiques point up is the nonideality of dialogue: there is no ideal model of "free and rational discussion" that we can call on that will provide transparent communication or an eventual agreement with others. But the absence of an ideal mechanism for resolving conflict or arriving at consensus hardly implies that one should now argue as if communication and agreement with everyone else were simply out of the question. Critical strategies that function as if agreement were impossible, or that get their power solely at the expense of others (positioning oneself in relation to an impure other or closing off one's ideas from scrutiny), do not follow from a brilliant rethinking of language or of Kant. Such habits of discussion are as common on the political and epistemological "Right" as on the "Left" and stem more from a crisis of confidence in the ideas being expressed than from any revolution in thinking. It is much easier to treat others as incapable of understanding than to actively engage their ideas; to open one's own thoughts as fully as possible to the scrutiny of others requires a high degree of clarity and of courage.

Yet if there is no philosophical basis for approaching the "other" as necessarily incapable of communication, understanding, or agreement, how do "they" approach "us"? In the summer of 1992, I was a Salvatori fellow at the Heritage Foundation.[10] A while before, the president of Hampshire College "rented" the Heritage Foundation to stage a debate defending Hampshire and political correctness from the evils of conservatism.[11] My battle with the president of Hampshire was the unspoken occasion for the debate, and although I was not invited to participate, by implication I was being aligned with the Heritage Foundation. When a few weeks later an application to be a Salvatori fellow arrived (some right-wing academics and journalists had taken up my cause), I welcomed the opportunity to find out more about the conservative world. What can be learned about the possibilities of dialogue from hanging out with Ed Meese?

✦

For most people I know, the Heritage Foundation epitomizes the nadir of intelligence, integrity, and reasoned discussion. They would not consider anyone from the foundation a worthy antagonist for an intellectual dispute, since they assume that such conservatives would do almost anything to advance the interests of the rich and powerful at the expense of the poor and disenfranchised and suspect that many of these people are also blinded by hatred (of the nonwhite, nonheterosexual, or non-Christian). There is even a fear of contamination, a feeling that any close contact would leave a taint of the malignant and evil forces in our society.

I went to the Heritage Foundation with a lot of curiosity about what goes on behind closed doors among the far Right. Several people at Heritage had wielded great influence in the Reagan administration. What do these people actually think? Is "think tank" an oxymoron, and is it a place of dogma rather than thought, where the gospel truth of Cold War, free-market conservatism is passed down to a cadre of young reactionaries? Are the people at the Heritage Foundation outside the pale of reason and discussion?

I had been happy when the *Wall Street Journal* editorial page ridiculed the president of my college. But are all the invocations of "freedom" that one hears among conservatives merely hypocritical, and had I indeed entered into a pact with the devil? Going to Heritage was like stepping through the looking glass, where words such as conservative, deconstruction, feminism, Freud, Nietzsche, Leo Strauss, and God would now have exactly opposite connotations. Was I entering a parallel or a hostile universe? Several years later, I still do not have any clear-cut answers to these questions. I will offer a few observations and vignettes that I hope shed light on the possibilities for dialogue.

In his opening remarks, the vice president for academic relations (they take education seriously at Heritage) exhorted us to battle for intellectual freedom and standards and to work toward arresting the decline of the university. He described universities today as "gulags of political correctness" and asked, "If the communists can be overthrown, why not the PC brigade?" Throughout my ten days at Heritage, universities were constantly described as under siege and corrupted by those who would politicize education and conflate power and truth. Yet we were also enjoined to engage actively in a political struggle over the future of the university. The abstract vision of a university that was worth saving, worth protecting from decay and corruption, was of a place above political struggle; a place where truth, intellectual standards, and freedom were uncorroded by ideological strife. We were studying "the foundations of American liberty" (including the founding of the University of Virginia by Jefferson) in order to help us confront the forces that have led American society away from its virtuous foundations.

The tension between an idyllic view of a realm transcending politics and power and a practical outlook on how to gain power and influence structured almost every narrative about contemporary American society. One Heritage resident scholar, in his analysis of the Supreme Court, argued that judicial activism from the Right is now needed to compensate for previous judicial activism from the Left; O'Connor would have been fine for a different era when justices followed tradition, but now, after the Warren court, we need the radical change of Scalia. Faced with contradictions between principle and pragmatism, between ideals and power, the response was not to deconstruct the oppositions (as many academics are wont to do), but to argue that liberals have corrupted the entire fabric of American society and that a partisan counterattack is now required to bring us back to a state of virtue and American greatness.[12]

The colloquium embodied these tensions. In the mornings, we met as a seminar (conducted by a professor from Claremont McKenna), and we read and discussed the founding documents of the United States (large chunks of The Federalist Papers, Jefferson, and so on). The seminar was quite similar to others I've participated in: a great deal of reading, often highly knowledgeable discussion, occasional good arguments about major and minor points — altogether it was highly informative and instructive. If the mornings were devoted to knowledge, the afternoons were devoted to power. We met with congressmen (Dick Armey), conservative power brokers and intellectuals (including Ed Meese, William Bennett, and Linda Chavez), and the heads of the National Endowments for the Arts and the Humanities (Anne-Imelda Radice and Lynne Cheney — these were the waning days of the Bush administration).

✦

Dick Armey was the most dynamic and least discreet of these power elite. He is a former college professor and has an extreme bitterness toward academia. His strongest animus is toward deans and administrators ("A dean is God's worst creation"), and he claims that universities are now almost worthless and have defaulted on their obligation to the community at large (only engineering schools are perhaps uncorrupted). Liberals, he argues, have taken over the university, and they have no methodological rigor (the most arrogant wins); are intellectually bankrupt (liberals are scared people will understand them; conservatives are worried that people will not understand them); are mean-spirited, intolerant, vicious, not fair-minded; and are relativists, for whom the ends justify the means (conservatives in contrast "have an ethical belief system"). Yet this trashing of the university is linked to a view of its extreme centrality. Armey asserts that if the universities fail, our culture will fail. The utter importance of the university is appealed to, even as all its current defects are cataloged. At this moment of crisis, however, Armey offers no elucidation of the idea of the university, no demonstration of its importance, and no thoughts about what an education ought to entail. A timeless ideal floats above the temporal decay, and it is this dichotomy that permits us to get very dirty in our fight for the university without tarnishing its cherished principles.

A similar vision structures Armey's portrayal of the differences between Republicans and Democrats. He paints Republicans as virtuous, natural, almost innocent, and Democrats as decadent, corrupt, and immoral. Yet he wants to seize power and is willing to use any of the other party's abusive tactics to do so: he says that if he were speaker, he would beat up on the Democrats (as opposed to them, "I would know I was doing wrong, but I would do it"). If Republicans had the majority, he says he would be just as ruthless as the Democrats: "If I had power, I would want to use it; my vision is morally just." On the one hand, there is an appeal to ethical beliefs, rights, virtue, principle, and the importance of ideas. But on the other, there is a claim that in our fallen era, having principle, morality, and the best ideas on one's side is not enough — one also has to adopt the tactics of the enemy, even their logic that the ends justify the means. Armey remarks that his job is to spread dissension on the other side, to blitz on every down, to get in the backfield and screw everything up. It was at about this time that he speculated (jokingly?) that perhaps there was a mole in the room.

"Who is the mole?" becomes a running joke over the next few days. Suspicion falls on me at one point, when my half-surreptitious attempt to jot down some of Lynne Cheney's remarks draws her eye, and she insists that everything she's saying is "off the record." (Cheney need hardly worry — her remarks are vacuous and hardly inflammatory; she's doing her best to be the skilled political bureaucrat.) I am, in some sense, a mole, but what is secret here? What might be revealed? Is something conspiratorial really going on? Are there secrets to be protected from the enemy? (No one would contemplate the possibility of a mole at any other colloquium I've attended.) The question of the mole, and the way it resonates, exemplifies the tension between the think tank mission of setting forth ideas (the tax exempt status of the Heritage Foundation depends on not lobbying, on not attempting "to aid or hinder the passage of any bill before Congress") and the belief that other routes to power and influence are necessary. Can the right-wing academic succeed through a better understanding of Jefferson, a greater "methodological rigor," an insistence on maintaining standards, and by developing networks of support, or is a more devious and underhanded strategy necessary? The question of secrecy versus openness is absolutely central to an ethics of dialogue and discussion, and at Heritage there is still a fundamental uncertainty about how much to rely on a free market of ideas. A narrative about fallenness and decay can be used to justify any appropriation of the corrupt tactics of the other side (along with a lot of denial — a Heritage vice president: "The Left uses ridicule effectively, but we're too gentlemanly to do it").

◆

Yet the idea of a mole was largely a joke, and the contradictions between the principles that are praised and the tactics employed are hardly peculiar to the Heritage Foundation or to conservatives; they do not provide a justification for debunking or dismissing these principles. When I reflect back on the breadth of opinion and level of disagreement, it was certainly as large as at most academic collo-quia. The Salvatori fellows ranged in background from fundamentalist Christian to principled libertarian, and many had no qualms about dis-agreeing with what appeared to be the Heritage line. A few spoke in favor of continuing funding for the National Endowment for the Arts (this was shortly after the Mapplethorpe controversy), and several had sharp criticism for some of the invited speakers. When Stephen Balch, the president of the National Association of Scholars, presented a long and boring talk explaining how the proliferation of course offerings and electives has led to a severe decline in the quality of undergrad-uate education, one of the fellows argued that Balch had actually presented strong evidence for the opposite position, that undergrad-uate education had greatly improved. He stressed the importance of specialized courses and of research for faculty (in schools where pro-fessors don't do research, the professors are often intellectually dead, he claimed). Whether the topic was single-parent families, Madonna and popular culture, or the triumphs of Ronald Reagan, there were always a few participants who expressed contrarian views.

In regard to the broader political spectrum, however, this was hardly a heterodox group, and the extremism of some (especially among the younger ones, still in graduate school) did not seem to have followed from a very strenuous thinking about history, education, po-litical theory, or American society. The strongest unifying theme, not surprisingly, was attacking those on the Left; during a bus trip to Mon-ticello, someone even began a chorus to the tune of "One Hundred Bottles of Beer on the Wall" about killing one hundred liberals (the whole experience was vaguely reminiscent of summer camp, includ-ing a picnic with the neighboring group [participants in the Institute of Humane Studies summer program at George Mason University],[13] but with a rather different ethos than the Socialist Zionist summer camps of my youth). Yet the quality of the discussions, especially at the morning sessions, was better than I had expected.

Each of these sessions began with a lecture going over the ma-terial we had read on such topics as "Empire and Liberty: The Pre-Revolutionary Debate," "The Principles of the Revolution," and "American Constitutionalism." The lectures, by Charles Kessler of Claremont McKenna, were quite straightforward and did not appear to be pushing an agenda. It was a thoroughly creditable professional performance, and it was not even clear what positions or ideology he was trying to promote with regard to debates about taxation and representation. There was a lot of give-and-take in the discussions — disagreement about key points, but also a real willingness to consider and respond to opposing ideas. The arguments were fairly "scholarly," but of interest to me were the criteria for scholarship here: strong appeals to the author's intentions, to manuscripts, and to historical details (nothing surprising—just different from my usual haunts). The basis for argument was often less hermeneutical than professional; almost as if the thinking were, "I've invested so much time learning this material that I need to make *my* knowledge the criterion for understanding and interpretation." There was very little attempt to explore or question these "great ideas"; the emphasis instead was on trying to understand what was happening at that time, to determine what people really meant, and to gauge correctly the significance of certain documents and certain words. Running through these discussions was a strong desire for foundations and for establishing ways to anchor the belief that one can truly know what these founding documents signify.

For several participants, a belief in God was essential for establishing a ground both for rights and for knowledge. One participant argued that we are lost without a religious compass and that we owe a "responsibility to a higher truth" (yet he often quoted Lacan, Bakhtin, and Levinas in making his arguments). There was heated discussion about the genesis and the significance of the phrase "the laws of nature and of nature's God" in the Declaration of Independence, and there was no unanimity concerning the foundations of American liberty (in conversation, a fundamentalist would use the term "nature" to ground his arguments when the ardent libertarian was around, "God" when he was not).

The most striking weakness in the discussions had nothing to do with the absolutism for which members of the Heritage Foundation are typically denounced (in the words of a past president of the Modern Language Association, "We live in the midst of a deep anger and intolerance that in large part have been brought about by...those who reject dialogue, rational discussion, and analysis of the issues because they know that they, and others who think in similar ways, are the sole possessors of the truth. Since to these critics there is only one truth, all other views must be either lies or mere ignorance").[14] The Salvatori fellows were not stupid, closed to the ideas of others, or unwilling or

unable to analyze the issues. Yet there was little real discussion of the
ideas themselves; no attempt, for example, to think about whether
Jefferson, Madison, or Adams had been right or wrong at the time
and why, or to speculate about what actually are the foundations for
liberty. Even when discussing Tom Paine, whose views are certainly
antithetical to many in the group, there was only an effort to position
him correctly in intellectual history, but not to take a position with
regard to his ideas. Within the confines of the topic, and within the
limits of this particular group, the discussion was as tolerant and as
rational as any an MLA president could hope for. The drawback of
confining thoughts to a narrow scope is not, however, a failing that is
unique to conservative academics. I did get the feeling that if a wide-
ranging discussion of all the implications of the founders' ideas were
to take place, an anxiety about being ideologically correct would arise;
it is easier and more comfortable to stay on a scholarly terrain.[15] Any
anxieties would have been greatly compounded if the forum were one
of confronting leftist academics about the foundations of American
liberty.

This weakness, of venerating ideas more than engaging them, of
wanting to establish the authority of an idea rather than wanting
to think with and against it, increased dramatically the higher one
went in conservative circles. Lynne Cheney, for instance, in evoking
her version of a good education in the humanities, could only pay
tribute to the value of teaching Keats's "To Autumn" (rather than a
newer or lesser text). Somehow the glory of this icon was supposed
to shine forth on its own, without need for any explanation of its
merits or beauty. Some of the most dismissive comments came from
William Bennett, despite his criticism of Dan Quayle for not going beyond labels and for not elucidating such buzzwords as "work ethic" by
shedding light on what they actually mean or where they come from
in our society. Bennett made the typical claim that the Stanford debates about a core curriculum had nothing to do with arguments, only
power, and that the Left is interested in propaganda, not scholarship.
He went on to describe ethnic studies courses at Harvard (many years
ago) as "ethnic thumb-sucking," racial group support for the insecure.
The strangest moment, however, had nothing to do with using ideas
as either idols or clubs. At the end of Anne-Imelda Radice's defense of
the NEA (she was selected by President Bush to chair the endowment
after he fired John Frohnmayer), someone from the Heritage Founda-

tion had theatrically been planted to ask a question about her reaction to attempts to "out" her in the gay press; for whatever reasons, here she was being "outed" to us in turn.

◆

If Lynne Cheney and Bill Bennett were not interested in thinking through the heritage of American democracy (or British poetry) with us, if Ed Meese, even while stressing the need for "ideas to compete, and extend the debate," offered only canned, simplistic, and entirely predictable remarks on judicial restraint, original intent, and faithfulness to the law, it had little to do with their capacity for dialogue or openness to persuasion. There are very few situations that encourage hard thinking or an interchange with the ideas of others, and these appearances to rally the conservative troops were not of that sort. But the academics I met at the Heritage Foundation were not "absolutists" whose epistemological, ideological, or religious outlook unsuited them for rational discussion. They did not "know that they . . . are the sole possessors of truth," and at a fundamental level, they are certainly capable of dialogue, even with those who hold widely divergent views.

Determining that the "other" is open to dialogue and persuasion does not imply, however, that there is much to be gained toward that end by staging public confrontations with the differently minded. While hanging out with people whose presumptions were so dissimilar from mine, I became acutely aware of how strongly both the ideas they expressed and their attitudes toward others were linked to the expectations of particular spaces and situations. Whereas the emphasis in the seminar and full-group gatherings of the Salvatori fellows had been on freedom and liberty, their talk in smaller groups, at night after a few drinks, sometimes switched to a desire for restrictions. One fellow (the group of twenty contained only one woman) spoke out stridently to a few others against the First Amendment, though he never expressed such thoughts when we were all assembled together discussing and praising the Constitution. Another spent our one free afternoon watching the entire Gay Pride parade. In recounting the details of each of the different groups, he seemed to be registering the degree to which each one had offended him. He was disappointed that Dykes on Bikes had not shown up, and he wondered why a group carrying a graphic poster of men having sex had not been arrested. He appeared to experience both titillation and a *frisson* of martyrdom, of being the lone Christian witness amid the decadent crowd. He too never expressed any intolerance in front of the entire group, which might easily have included nonheterosexuals.

I do not think that the ideas articulated in more open settings were just a sham, covering over a core of prejudice and intolerance. Attitudes towards others also depend to some extent on the setting; spaces of tolerance — much less of thinking or consideration of opposing ideas — are few and fragile. While the "seminar" encouraged at least a modicum of engagement with the ideas of others, this was much less the case in the "private" space of conversation with those who had very similar views and would not be the case at all in a more "public" confrontation with those who hold radically divergent opinions. It is a daunting but important task to create more spaces that encourage both critical thinking and dialogues that go beyond a mere stating of each person's views. I think it likely that any such spaces will be some intermediary between the classically "public" or "private." In our mass media tabloid society, the broadest public and political spaces often perversely mirror the private ones; television is a better medium for communicating the emotional posture of a political candidate than for conveying his or her ideas.

The seminar room is not universalizable; there is no model of dialogue that universities can hope to export and project onto the rest of society. Academic and political dialogues often have different goals, and our political institutions would not be improved if every representative began to speak and act like a professor. What is needed is a refashioning of many different spaces for dialogue, especially in light of the rapid proliferation of new forms of connecting to others, rather than more seminar rooms or additional ways to merge the academic and the political. The dynamics of any social space depend greatly on the expectations we bring to our interactions with others. Academic critics play an important role in crafting what we expect from discussion. Not only do acts of criticism diagnose the perturbations and significant features of our discursive fields, but they always also shape the array of possible responses. Recognizing that there is the potential for thought, openness, and persuasion in whatever "others" we hope to engage and, more importantly, incorporating this recognition into our critical strategies would already begin a reshaping of our future dialogues. I do not always want to be either a mole or a fellow traveler.

NOTES

◆

Introduction

1. "I am only imparting knowledge, I am only making a report. To you also, honored Members of the Academy, I have only made a report" (from Franz Kafka, "A Report to an Academy," in *Franz Kafka: The Complete Stories,* ed. Nahum N. Glatzer [New York: Schocken, 1971], 259). "Herein lies the crowning achievement of a Jesuitical education; the formation of a habit of paying no attention to those things which are clearer than daylight" (from Stendhal, *The Charterhouse of Parma,* trans. Margaret Shaw [New York: Penguin, 1958], 209).

2. There is a well-worn genre of books analyzing and bemoaning the split between the academic and the "public" critic; Morris Dickstein's *Double Agent: The Critic and Society* (New York: Oxford University Press, 1992) is a typical recent example. Such books as Russell Jacoby's *Dogmatic Wisdom: How the Culture Wars Divert Education and Distract America* (New York: Doubleday, 1994) and Christopher Lasch's *The Revolt of the Elites and the Betrayal of Democracy* (New York: Norton, 1995) take contemporary "progressive" academics to task for diverting attention from the ailments of society and for betraying democracy, whereas Gerald Graff, in contrast, offers academia as a potential model for political debate in his *Beyond the Culture Wars: How Teaching the Conflicts Can Revitalize American Education* (New York: Norton, 1992). Todd Gitlin, in *The Twilight of Common Dreams: Why America Is Wracked by Culture Wars* (New York: Henry Holt, 1995), argues that both the academic and the nonacademic Left need to return to "common dreams" in order to overcome "the breakdown of the idea of a common Left" and to offer a model of progressive reform for the rest of society.

3. Stanley Fish, in *Professional Correctness: Literary Studies and Political Change* (Oxford: Oxford University Press, 1995), argues against "the possibility of transforming literary study so that it is more immediately engaged with the political issues that are today so urgent." He states: "It is not so much that literary critics have nothing to say about these issues, but that so long as they say it *as* literary critics no one but a few of their friends will be listening, and, conversely, if they say it in ways unrelated to the practices of literary criticism, and thereby manage to give it a political effectiveness, they will no longer be literary critics" (1). In contrast, I am stressing less the institutional criteria — that literary criticism is limited to the small circle of literature professors and that politically effective discourse necessarily takes place in different institutional settings — than the critical ones: the dominant forms of literary analysis and argument are actually often at odds with the social, political, and institutional goals that underlie them. But I do not want to narrow the gap between political goal and literary critique (this is the frequent plea from those on the Right and the Left

195

who reject any thinking that they do not see as leading to the desired end); rather, I want to explore the problems that arise from suppressing the incompatibilities between academic thought and political hope.

4. Richard Rorty, *Contingency, Irony, and Solidarity* (New York: Cambridge University Press, 1989), 67. I discuss the repercussions of this claim in chapter 1. For Fish's version, see *Doing What Comes Naturally: Change, Rhetoric, and the Practice of Theory in Literary and Legal Studies* (Durham, N.C.: Duke University Press, 1989).

5. Twentieth-century criticism is tremendously indebted to Nietzsche, and it would be a very worthwhile project to trace out not simply the influence, but the very different interpretations of Nietzsche that are at play among many of the most important critics. Agreeing or disagreeing with Rorty's (or Nietzsche's) philosophical critique is not, however, the primary issue in assessing the institutional consequences of such a critique or in questioning whether these consequences are in line with Rorty's hopes for persuasion and communication.

6. Each of these adjectives, "rich, white, male," now serves to discredit, and to disqualify from consideration, the ideas of the person whom they describe. The substantive "slaveholders" provides the coup de grace, the ultimate disqualification. In an argument about free expression, this is typical: try to smear by association those who hold different views. The debate around freedom of expression was provoked by student demands to shut down an installation by the African American artist James Montford, which some students of color found racist and offensive. The president of the college — while siding with those who were for restricting and prescreening future exhibitions and for voting down the resolution affirming the college's support for freedom of expression and speech in the arts and in public and scholarly fora — concluded the meeting by saying that we shouldn't tell people what we just voted about, as "It would send the wrong message."

7. Not all of the critiques of liberalism have overtly political aims. Stanley Fish, offering as usual a clear condensation of tendencies in contemporary criticism, writes in the introduction to *There's No Such Thing as Free Speech, and It's a Good Thing, Too* (New York: Oxford University Press, 1994), "[I]t is the structure of liberal thought that is my target in every one of these essays" (16).

8. As Bill Readings notes in *The University in Ruins* (Cambridge, Mass.: Harvard University Press, 1996), "More precisely, the concept of a public sphere is anchored upon the notion of a liberal individual who participates in it" (140). Readings goes on to offer a very astute discussion of Habermas's notion that "public life becomes the possibility of open democratic discussion and the establishment of consensus among subjects" (141). Readings offers the most perceptive recent discussion of the university, and I could cite his book at many points, either to embellish or to counterpoint my own arguments. Not all critics, of course, are blind to the tensions between critiquing and invoking liberalism. Ernesto Laclau and Chantal Mouffe, for example, write in *Hegemony and Socialist Strategy: Towards a Radical Democratic Politics* (London: Verso, 1985): "It is not liberalism as such which should be called into question, for as an ethical principle which defends the liberty of the individual to fulfill his or her human capacities, it is more valid today than ever. But if this dimension of liberty is constitutive of every democratic and emancipatory project, it should not lead us, in reaction to certain 'holistic' excesses, to return purely and simply to the defence of 'bourgeois' individualism" (184). Yet despite their claim that "the demand for *equality* is not sufficient, but needs to be balanced by the demand for *liberty*," and that

"the project for a plural democracy can link up with the logic of liberalism," their work strips liberalism of much of its logic and does not provide a basis on which this balancing act might be carried out.

9. Friedrich Nietzsche, *On the Genealogy of Morals*, trans. Walter Kaufmann and R. J. Hollingdale (New York: Vintage, 1989), 119. As mentioned above, much of contemporary theory (Heidegger, Derrida, Foucault, Deleuze, and so on) involves a reading of Nietzsche. Here I am interested in processes of applying theory and in the underscrutinized gaps between theory and its administration (and theorizing, when disseminated in academic institutions, also ends up being administered, transformed into institutional policy).

10. Nietzsche continues: "[A]nd the *more* affects we allow to speak about one thing, the *more* eyes, different eyes, we can use to observe one thing, the more complete will our 'concept' of this thing, our 'objectivity,' be" (119).

11. Bill Readings, in *The University in Ruins*, analyzes "the way in which the community of scholars in the University is presumed to serve as a model for rational political community at large" (180) and argues against the attempts to view the university as either a model community or a model of community. At Hampshire College, the desire to view the institution as a model is more extreme and more desperate than elsewhere, as its financial existence depends on offering an alternative community and a prescient model.

12. Samuel Weber, *Institution and Interpretation* (Minneapolis: University of Minnesota Press, 1987), and Gerald Graff, *Professing Literature: An Institutional History* (Chicago: University of Chicago Press, 1987).

13. These are the titles of recent books by Roger Kimball, Dinesh D'Souza, Russell Jacoby, and Christopher Lasch. See Roger Kimball, *Tenured Radicals: How Politics Has Corrupted Our Higher Education* (New York: Harper, 1990) (I love that "our," which presents the so-called radicals as aliens); Dinesh D'Souza, *Illiberal Education: The Politics of Race and Sex on Campus* (New York: Free Press, 1991); Jacoby, *Dogmatic Wisdom*; Lasch, *Revolt of the Elites*.

14. Paul de Man, *The Resistance to Theory* (Minneapolis: University of Minnesota Press, 1986), 25; all further citations appear in the text.

15. This is Terry Eagleton's description of a "bourgeois 'public sphere,' as Jürgen Habermas has termed it," "a distinct discursive space, one of rational judgement and enlightened critique rather than of the brutal ukases of an authoritarian politics," carved out by the European bourgeoisie in the seventeenth and eighteenth centuries. See *The Function of Criticism: From "The Spectator" to Post-structuralism* (London: Verso, 1984), 9.

16. Such questions are addressed in many of the recent books exploring the relations between "university-based intellectuals" (humanities professors) and the public. See, for instance, Bruce Robbins, *Secular Vocations: Intellectuals, Professionalism, Culture* (New York: Verso, 1993), and Michael Bérubé, *Public Access: Literary Theory and American Cultural Politics* (New York: Verso, 1994).

17. These examples have been selected almost at random. Especially when academic critics write for a broader audience, there is almost always an injunction to refashion a "critical dialogue." These quotes come from an op-ed piece by Henry Louis Gates Jr., a best-selling book by Cornel West, and a magazine article by Leon Wieseltier quoting Hillary Clinton. I am not suggesting that Hillary Clinton is an academic critic; rather, the call for a "new conversation," especially with the appointment of Sheldon Hackney as director of the National Endowment for the Humanities,

became a common political theme. See Henry Louis Gates Jr., "Black Intellectuals, Jewish Tensions," *New York Times*, 14 April 1993, A15; Cornel West, *Race Matters* (Boston: Beacon, 1993), 105; and Leon Wieseltier, "Total Quality Meaning," *New Republic*, 19 and 26 July 1993, 17.

18. Jürgen Habermas, *The Structural Transformation of the Public Sphere: An Inquiry into a Category of Bourgeois Society*, trans. Thomas Burger (Cambridge, Mass.: MIT Press, 1989), 82.

1. Political Correctness

1. Thomas Palmer, "At Harvard, Dissent on the State of Dissent," *Boston Globe*, 11 April 1991, 29, 32.

2. Catharine Stimpson, for example, in an appearance on the *McLaughlin Report* filmed in January 1991, argued that the "political" controversies on college campuses are signs of a "healthy debate."

3. Alexander Reid, "Bok Report Cites Threats to Colleges," *Boston Globe*, 12 April 1991.

4. This statement has been widely quoted, such as in a *Wall Street Journal* piece of 13 November 1990 and a *Newsweek* story of 24 December 1990. There is apparently some disagreement about exactly what Fish wrote, in which memo, but in the *McLaughlin Report* show on political correctness, he reiterated the assertion that members of the National Association of Scholars are known to be "racist, sexist, and homophobic."

5. Louis Joughin, ed., *Academic Freedom and Tenure: A Handbook of the American Association of University Professors* (Madison: University of Wisconsin Press, 1967), 50.

6. H. Keith H. Brodie and Leslie Banner, "Opening Remarks," *South Atlantic Quarterly* 89, no. 1 (1990): 4. The word "subversion" is one of the most frequently used terms today in literary criticism. It often serves only as a more charged synonym to "challenge," but the idea that education, reading, and the university should be subversive is well worth pondering and should also be considered in regard to the function of "subversion" in the historical tradition of Socrates to the present, the tradition that is one of the most common targets of subversion.

7. In an essay on academic freedom, law professor J. Peter Byrne offers an unconvincing account of "academic speech": "The speaker cannot persuade her colleagues by her social standing, physical strength or the raw vehemence of her argument; she must persuade on the basis of reason and evidence (concepts vouchsafed, if only contingently, by her discipline)" ("Academic Freedom: A 'Special Concern of the First Amendment,'" *Yale Law Journal* 99 [1989]: 258). Such a disembodied notion of academic speech ignores the institutional context it purports to describe. Stanley Fish is one of the more persistent advocates of an opposing view of academic speech. See, in particular, "No Bias, No Merit: The Case against Blind Submission," in *Doing What Comes Naturally* (Durham, N.C.: Duke University Press, 1989), 163–79.

8. Carl Schmitt, in his critique of liberalism and of "parliamentarism" (the institutional mode of political liberalism), makes exactly this point. I will be discussing Schmitt more directly later in this chapter, and in chapter 7 as well. I am thinking here especially of the preface to the second edition of *The Crisis of Parliamentary Democracy* (*Die geistesgeschichtliche Lage des heutigen Parlamentarismus*), trans. Ellen Kennedy (Cambridge, Mass.: MIT Press, 1985).

9. Richard Rorty, *Contingency, Irony, Solidarity* (Cambridge: Cambridge University Press, 1989), 67. As Rorty points out, the notion of a "free and open encounter" is employed by Milton (in *Areopagitica*): "And now the time in special is, by privilege to write and speak what may help to the further discussing of matters in agitation. The temple of Janus, with his two controversial faces, might now not unsignificantly be set open. And though all the winds of doctrine were let loose to play upon the earth, so truth be in the field, we do injuriously by licensing and prohibiting to misdoubt her strength. Let her and falsehood grapple; who ever knew truth put to the worse, in a free and open encounter? Her confuting is the best and surest suppressing" (*The Portable Milton*, ed. Douglas Bush [New York: Viking, 1949], 198–99). Rorty, however, differentiates his argument from Milton's: "It is central to the idea of a liberal society that, in respect to words as opposed to deeds, persuasion as opposed to force, anything goes. This open-mindedness should not be fostered because, as Scripture teaches, Truth is great and will prevail, nor because, as Milton suggests, Truth will always win in a free and open encounter. It should be fostered for its own sake. *A liberal society is one which is content to call 'true' whatever the upshot of such encounters turns out to be*" (52; emphasis in the original).

10. Dinesh D'Souza, American Enterprise Institute fellow and former editor of the *Dartmouth Review*, makes these arguments in *Illiberal Education: The Politics of Race and Sex on Campus* (New York: Free Press, 1991). The book was excerpted as the cover story for the March 1991 issue of the *Atlantic*, and a review of the book was featured as the cover story by the *New Republic* (15 April 1991 — Eugene Genovese wrote the [highly positive] review).

11. On television in particular, people usually attempt to defend positions, rather than to explore or understand a problem; in one sense of the term, they rarely act "academic." One can always easily undermine this opposition between exploring and defending positions, yet professors often talk quite differently on television than they do in the classroom or the lecture hall.

12. I have borrowed these definitions, almost at random, from Richard Rorty, Samuel Weber, and Renato Rosaldo. For Rorty, see *Contingency, Irony, and Solidarity*, 3, although the entire book, and especially the first section on contingency, is a response to this critique of truth. For Weber, see the introduction to *Institution and Interpretation* (Minneapolis: University of Minnesota Press, 1987), ix. For Rosaldo, see *Culture and Truth: The Remaking of Social Analysis* (Boston: Beacon, 1989), 21.

13. I am citing the phrase "extrinsic conditions" from Jacques Derrida, both to point to the work of one of the most important thinkers about the institution (see in particular his collection, *Du droit à la philosophie*) and also to indicate some of the directions of this critique. Samuel Weber, in *Institution and Interpretation*, states that in "Le parergon" Derrida argues that deconstruction "would have to occupy itself increasingly with the institutional conditions of its own practice" (19) and (in Derrida's words) "with what is generally, and wrongly, considered as philosophy's external habitat, as the extrinsic conditions of its exercise — that is, the historical forms of its pedagogy, the social, economic, or political structures of this pedagogical institution. It is by touching solid structures, 'material' institutions, and not merely discourses or significant representations, that deconstruction distinguishes itself from analysis or 'criticism'" (from *La vérité en peinture* [Paris: Flammarion, 1978], 23–24, this passage trans. Samuel Weber).

14. It is this difficulty of stabilizing the relation of the university to its contents that people such as Allan Bloom find most troubling today. See the epigraph to this

chapter, where Bloom claims "the university...is after all only a vehicle for contents in principle separable from it" (*The Closing of the American Mind* [New York: Simon & Schuster, 1987], 245).

15. Weber, *Institution and Interpretation*, 42, 44. In his insightful analysis of academic disciplines, Weber argues that they "must exclude or at least reduce the purport of their own inner disunity and internal conflictuality, and above all, of the inevitably conflictual process by which, *through exclusion and subordination*, disciplines define their borders and constitute their fields" (44; emphasis added). What I wish to call attention to here is the impossibility of simply eliminating all "exclusion and subordination" through some reform of the university or through some interdisciplinary curriculum.

16. This idea that all the new developments in scholarship tend toward a greater openness and inclusiveness is presented by Lawrence Levine in *The Opening of the American Mind: Canons, Culture, and History* (Boston: Beacon, 1996). In this weakly argued book, Levine claims, on the one hand, that there have always been battles over the structure and content of education, and the current fuss arises from conservative critics who are ignorant of the very history they claim to cherish; yet, on the other hand, he asserts that contemporary scholars have produced a genuine "opening" of the scholarly, even of the American mind (this is yet another version of American triumphalism — our generation has truly opened up American intellectual life).

17. Jane Tompkins, "An Introduction to Reader-Response Criticism," in *Reader-Response Criticism: From Formalism to Post-Structuralism*, ed. Jane Tompkins (Baltimore: Johns Hopkins University Press, 1980), xxv. I have selected Tompkins here not for the originality of the thought (these ideas have become widely espoused in the years following the publication of the piece), but for its very representativeness. Also, Duke (where Tompkins teaches) has been at the center of a lot of the debates around political correctness (see especially D'Souza's *Illiberal Education*). A document that echoes Tompkins, and that offers a representative view (and unintentional caricature) of some recent trends in the humanities, is *Speaking for the Humanities*, co-written by George Levine, Peter Brooks, Jonathan Culler, Marjorie Garber, E. Ann Kaplan, and Catharine Stimpson (New York: ACLS, 1989). This paper has been lambasted especially by neoconservative critics such as Roger Kimball (author of *Tenured Radicals* [New York: Harper & Row, 1990]).

18. Carl Schmitt, "Preface to the Second Edition (1926): On the Contradiction between Parliamentarism and Democracy," in *The Crisis of Parliamentary Democracy*, trans. Ellen Kennedy (Cambridge, Mass.: MIT Press, 1985), 3 and 5; emphasis added. Schmitt's writings on the crisis of liberalism, and parliamentarism, are historical; Schmitt points out that the parliamentary emphasis on "openness" and "discussion" arose in reaction to earlier political systems, and for him, the crisis arises out of the contradictions between twentieth-century "mass democracy" and parliamentary liberalism. Invoking Schmitt always has its risks. After the collapse of the Weimar Republic, Schmitt became a leading Nazi ideologue. Nevertheless, I think he still offers one of the most incisive critiques of liberalism, and his own career illustrates some of the potential dangers of this critique. I elaborate some of the implications of Schmitt's analyses, with regard to current pleas for "openness" and "discussion" in the university and in the political realm, in chapter 7.

19. Immanuel Kant, *The Critique of Judgement*, trans. James Creed Meredith (Oxford: Oxford University Press, 1952), 50.

20. Rorty, *Irony, Contingency, and Solidarity*, 56. Richard Thoma makes a similar point in his response to Carl Schmitt: "The worth and vitality of a political institution

in no way depends on the quality and persuasiveness of the ideologies advanced for its justification" ("On the Ideology of Parliamentarism," in *The Crisis of Parliamentary Democracy*, 80).

21.   In the next chapter, I will analyze (and vigorously disagree with) Rorty's arguments, specifically that debates about truth have absolutely no significance for or effect on academic freedom.

22.   When, after many months, my appeal on the grounds of procedural irregularities and abuses of academic freedom was successful, the president sought to have that judgment overturned by a five-college appeal committee (Hampshire is part of a five-college consortium, along with Smith, Amherst, Mt. Holyoke, and the University of Massachusetts, Amherst). During this period, my case and that of another colleague (Norman Holland) received a great deal of local and national media coverage. For some examples, see *Village Voice*, 9 October 1990, 49; *Wall Street Journal*, 4 January 1991, A6; and *Boston Globe*, 20 December 1990, 97, 100–101.

23.   Hampshire, in place of tenure, has a contract system: one is appointed for a three-year contract, then a four-year contract, and if all goes well, one finally receives a ten-year contract (tenure has been turned into a ten-year position).

24.   These comments are direct transcriptions from the ballots of those who voted against my reappointment. I received transcriptions of these comments from the administration after a nine-month battle, when an appeals committee ruled that I was entitled to them. An irony of Hampshire's insistence on "openness" and very limited confidentiality in the reappointment process was that the administration finally had to provide me with these written comments. Three people in almost identical language accused me of failing to think independently.

25.   Hampshire adopted a "Third World Expectation" in 1985, shortly before I arrived. During the course of their education, students are "expected" (Hampshire frowns on "requirements") "to present tangible evidence, prior to graduation," that they have had "an intellectually substantive engagement with the experience of the peoples of Asia, Africa, and Latin America (including North America's own domestic 'third world')." This has been translated into a demand that almost every course address the Third World and challenge the hegemony of Europe and the United States. As Stanley Aronowitz remarks, "in the late 1960s and early 1970s ... a considerable fraction of the New Left, inspired by the Cuban and Vietnamese revolutions and independence movements, especially in Angola and Mozambique, theorized the Third World as the new collective proletariat and the key site of revolutionary upsurge." Aronowitz also goes on to note in the 1980s, "among Marxists and other socialists," a "certain anti-Third Worldism that is, on the one hand, a healthy counterpoint to the almost slavish subordination of one part of the left to this doctrine and the movement it 'represents'" ("On Intellectuals," in *Intellectuals: Aesthetics, Politics, Academics*, ed. Bruce Robbins [Minneapolis: University of Minnesota Press, 1990], 5, 6).

26.   This version of Third World studies is fostered by an administration that tallies the number of courses having a "Third World component." When I was on the faculty senate, the dean of faculty encouraged all courses to contain a "Third World component" and presented statistics breaking down the current achievement toward this goal for each area of the college (my recollection is that the overall percentage was in the 70s).

27.   Louis Menand, "The Limits of Academic Freedom," in *The Future of Academic Freedom*, ed. Menand (Chicago: University of Chicago Press, 1996), 15–16.

28.   In June 1995, the "Conference on the Role of Advocacy in the Classroom"

was held in Pittsburgh. The conference was sponsored by the University of Pittsburgh and fifteen academic organizations (American Academy of Religion, American Anthropological Association, American Association of University Professors, American Council of Learned Societies, American Historical Association, American Philosophical Association, American Society for Aesthetics, American Sociological Association, American Studies Association, Association of American Geographers, Association of American Law Schools, College Art Association, Middle East Studies Association, Modern Language Association of America, Organization of American Historians). A volume of selected papers from the conference has been published (and includes my contribution to the conference, "Teachers, Not Advocates: Towards an Open Classroom): *Advocacy in the Classroom: Problems and Possibilities*, ed. Patricia Meyer Spacks (New York: St. Martin's Press, 1996).

29. This language comes from the primary AAUP (American Association of University Professors) document on academic freedom, and is part of the explanation of the mission of institutions of higher education. See "1940 Statement of Principles on Academic Freedom and Tenure," in *Academic Freedom and Tenure*: "Institutions of higher education are conducted for the common good and not to further the interest of either the individual teacher or the institution as a whole. The common good depends upon the free search for truth and its free exposition" (34).

30. Max Weber, "Science as a Vocation," in *From Max Weber: Essays in Sociology*, ed. H. H. Gerth and C. Wright Mills (New York: Oxford University Press, 1958), 145.

31. See J. L. Austin, *How to Do Things with Words*, ed. J. O. Urmson and Marina Sbisà (Cambridge, Mass.: Harvard University Press, 1975).

32. Max Weber, in "Science as a Vocation," also states: "One can only demand of the teacher that he have the intellectual integrity to see that it is one thing to state facts, to determine mathematical or logical relations or the internal structure of cultural values, while it is another thing to answer questions of the *value* of culture and its individual contents and the question of how one should act in the cultural community and in political associations" (146). Wayne Booth provides an insightful discussion of these passages from Weber in *Modern Dogma and the Rhetoric of Assent* (Notre Dame, Ind.: University of Notre Dame Press, 1974), 18–21.

33. The German university that Weber describes was not an arena for discussion: "In the lecture-room we stand opposite our audience, and it has to remain silent. I deem it irresponsible to exploit the circumstance that for the sake of their career the students have to attend a teacher's course while there is nobody present to oppose him with criticism. The task of the teacher is to serve the students with his knowledge and scientific experience and not to imprint upon them his personal political views" (146).

34. Louis Menand, "Culture and Advocacy," in *Advocacy in the Classroom*, 122; all further references will be cited parenthetically in the text.

35. Tompkins, "Introduction to Reader-Response Criticism," xxv. Or in the words of the ACLS (American Council for Learned Societies) manifesto, "all stances in scholarly research, as in the choice of values, imply a prior commitment to some basic belief system" (11). The course of academic arguments will thus be determined by the coincidence or clash of basic belief systems, rather than by the choice between different ideas.

36. Gerald Graff, "Other Voices, Other Rooms: Organizing and Teaching the Humanities Conflict," *New Literary History* 21 (1990): 827. I think that Graff is motivated as much by the feeling that the important conflicts are always taking place *somewhere else* as by a desire to improve undergraduate education (graduate students are already

well aware of ideological conflicts). I will provide a fuller critique of Graff's suggestions in chapters 6 and 7.

37. Ibid., 837.

38. Mark Starr made this comment at a student-sponsored forum on political correctness at Dartmouth College on 15 April 1991. He was invited to this forum since he had played a major role in the *Newsweek* cover story on political correctness (24 December 1990). I was the other speaker who had been brought in from outside the Dartmouth community, and we were both placed in the role of the bad guys complaining about political correctness, in juxtaposition to the good Dartmouth faculty defending academia.

2. Is Academic Freedom in Trouble?

1. Louis Menand, ed., *The Future of Academic Freedom* (Chicago: University of Chicago Press, 1996). I will be discussing in particular two essays in this volume, Menand's "The Limits of Academic Freedom" and Richard Rorty's "Does Academic Freedom Have Philosophical Presuppositions?" Further references to these essays will be included parenthetically in the text. In her foreword to this volume Linda Ray Pratt, a past president of the AAUP, writes: "This collection of essays grew out of confusion and need. By 1990, the growing controversies within the academic disciplines had spilled into the popular press and the political arena.... The academy could not get control of the 'PC' problem because it was deeply embedded in philosophical questions that had been developing for many years rather than in the politics of a particular season.... In 1915 many of the leading scholars and intellectuals of the day had met to draft the first 'General Declaration of Principles' of the fledgling association of university professors. Now, with almost eighty years of history behind it, it seemed appropriate for the AAUP again to bring some of the best minds to bear on these issues. Was the practice of academic freedom consistent with the principles? Could the principles be defended in the context of poststructuralist philosophy? Was the traditional practice possible in a charged political climate?" (vii–viii).

2. The AAUP's "1940 Statement of Principles on Academic Freedom and Tenure" includes the following statements on academic freedom: "The teacher is entitled to full freedom in research and in the publication of the results.... The teacher is entitled to freedom in the classroom in discussing his subject, but he should be careful not to introduce into his teaching controversial matter which has no relation to his subject.... The college or university teacher is a citizen, a member of a learned profession, and an officer of an educational institution. When he speaks or writes as a citizen, he should be free from institutional censorship or discipline" (in Louis Joughin, ed., *Academic Freedom and Tenure: A Handbook of the American Association of University Professors* [Madison: University of Wisconsin Press, 1967], 35–36). A version of this language is codified in many university policies on academic freedom.

3. John Dewey, "Academic Freedom," in *John Dewey: The Middle Works, 1899–1924*, vol. 2 (Carbondale: Southern Illinois University Press, 1976), 55. Dewey, one of the founders of the AAUP, first published this essay in 1902 (the AAUP was founded in 1915). In the sentences preceding these claims Dewey writes: "To investigate truth; critically to verify fact; to reach conclusions by means of the best methods at command, untrammeled by external fear or favor, to communicate this truth to the student; to interpret to him its bearing on the questions he will have to face in life — this is precisely the aim and object of the university. To aim a blow at any one of these

operations is to deal a vital wound to the university itself." Rorty discusses Dewey's ideas about truth and their bearing on academic freedom in "Does Academic Freedom Have Philosophical Presuppositions?"

4. A few of the many instances where a lack of tenure has contributed to an in-adequate protection of academic freedom are the mass firings of faculty at Bennington College a few years ago, my own experiences at Hampshire College (contrary to John Silber's claim in *Straight Shooting: What's Wrong with America and How to Fix it* [New York: Harper & Row, 1989] that "academic freedom can clearly exist on a campus where there is not tenure, as shown by Hampshire College" [153]), and the recent case of Kalí Tal at the new Arizona International Campus, founded without tenure and without basic procedural safeguards for reappointment and academic freedom. Kalí Tal was fired ("not renewed," despite promises of a long-term contract) for rais-ing criticisms about what she saw as AIC's shortcomings. For an account of the case, see Margaret Regan, "Tenure Bender," *Tucson Weekly*, 17–23 July, 14–19. Tenure was promulgated primarily as a means to protect academic freedom, but with the increas-ing use of part-time workers, fewer and fewer of the people teaching classes now have tenure. Moreover, some institutions are speaking of getting rid of tenure altogether, and new institutions are being developed without tenure. For examples of some of the recent efforts to argue that academic freedom can be adequately protected without tenure, see the American Association of Higher Education's "New Pathways: Faculty Careers and Employment for the 21st Century Project" and especially the working pa-pers "Academic Freedom without Tenure?" by J. Peter Byrne and "Where Tenure Does Not Reign: Colleges with Contract Systems" by Richard Chait and Cathy A. Trower.

5. The declining prospects for good jobs in universities has drawn a lot of at-tention to employment conditions in higher education. One recent example is Cary Nelson, ed., *Will Work for Food: Academic Labor in Crisis* (Minneapolis: University of Minnesota Press, 1997).

6. Joughin, ed., *Academic Freedom and Tenure*, 34.

7. The literature on academic freedom is immense. Some of the writings that I have found especially informative, in addition to the AAUP's *Academic Freedom and Tenure* and Dewey's writings, are Richard Hofstadter and Walter P. Metzger, *The Development of Academic Freedom in the United States* (New York: Columbia Univer-sity Press, 1955); William Van Alstyne, ed., *Freedom and Tenure in the Academy: The Fiftieth Anniversary of the 1940 Statement of Principles*, special issue, *Law and Contem-porary Problems* 53 (summer 1990); and for the McCarthy period, Ellen Schrecker's *No Ivory Tower: McCarthyism and the Universities* (New York: Oxford University Press, 1986). Thomas Haskell's contribution to *The Future of Academic Freedom*, "Justifying the Rights of Academic Freedom in the Era of 'Power/Knowledge,'" also contains a good early history of the controversies that prompted the founding of the AAUP.

8. There are many discussions of the rise of a "new class" after World War II. See in particular Alvin Gouldner, *The Future of Intellectuals and the Rise of the New Class* (New York: Seabury, 1979), and Andrew Ross, "Defenders of the Faith and the New Class," in *Intellectuals: Aesthetics, Politics, Academics*, ed. Bruce Robbins (Minneapolis: University of Minnesota Press, 1990), 101–32.

9. Many scholars are now in fact theorizing these possibilities of crossing, mixing, contamination, and infiltration, and a widespread literature on such ideas as "border crossings" and "contact zones" is emerging.

10. A Panamanian-born professor of Latin American literature was not reap-pointed (though he did finally regain his position after a long battle) amid charges

that his teaching was too "Eurocentric" and that he did not provide the proper mentorship for Latino students (see note 22 to chapter 1). Another disgruntled African American professor talked of making a T-shirt for herself stating, "I Am Your Third World Expectation."

11. John Searle, "Rationality and Realism: What Is at Stake?" *Daedalus* 122 (fall 1992): 56, 69.

12. Although Rorty, Kuhn, Davidson, and Derrida all question correspondence theories of truth, there are huge differences in their philosophies, and they by no means hold an identical view about the nature of truth. Rorty speaks of "we Davidsonians," but Donald Davidson often takes great care to distinguish his views from Rorty's.

13. Rorty is referring to Donald Davidson's essay "The Structure and Content of Truth," *Journal of Philosophy* 87 (June 1990): 279–328. For some of Davidson's earlier writings about truth, see *Inquiries into Truth and Interpretation* (New York: Oxford University Press, 1984). In this essay, Davidson rejects both "epistemic" and "realist" views of truth: "[T]he assertion of an essential tie to epistemology introduces a dependence of truth on what can somehow be verified by finite rational creatures, while the denial of any dependence of truth on belief or other human attitudes defines one philosophical use of the word 'realism'" (298). Davidson argues: "Realism, with its insistence on radically nonepistemic correspondence, asks more of truth than we can understand; antirealism, with its limitation of truth to what can be ascertained, deprives truth of its role as an intersubjective standard. We must find another way of viewing the matter" (309). Searle attacks "philosophers who make an explicit point of rejecting the Western Rationalistic Tradition, such as Richard Rorty or Jacques Derrida" ("Rationality and Realism," 77), but I doubt very much that he would include Davidson in this category.

14. Davidson, "Structure and Content of Truth," 325.

15. Thomas Haskell explores (and deplores) "the consequences of doing away with truth (or shrinking it to a vestigial synonym for whatever we want to believe, which comes to the same thing)," and he argues that Rorty shrinks truth in this way ("Justifying the Rights of Academic Freedom," 72).

16. Rorty is referring here to Searle's citation of the ACLS report *Speaking to the Humanities* (New York: ACLS, 1989). I discuss this report further in chapters 1 and 3.

17. Rorty, "Academic Freedom," 39n.1. The definition of "folkways" is from *The Random House Dictionary of the English Language* (New York: Random House, 1967), emphasis added.

18. Richard Rorty, *Objectivity, Relativism, and Truth: Philosophical Papers*, vol. 1 (Cambridge: Cambridge University Press, 1991), 27.

19. Lewis Carroll, *Through the Looking-Glass* (New York: Random House, 1946), 94, 95.

20. Richard Rorty, *Consequences of Pragmatism: Essays 1972–1980* (Minneapolis: University of Minnesota Press, 1982), xiv.

21. Barbara Herrnstein Smith, *Belief and Resistance: Dynamics of Contemporary Intellectual Controversy* (Cambridge, Mass.: Harvard University Press, 1997).

22. The quotation is from the Israeli historian Ilan Pappe and appears in Jonathan Mahler, "Uprooting the Past," *Lingua Franca* 7, no. 6 (1997): 31. Pappe qualifies this assertion with "at least in the Israeli-Palestinian context." Mahler continues, "According to him [Pappe], the historical documents speak in different ways to different people; call him a postmodern post-Zionist." I picked this quotation almost at random and simply to demonstrate how widespread are challenges not only to the idea that

the historian (or scholar) could achieve absolute objectivity, but to the idea that the scholar should strive to be objective, should attempt to overcome his or her biases and prejudices, or should work toward a stance of neutrality. Of course, the debates about "objectivity" in history are just as large as they are in philosophy. For an interesting overview, see Peter Novick, *That Noble Dream: The "Objectivity Question" and the American Historical Profession* (Cambridge: Cambridge University Press, 1988).

23. Menand, in "Limits of Academic Freedom," offers some very insightful remarks about why the concept of academic freedom is inherently problematic, about "how academic freedom operates simultaneously as a liberty and a restriction" (7), and about the ways in which "the meltdown in disciplinary boundaries" threatens "the machinery of self-governance": "Academic freedom, as it is now structured, depends crucially on the autonomy and integrity of the disciplines. For it is the departments, and the disciplines to which they belong, that constitute the spaces in which rival scholarly and pedagogical positions are negotiated" (17). Yet academic freedom also depends on a university-wide presumption that all professors are entitled to express their views about educational matters without fearing retribution. In portraying any threats to academic freedom as emerging primarily from changes in institutional structures, Menand finally relieves professors of most of the responsibility for justifying, protecting, and respecting the academic freedom of themselves and their colleagues.

24. Franz Kafka, *Sämtliche Erzählungen* (Frankfurt am Main: Fischer Taschenbuch Verlag, 1977), 100. For the English translation of "In the Penal Colony," see *Franz Kafka: The Complete Stories*, ed. Nahum N. Glatzer (New York: Schocken Books, 1971), 140.

25. *Cassell's German-English/English-German Dictionary* (New York: Macmillan, 1978).

3. Forging a Public Voice for Academic Critics

1. Russell Jacoby, *The Last Intellectuals: American Culture in the Age of Academe* (New York: Basic Books, 1987), and Morris Dickstein, *Double Agent: The Critic and Society* (New York: Oxford University Press, 1992). See also Jacoby's more recent book, *Dogmatic Wisdom: How the Culture Wars Divert Education and Distract America* (New York: Doubleday, 1994). There are now a plethora of books on the relations between academics and the public, some of which defend or celebrate the current state of academic criticism (such as Bruce Robbins, *Secular Vocations: Intellectuals, Professionalism, Culture* [London: Verso, 1993] and Gerald Graff, *Beyond the Culture Wars: How Teaching the Conflicts Can Revitalize American Education* [New York: Norton, 1992]).

2. T. W. Heyck, *The Transformation of Intellectual Life in Victorian England* (New York: St. Martin's, 1982), 11. Heyck argues that only "in the late-Victorian years (1870–1900)" did the English generally adopt this concept of intellectuals as a "self-conscious, distinct group with common attitudes." Many of Huxley's most important essays appeared in the 1860s, but he remained an active essayist and public figure until his death in 1895.

3. Such claims for the widespread influence of academic criticism come not only from the Right. Thomas McLaughlin, for example, in his introduction to *Critical Terms for Literary Study* (ed. Frank Lentricchia and Thomas McLaughlin [Chicago: University of Chicago Press, 1990], 1), states: "Literary theory has permeated our thinking to the point that it has defined for our times how discourse about literature, as well as about culture in general, shall proceed." Bruce Robbins, in *Secular Vocations*, also

argues that university-based intellectuals are beginning to have a large impact outside of the university.

4. Recently, I saw a billboard in the Palms neighborhood of Los Angeles (middle-class and mostly white), with two black adults and the slogan: "It's a black thing." This was an advertisement for a brand of condoms. Although the message seems designed to overcome blacks' resistance to condom use, the location of the billboard suggests that whites, too, can understand the "black thing" of sexuality — consumerism, yet again, performs a feat of cross-cultural understanding.

5. Thomas Henry Huxley, *Essays*, ed. Frederick Barry (New York: Macmillan, 1929), 35; all further references to Huxley will be included parenthetically in the text.

6. Patrick Brantlinger, "Introduction: Zadig's Method Re-visited," in *Energy and Entropy: Science and Culture in Victorian Britain*, ed. Patrick Brantlinger (Bloomington: Indiana University Press, 1989), xv–xxii.

7. James H. Kavanagh, "Ideology," in *Critical Terms for Literary Study*, 311; emphasis added. "Ideology" has been a prominent term since the eighteenth century; many of its more modern connotations derive from Marx, especially from his *German Ideology* (coauthored with Engels). I do not want to trace here the history of "ideology critique" from Marx to Mannheim to Althusser, but only to focus on some of its current uses as an academic strategy for eviscerating the arguments of others (chapter 2 of Karl Mannheim's *Ideology and Utopia*, trans. Louis Wirth and Edward Shils [New York: Harcourt Brace Jovanovich, 1936], provides an excellent discussion of the early history and the concept of ideology).

8. This insight is also central to the antifoundationalism of critics such as Stanley Fish and Richard Rorty, who rarely invoke "ideology." But the repercussions of such an outlook are highly debatable. Many leftists argue that the constructedness and contingency of the social world offer tremendous hope for progressive change; Fish, in contrast, argues that the adoption of this outlook has no consequences whatsoever.

9. Kavanagh, "Ideology," 312.

10. The word "sensitized" is now often paired with "ideology." See, for example, Stanley Fish, "Rhetoric," in *Critical Terms for Literary Study*, where he writes that the hope of some critics is to become "sensitized to the effects of ideology," in order to begin "to clear a space in which those effects can be combatted" (217). In *Speaking for the Humanities*, which I analyze below, the writers also claim that the best "contemporary humanistic thinking... attempts to sensitize us to the presence of ideology in our work" (George Levine et al., *Speaking for the Humanities* [New York: American Council of Learned Societies, 1989], 11). The popularity of the word "sensitize" speaks volumes about contemporary academia, in which the mission is now to "sensitize" our students to the ills of the world and to the harm that words can inflict.

11. Levine et al., *Speaking for the Humanities*, 11.

12. See the preface to *Speaking for the Humanities*. Christopher Lasch, in *The Revolt of the Elites and the Betrayal of Democracy* (New York: Norton, 1995), 181, provides a scathing critique of this defense of "recent trends in the humanities."

13. The authors appear to embrace the traditional critical goal of rising above one's own interests, even as they claim to perform a radical critique of the notion of "disinterestedness."

14. For a very different notion of "ideology critique" than the one described above, see Theodor Adorno's 1957 essay "On Lyric Poetry and Society" (*Notes to Literature*, vol. 1, trans. Shierry Weber Nicholsen [New York: Columbia University Press, 1991], 39): "Special vigilance is required when it comes to the concept of ideology, which

these days is belabored to the point of intolerability. For ideology is untruth, false consciousness, deceit. It manifests itself in the failure of works of art, in their inherent falseness, and it is countered by criticism. To repeat mechanically, however, that great works of art, whose essence consists in giving form to the crucial contradictions in real existence, and only in that sense in a tendency to reconcile them, are ideology, not only does an injustice to their truth content but also misrepresents the concept of ideology. That concept does not maintain that all spirit serves only for some human beings to falsely present some particular values as general ones; rather, it is intended to unmask spirit that is specifically false and at the same time to grasp it in its necessity. The greatness of works of art, however, consists solely in the fact that they give voice to what ideology hides. Their very success moves beyond false consciousness, whether intentionally or not." The "special vigilance" that Adorno calls for is needed even more today.

15. For an example of the former, see Christine Stansell's discussion of Catharine MacKinnon's views of Clarence Thomas (before the Anita Hill charges), "White Feminists and Black Realities: The Politics of Authenticity," in *Race-ing Justice, Engendering Power: Essays on Anita Hill, Clarence Thomas, and the Construction of Social Reality*, ed. Toni Morrison (New York: Pantheon, 1992), 250–68. In a talk at Harvard's Center for Literary and Cultural Studies in March 1992, Kendall Thomas, a law professor at Columbia University, analyzed the ways in which Clarence Thomas was a victim of the dominant ideology.

16. In the nineteen essays of the Morrison volume, there is very little attempt to explain why we should disagree with Thomas's views. The contrast between the way Thomas and Scalia (the justice with whom he most often votes) are treated is stunning. Scalia is usually described as "brilliant," and there seems to be little difficulty accepting how an Italian American could hold such conservative views (only a generation ago, it was very difficult for an Italian American to make his [much less her] way into the major law firms — Mario Cuomo, for instance, has talked about his difficulties getting a job due to his ethnic background).

17. William V. Spanos, *Repetitions: The Postmodern Occasion in Literature and Culture* (Baton Rouge: Louisiana State University Press, 1987), 302.

18. Fish's comment about being an "outsider" is missing from the published version of his talk, "On the Unbearable Ugliness of Volvos," in *English Inside and Out: The Places of Literary Criticism*, ed. Susan Gubar and Jonathan Kamholtz (New York: Routledge, 1993), 105. Confessing to feel like an outsider is another gesture toward bolstering his (considerable) authority, his right to speak, and the value of his thoughts. In the talk, Fish offers some insight into this posture: "In the psychic economy of the academic, oppression is the sign of virtue" (105). And being on the margins is a sign of oppression.

19. Graff's essay is published in the same volume, *English Inside and Out* (109–21). In the published version he preserved, without discussion, the use of "Professor Redneck."

20. *Boston Globe*, 7 April 1991, A23.

21. The executive committee of the MLA came out against the nomination of Carole Iannone to the National Humanities Council, an advisory body to the National Endowment of the Humanities. In turn, the MLA was widely attacked in the press (though Iannone's nomination was defeated). This panel discussion took place at the MLA convention in December 1991. Even in the title of the panel we get the defensive gesture ("answering back" to the media) conflated with or envisioned

as "the future of the profession." Needless to say, there was a narrow range of views on this panel, and nobody sympathetic with any of the criticisms of the MLA hierarchy was included. Questioners from the floor who disagreed with the members of the panel were treated as if they just somehow didn't get the point (that *we* were misrepresented and unfairly attacked by the media). The idea that some of the views expressed in the media might also be held by (many) members of the MLA seems not to have occurred to them; this would interfere with the (too easy) positioning of the media, and of the public, as "outside" our academic discourse, even at moments when we directly enter the political sphere. It would also interfere with characterizing any attacks on the MLA and on political correctness as coming exclusively from right-wing conservatives, that is, from those who are easy to caricature as outside the purview of reasonable discussion.

22. This was the term used by Stephen Greenblatt, also a speaker on the panel. He writes: "But, in our defense, we have found ourselves in a debate in which the dominant terms, the language and concepts through which we might hope to achieve clear-eyed understanding, have been systematically poisoned." Yet in the next sentence he states: "David Duke was asked how he would link his years as a Nazi and a leader of the Ku Klux Klan with his campaign for the governorship of Louisiana: 'The common strain is my love for Western civilization,' he replied. 'That's what I've always been about.'" Greenblatt's talk, "The MLA on Trial," was published in *Profession 92* (New York: Modern Language Association of America, 1992), 39–41. Critics of contemporary academia who invoke Western civilization are heavy-handedly linked to Duke, the Nazis, and the Klan, despite Greenblatt's own denunciation of the *Wall Street Journal* for "slyly" implying that Ted Kennedy's vote against Carol Iannone and the drowning of Mary Jo Kopechne "both were murders." While Greenblatt rails against "the sheer nastiness of Washington politics" and the "swelling current of contempt for academic work, and particularly for work in the humanities," he does not finally present a more reasoned or less "poisonous" discourse. He makes no attempt at all to consider the possible merits of criticisms of academia, but simply dismisses them: "[T]hese critiques have no intellectual content. . . . [T]he characterizations are crude, the charges inherently implausible, the so-called evidence a handful of endlessly recycled, shamelessly oversimplified scare stories." This does not offer any basis for "a debate . . . through which we might hope to achieve clear-eyed understanding."

23. Houston Baker, "President's Column," *MLA Newsletter* 24, no. 1 (1992): 3.

24. Baker quotes a stanza from Césaire's *Return to My Native Land:* "I give you my quick words / consume and wrap / and as you wrap kiss me with a violent trembling / kiss me until I am the furious WE / kiss, kiss US." Milton ends *Paradise Lost* with the words: "The world was all before them, where to choose / Their place of rest, and Providence their guide. / They hand in hand with wandering steps and slow, / Through Eden took their solitary way." As they face "a New World future," Adam and Eve are not presented with a binary choice between opposing ways.

25. The first instance is exemplified by Michael Bérubé's *Public Access: Literary Theory and American Cultural Politics* (London: Verso, 1994); the second by Russell Jacoby's *Dogmatic Wisdom;* and the third by Gerald Graff's *Beyond the Culture Wars.*

26. Foucault makes this remark in an interview, "Revolutionary Action: 'Until Now,'" in *Language, Counter-memory, Practice,* ed. Donald F. Bouchard (Ithaca, N.Y.: Cornell University Press, 1977), 230. Richard Rorty, in "Two Cheers for the Cultural Left," discusses this comment by Foucault and makes an argument (with which I agree) for reforming rather than revolutionizing current institutions (in *The Politics*

of Liberal Education, ed. Darryl J. Gless and Barbara Herrnstein Smith [Durham, N.C.: Duke University Press, 1992], 235).

27. "Community" has become an extremely prominent word in academic discourse and is often used to denote a group bound by common interests or background. Although providing a sense of inclusion and of extension beyond the individual, "community" is nevertheless most often defined by criteria of difference from other groups.

28. Paul de Man, in "The Resistance to Theory" (in *The Resistance to Theory* [Minneapolis: University of Minnesota Press, 1986], 17), applies this description to "the undoing of theory." It is also exemplary of the "undoing" of deconstruction.

29. The seminal work is Jürgen Habermas's *The Structural Transformation of the Public Sphere: An Inquiry into a Category of Bourgeois Society,* trans. Thomas Burger (Cambridge, Mass.: MIT Press, 1989). The enormous literature on so many aspects of Habermas's thought (not just his conception of *Öffentlichkeit* or the "public sphere") is far too lengthy to be discussed here.

30. Stanley Fish, *Doing What Comes Naturally: Change, Rhetoric, and the Practice of Theory in Literary and Legal Studies* (Durham, N.C.: Duke University Press, 1989), 141.

31. Jacques Derrida discusses this fragment at length in *Spurs: Nietzsche's Styles,* trans. Barbara Harlow (Chicago: University of Chicago Press, 1978).

4. Why I'd Rather Be Talking to a TV Camera

1. An earlier version of this chapter was presented at a panel entitled "The Public Relations of Literary Criticism" at the 1993 MLA convention in Toronto. A first version of the previous chapter was given at a 1992 MLA panel on popularizing literary criticism, chaired by Gerald Graff. While giving that talk, I had the strong feeling that I would rather be speaking to a TV camera than to an MLA audience. The expectations of an academic audience, even for a talk about popularizing criticism or about public relations, are that one will undermine or call into question — rather than appeal to — any commonly espoused principles and that one will also blame the misguided representatives of the public (ignorant or malfeasant journalists and politicians) for any negative publicity about professors and academic practices. In our media age, the title of my talk drew the interest of journalists who were covering the convention for Canadian and Dutch media, and I was also contacted later by a reporter from the *Chronicle of Higher Education.*

2. I have in mind, of course, Michel Foucault's ideas, especially from *Discipline and Punish: The Birth of the Prison,* trans. Alan Sheridan (New York: Vintage Books, 1979). I do not want to attack Foucault's arguments, but rather to offer an example of someone whose ideas have been too easily, and now almost unthinkingly, institutionalized. It is the paradoxes around the institutionalization of a "Foucauldian" criticism that I wish to question.

3. In their essay "Cultural Criticism" (in *Redrawing the Boundaries: The Transformation of English and American Literary Studies,* ed. Stephen Greenblatt and Giles Gunn [New York: Modern Language Association, 1992] 419–36), Gerald Graff and Bruce Robbins, while discussing Raymond Williams's work, define the "critical" component of "cultural criticism" as "opposing the social mainstream": "Together, these two adjectives define the heroic project of cultural criticism, which claims to be 'critical' in opposing the social mainstream and yet 'cultural' in speaking for that

mainstream" (419). This equation of "critical" and "oppositional" is often taken for granted in contemporary criticism.

4. This phrase comes from Miller's "An Open Letter to Professor Jon Wiener," written in response to the attacks on Paul de Man following the revelations of his wartime journalism (in *Responses: On Paul de Man's Wartime Journalism*, ed. Werner Hamacher, Neil Hertz, and Thomas Keenan [Lincoln: University of Nebraska Press, 1989], 334–42).

5. Paul de Man, *The Resistance to Theory* (Minneapolis: University of Minnesota Press, 1986), 26.

6. Homi K. Bhabha, "Postcolonial Criticism," in *Redrawing the Boundaries*, 438.

5. Crossing Over

1. Matthew Arnold, *Culture and Anarchy and Other Writings*, ed. Stefan Collini (Cambridge: Cambridge University Press, 1993), 50.

2. Catharine MacKinnon, *Only Words* (Cambridge, Mass.: Harvard University Press, 1993). MacKinnon begins the book: "Imagine that for hundreds of years your most formative traumas, your daily suffering and pain, the abuse you live through, the terror you live with, are unspeakable — not the basis of literature. You grow up with your father holding you down and covering your mouth so another man can make a horrible searing pain between your legs. When you are older, your husband ties you to the bed and drips hot wax on your nipples and brings in other men to watch and makes you smile through it. Your doctor will not give you drugs he has addicted you to unless you suck his penis" (3). MacKinnon states that "these facts are taken from years of confidential consultations with women who have been used in pornography" or adapted from judicial cases (113). The closing paragraph of the book concludes with the hope for "a new conversation" (see chapter 7 below, "The Poverty of Conversation," in which I discuss such appeals): "In a society in which equality is a fact, not merely a word, words of racial or sexual assault and humiliation will be nonsense syllables. Sex between people and things, human beings and pieces of paper, real men and unreal women, will be a turn-off....When this day comes, silence will be neither an act of power, as it is now for those who hide behind it, nor an experience of imposed powerlessness, as it is now for those who are submerged in it, but a context of repose into which thought can expand, an invitation that gives speech its shape, an opening to a new conversation" (110).

3. For an overview of some recent academic feminist work on hard-core pornography, see M. G. Lord, "Pornutopia: How Feminist Scholars Learned to Love Dirty Pictures," *Lingua Franca* 7, no. 4 (1997): 40–48, which discusses Constance Penley, Linda Williams, Laura Kipnis, and Joanna Frueh. There is a broad academic interest in pornography, and this extends well beyond the study of hard-core films.

4. John M. Woolsey, "Decision of the United States District Court Rendered December 6, 1933," in *Ulysses*, by James Joyce (New York: Vintage-Random, 1961), ix; all further references will be included parenthetically in the text.

5. Recently there has been controversy around the suppression and destruction, by Joyce's family, of letters that reveal Joyce's own "too poignant preoccupation with sex."

6. Throughout the Nausicaa episode, Joyce is parodying Maria Cummins's *The Lamplighter* and the style of cheap romantic magazines that probably form the bulk of Gerty MacDowell's reading. In 1920, this episode was published in the *Little Review,*

and the editors were convicted of publishing obscenity in 1921, and fined fifty dollars. See Richard Ellmann, *James Joyce*, rev. ed. (New York: Oxford University Press, 1983), 500–502.

7. Arnold, *Culture and Anarchy and Other Writings*, 110. In debates about the canon in English departments, Matthew Arnold is often taken to be the epitome of conventional humanism and portrayed as the precursor of traditionalists and conservatives. This portrayal of Arnold ignores the context in which Arnold was writing, and current efforts at reform could usefully be compared with Arnold's own efforts at educational reform.

8. One example of the risks professors face is the case of Dean Cohen, an English professor at San Bernadino Valley College, who was found guilty of sexual harassment by the college after he required students to write an essay defining pornography and after occasionally reading from *Hustler* and *Playboy* in class. A federal appeals court later ruled that the college violated his First Amendment rights. See Courtney Leatherman, "Court Finds College Violated First Amendment," *Chronicle of Higher Education*, 6 June 1996.

9. This is from an epigraph (from Aaron Travis's "Blue Light") in a paper that was circulated and discussed at one of the seminars at Harvard's Center for Literary and Cultural Studies.

10. Michel de Montaigne, *Oeuvres complètes* (Paris: Gallimard, 1962), 508.

11. Some works on pornography, such as MacKinnon's *Only Words* and Laura Kipnis's *Bound and Gagged: Pornography and the Politics of Fantasy in America* (New York: Grove Press, 1996), do reach a nonacademic audience, but what especially interests me is how little the pornographic discourse usually disturbs the academic one. It would also be worthwhile to pursue the additional paradox of why it is sometimes now easier to incorporate queer rather than hetero sexuality into academic discourse. The quotation given in the text is not simply pornographic, sadomasochistic, and/or erotic writing, but writing aimed at a gay male readership. In the post–Anita Hill age, in which the "analysis" of pornography always runs the risk of slipping over into the "performance" of harassment, it is occasionally safer to use homosexual examples. More than this, the tension of policing heterosexual relations, and the fear of politically incorrect attitudes, has itself contributed to the rise of queer theory/gay studies as a place in which sexuality can be more openly, aggressively, and intimately explored. There is a frequent undercurrent of possible arousal in queer discourse, of initiation, of being in the know, and of possible contact with the audience, that is now more suppressed and regulated in nonqueer studies of gender. And at a time when any conceptualization of an "other" is becoming increasingly problematic, queer sexuality more easily permits one's own experiences to serve as a ground for critical authority. The post–Cold War emergence of homosexuality as a favorite political and fund-raising issue for the far Right also adds to the urgency and the power of queer discourse in the university. An analysis of the erotics of academia would require a substantial inquiry into the rise of gay studies.

12. Sigmund Freud, "On Negation," in *General Psychological Theory*, ed. Philip Rieff (New York: Collier-Macmillan, 1963), 214–15.

13. Eve Kosofsky Sedgwick, "Socratic Raptures, Socratic Ruptures: Notes Toward Queer Performativity," in *English Inside and Out: The Places of Literary Criticism*, ed. Susan Gubar and Jonathan Kamholtz (New York: Routledge, 1993), 129. This essay is an excellent example of the attempt to theorize the performative potential of literary criticism and pedagogy. See also the volume that Kosofsky Sedgwick co-

edited with Andrew Parker, *Performativity and Performance* (New York: Routledge, 1995).

14. The theoretical foundation for recent explorations of the "performative" power of language is the work of J. L. Austin. He states, for example: "We said that the idea of a performative utterance was that it was to be (or to be included as part of) the performance of an action" (*How to Do Things with Words,* ed. J. O. Urmson and Marina Sbisà [Cambridge: Cambridge University Press, 1975], 60).

15. Paul de Man, "The Resistance to Theory," in *The Resistance to Theory* (Minneapolis: University of Minnesota Press, 1986), 4.

16. Sedgwick, "Socratic Raptures," 129.

17. Ibid., 129.

18. Judith Butler, *Bodies That Matter: On the Discursive Limits of "Sex"* (New York: Routledge, 1993), 30. Here is the full paragraph: "Here it is of course necessary to state quite plainly that the options for theory are not exhausted by *presuming* materiality, on the one hand, and *negating* materiality, on the other. It is my purpose to do precisely neither of these. To call a presupposition into question is not the same as doing away with it; rather, it is to free it from its metaphysical lodgings in order to understand what political interests were secured in and by that metaphysical placing, and thereby to permit the term to occupy and to serve very different political aims. To problematize the matter of bodies may entail an initial loss of epistemological certainty, but a loss of certainty is not the same as political nihilism. On the contrary, such a loss may well indicate a significant and promising shift in political thinking. This unsettling of 'matter' can be understood as initiating new possibilities, new ways for bodies to matter." This paragraph expresses what is envisaged in Butler's very ambitious project: a social and political, as well as theoretical, power in the critical acts of the humanities professor.

19. The responses of critics who feel called on either to attack or to defend the "person" of the critic are themselves interesting in their dramatization of the relation between the critical and the personal. The essays in the volume around Paul de Man (Werner Hamacher, Neil Hertz, and Thomas Keenan, eds., *Responses: On Paul de Man's Wartime Journalism* [Lincoln: University of Nebraska Press, 1989]) are extremely troubling for anyone interested in the state of contemporary criticism. With few exceptions, the essays reveal the weaknesses rather than strengths of the critical methods employed; this is especially true for the deconstructionist defenders of de Man. The ways in which the "personal" stake of many of the writers interferes with their critical acuity (in comparison with their other writings) are worth exploring.

20. There are many recent examples of autobiographical and performative criticism (such as works by Jane Gallop, Jane Tompkins, D. A. Miller, Nancy K. Miller, and so on). I mention Sedgwick here mainly for the earliness of her essay "A Poem Is Being Beaten," which she introduces with the remark: "Part of the motivation behind my work on it has been a fantasy that readers or hearers would be variously — in anger, identification, pleasure, envy, 'permission,' exclusion — stimulated to write accounts 'like' this one (whatever that means) of their own, and share those" (*Representations* 17 [1987]: 110). Her fantasy has come true.

21. Moreover, the institutional sanctioning and rewarding of "transgression" in academia also insulate the professor from the public consequences of his or her discourse. As I discussed at the end of the previous chapter, the strategies by which academics are rewarded are sometimes in direct contrast to those by which others must regulate their behavior.

22. This is what Cornel West envisages to be one of the key roles of the intellectual (and of the "jazz freedom fighter"): "to attempt to galvanize and energize world-weary people into forms of organization with accountable leadership that promote critical exchange and broad reflection" (*Race Matters* [Boston: Beacon, 1993], 105).

23. See Bruce Robbins, *Secular Vocations: Intellectuals, Professionalism, Culture* (London: Verso, 1993) and Russell Jacoby, *Dogmatic Wisdom: How the Culture Wars Divert Education and Distract America* (New York: Doubleday, 1994). What many recent books about academia have in common, ranging from Terry Eagleton's *The Function of Criticism: From "The Spectator" to Post-structuralism* (London: Verso, 1984) to Roger Kimball's *Tenured Radicals: How Politics Has Corrupted Our Higher Education* (New York: Harper, 1990), is their anxiety about the role of the intellectual, and especially of the professor of humanities (and even more particularly, of English), in contemporary society.

24. For Edwin Meese's views on pornography, see the *Attorney General's Commission on Pornography* (Washington, D.C.: United States Department of Justice, 1986).

6. Criticism as Displacement

1. Some may object to the word "apply" and prefer "deploy," or another word that sounds less mechanical or more interactive. But the well-trained critic does not approach the work in some naive or pure state and develop critical insights in response to the "internal" qualities of the work, apart from the institutional norms of the discipline. Pretending that frameworks of interpretation are arbitrary ("Today, I will read *Bleak House* in a 'deconstructive,' rather than a 'post-Marxist' mode") or ought to be avoided ("The critic should bow before the primacy of the literary work") only attests to the professional anxieties of academic literary criticism.

2. *The Poem Itself* (the word "text" already displaces the emphasis on a unique work) was a popular anthology of modern poetry in translation, published in 1960 (ed. Stanley Burnshaw [New York: Schocken]). The hope was to enable the reader (ignorant of foreign languages) to *experience* the original poem, by offering a literal translation plus commentary, rather than a verse translation of the poem. The notion of "the poem itself" follows from the ideology of the New Criticism. With regard to the idea of achieving the final interpretation of a work, David Lodge offers a wonderful parody of this aspiration in his novel *Changing Places: A Tale of Two Campuses* (London: Secker and Warburg, 1970). I could add a note after nearly every sentence of this essay, in order to support every point, provide its lineage, demonstrate its relation to the arguments of others, and so on. Such rampant footnoting would not help to prove my arguments; it would only demonstrate that I am properly cognizant of the work of other critics and am able to situate my ideas amid a historical or contemporary scene. Since one of my complaints about literary criticism will be that it displaces discussion away from what most needs to be argued, I will try to avoid the usual practice of providing lots of notes that do little to substantiate the actual arguments.

3. Edward Said begins his book *Representations of the Intellectual* with a discussion of Gramsci's distinction between "traditional intellectuals" ("who continue to do the same thing from generation to generation") and "organic intellectuals, whom Gramsci saw as directly connected to classes or enterprises that used intellectuals to organize

interests, gain more power, get more control" (*Representations of the Intellectual* [New York: Pantheon, 1994], 4). Said contrasts Gramsci to Julien Benda's ideal of the disengaged, otherworldly intellectual and concludes that "[t]oday, everyone who works in any field connected with either the production or distribution of knowledge is an intellectual in Gramsci's sense" (9). For Said, the positive side of the organic intellectual (and this opposition between the traditional and the organic intellectual [and between Matthew Arnold and Oscar Wilde] formed the basis for a class titled "The Role of the Intellectual" that I took with Said in 1979) is the *connection* to the issues, problems, and pains of the contemporary world. Said states eloquently: "I also want to insist that the intellectual is an individual with a specific public role in society that cannot be reduced simply to being a faceless professional, a competent member of a class just going about her/his business. The central fact for me is, I think, that the intellectual is an individual endowed with a faculty for representing, embodying, articulating a message, a view, an attitude, philosophy or opinion to, as well as for, a public. And this role has an edge to it, and cannot be played without a sense of being someone whose place it is publicly to raise embarrassing questions, to confront orthodoxy and dogma (rather than to produce them), to be someone who cannot easily be co-opted by governments or corporations, and whose *raison d'être* is to represent all those people and issues that are routinely forgotten or swept under the rug" (11).

4. Edward Said, *Culture and Imperialism* (New York: Knopf, 1993), 303; all further references will be included parenthetically in the text.

5. Said elaborates his antiprofessional stance in chapter 4, "Professionals and Amateurs," of his newer book *Representations of the Intellectual.*

6. See particularly "Profession Despise Thyself: Fear and Self-Loathing in Literary Studies" and "Anti-professionalism," in *Doing What Comes Naturally: Change, Rhetoric, and the Practice of Theory in Literary and Legal Studies* (Durham, N.C.: Duke University Press, 1989). In the latter essay Fish states: "A professional must find a way to operate in the context of purposes, motivations, and possibilities that precede and even define him and yet maintain the conviction that he is 'essentially the proprietor of his own person and capacities.' *The way he finds is anti-professionalism.*" And he concludes: "Anti-professionalism is professionalism in its purest form" (244, 245).

7. Bruce Robbins, *Secular Vocations: Intellectuals, Professionalism, Culture* (London: Verso, 1993), x. Robbins speaks extremely highly of Said (see chapter 5 of *Secular Vocations*, "The East Is a Career: Edward Said"), but attempts to "bring the perspective of professionalism to bear on this exemplary leftist career" (153). Robbins states that "my own project is visibly indebted" to Fish's "Anti-Professionalism" essay (103), and his book attempts to find a path to reconcile the "anti-democratic" tendencies of professionalism with his desire for progressive, socially responsive, oppositional criticism, or as he puts it at the end of the book: "To do culture [professionally] has thus meant to be in public, linked to real groups struggling in the real world, groups that make their demands not only in terms of culture, but to the state" (224). Despite the use of the past tense, this statement (and much of the book) reads more as a desideratum than as a description of the current state of "cultural politics" and academic professionalism.

8. In recent criticism, conflict and "dissensus," rather than reconciliation and consensus, have become the privileged terms for describing the state and the aims of criticism. A new conceptualization of criticism has not, however, produced better critical dialogue. I discuss this at length in the next chapter, "The Poverty of Conversation."

9. See Terry Eagleton, *The Function of Criticism: From "The Spectator" to Post-structuralism* (London: Verso, 1984), 107.

10. In the next couple of pages, I am alluding to Mary Poovey's essay "Reading History in Literature: Speculation and Virtue in *Our Mutual Friend*" (in *Historical Criticism and the Challenge of Theory*, ed. Janet Levarie Smarr [Urbana: University of Illinois Press, 1993]; the quotes above are from page 67). I am using this essay here only to illustrate some of the typical strategies for analyzing inequality and race. Poovey's essay challenges certain features of new historicism, and her discussion of inequality focuses more on money ("speculation") and gender than on race. A full (and perhaps a fair) discussion of her essay would have to confront her central arguments, but I am interested in the almost offhand ("textually marginal" yet "ideologically central") way that race functions in this essay and in the exemplarity of the critical strategies, regardless of the particular aims of the essay.

11. Poovey writes: "In part, however, the threat posed by the possibility that difference might not be anchored in sexual nature could be symbolically managed even as it was exposed because another principle of differentiation had become available by the 1860s to compensate for — and complicate — the difference of sex. This difference was the difference of race..." (67). Amidst the indeterminacies opened up by speculation and the analysis of gender, race provides the best anchor.

12. This is the tack taken by D. A. Miller in his analyses of Dickens in *The Novel and the Police* (Berkeley: University of California Press, 1988). Poovey does not at all endorse this Foucauldian interpretation. My point is that the strategies of reading, despite the different conclusions, similarly shield their most arguable suppositions and political aspirations from debate.

13. Poovey, "Reading History in Literature," 72.

14. Throughout his book *There's No Such Thing as Free Speech, and It's a Good Thing, Too* (New York: Oxford University Press, 1994), Stanley Fish presents those who disagree with his views as blind to history, preferring an a-contextual, homogenizing, and pseudo-transcendental perspective that hides their own partisanship and interests. But an appeal to "history" only begins the discussion on the contentious issues about which he is arguing (and "debating" with Dinesh D'Souza); it does not put an end to it. Fish acts as if "knowledge" alone will solve political disagreement; this is the attitude I am criticizing.

15. In his essay "The Politics of Recognition," Charles Taylor states that a "crucial feature of human life is its fundamentally *dialogical* character" (in *Multiculturalism: Examining the Politics of Recognition*, ed. Amy Guttman [Princeton, N.J.: Princeton University Press, 1994], 32). He states that acknowledging this "crucial feature of the human condition" is essential for understanding "the close connection between identity and recognition." I am making a more limited claim: questions that depend on the assent and interaction of others (a theory of equality that is closed to the opinions of others is a recipe for totalitarianism) are fundamentally dialogical and cannot be answered simply through philosophical inquiry, textual exegesis, or historical analysis.

16. Eve Kosofsky Sedgwick, *Between Men: English Literature and Male Homosocial Desire* (New York: Columbia University Press, 1985) and *Epistemology of the Closet* (Berkeley: University of California Press, 1990).

17. Said's *Culture and Imperialism* has been attacked in England for besmirching the honor and purity of Jane Austen (and synecdochally, of pastoral Albion). As Said puts it, he committed the "unforgivable sin" of arguing that *Mansfield Park* "also had something to do with slavery and British-owned sugar plantations in Antigua" (*Repre-*

sentations of the Intellectual, xi). Susan Fraiman, in her essay "Jane Austen and Edward Said," *Critical Inquiry* 21 (1995): 805–21, provides a list of the many responses to Said's reading of *Mansfield Park* and then goes on to argue that "Said's typing of Austen is . . . symptomatic of a more general gender politics underlying his postcolonial project" (807). I have no interest in defending Austen or protecting the aesthetic pleasures of reading her work, nor do I want to focus on whether Said's reading is fair to Austen, to England, or to imperialism. I have chosen this section of Said's book since it offers a good opportunity for examining the possibilities and the results of the new awareness of colonialism for literary criticism.

18. Said writes, "Imperialism and the culture associated with it affirm both the primacy of geography and an ideology about control of territory" (*Culture and Imperialism,* 78), and he claims, "After Lukács and Proust, we have become so accustomed to thinking of the novel's plot and structure as constituted mainly by temporality that we have overlooked the function of space, geography, and location" (84). Yet in the last fifteen years, there has been a tremendous interest in geography, cartography, and "space" in literary and cultural analysis. In our "postmodern" critical era, attentiveness to geography and space has superseded the concentration on history and time.

19. Said slightly misquotes this passage, leaving out the exclamation mark after "silence" and presenting "there was such a dead silence" as a complete sentence. Said writes: "Fanny Price reminds her cousin that after asking Sir Thomas about the slave trade, 'There was such a dead silence.' " The Penguin edition from which he is quoting reads:

"Did not you hear me ask him about the slave-trade last night?" [Fanny]

"I did — and was in hopes the question would be followed up by others. It would have pleased your uncle to be inquired of farther." [Edward]

"And I longed to do it — but there was such a dead silence! And while my cousins . . . " [Fanny]

See Jane Austen, *Mansfield Park* (Harmondsworth, England: Penguin, 1966), 213. Fanny, to enter into the world of Mansfield Park, must constantly regulate and suppress her desires and interests (in contrast to Miss Crawford). The "dead silence" is that of the other characters who are everywhere being critiqued in the novel.

20. Here is part of the article on slavery from the *Encyclopedia Britannica* (15th ed., 1991): "Slavery in England was formally abolished by judicial fiat in 1772, when Chief Justice Mansfield held that the captured fugitive slave James Somersett, from Virginia, could not be claimed by his owner and that furthermore any slave by the act of walking on English soil became free. The fate of slavery in most of the rest of the world depended on the British abolition movement, which was initiated by the English Quakers in 1783, when they presented the first important antislavery petition to Parliament. . . . An act of March 2, 1807, forbade trading in slaves with Africa. . . . In 1807 the British abolished the slave trade with their colonies. In the Caribbean, slavery was abolished by British Parliamentary fiat, effective July 31, 1834, when 776,000 slaves in the British plantation colonies were freed. The British imperial emancipation can be attributed to the growing power of the philanthropic movement and a double switch in the focus of the British Empire, geographically from west (the Caribbean) to east (India) and economically from protectionism to laissez-faire." Although the Bertrams may have been silent, this was not the case for many others at the time of the novel.

21. If one is going to attack the complicity of Western culture in imperialism, it is better to do so straightforwardly. Said, to his credit, does not try to rescue Austen by claiming that she in fact "subverts" imperialism in *Mansfield Park*. It is now common, in a gesture that justifies our profession and our research, for critics to demonstrate how their favored texts subvert the evils of our culture. The particular work, like the critic him- or herself, then becomes the exception to the oppressive culture; one need not even extend the range of one's reading to adopt a stance of resistance. It is easy to come up with a "subversive" reading for almost any work (and for that matter, a "complicitous" one as well), but such readings usually beg the question of why the work has had so little of the desired subversive effect. Said's project, in contrast, is to emphasize the affirming, sanctioning, and legitimating functions of the bourgeois novel with regard to imperialism.

22. Said continues: "In the counterpoint of Western classical music, various themes play off one another, with only a *provisional privilege* being given to any particular one; yet in the resulting polyphony there is concert and order, an organized interplay that derives from the themes, not from a rigorous melodic or formal principle outside the work. In the same way, I believe, we can read and interpret English novels, for example, whose engagement (usually suppressed for the most part) with the West Indies or India, say, is shaped and perhaps even determined by the specific history of colonization, resistance, and finally native nationalism. At this point alternative or new narratives emerge, and they become institutionalized or discursively stable entities" (*Culture and Imperialism*, 51; emphasis added). One of Said's key aims is to supply this "contrapuntal perspective."

23. I do not think that the only good reading is a resistant reading, nor that political justice or freedom come only from resistance to dominant power. And I certainly do not think that "critical" reading is the primary path for achieving justice and freedom (as if all good readers will be good people). I also want to challenge any easy equation of "resistance" in reading to political resistance. When "resistance" (to hegemony, imperialism, the dominant culture, and so on) becomes the only intellectually and politically acceptable stance, there is no longer any room for engaging other opinions and no need for open theorizing about equality. Criticism then provides the model for foreclosing dialogue.

24. It is no accident that we now have William Bennett's reading for virtue, which is just the flip side of reading for evil. Yet virtue is at least a better model: it offers the possibility of imitation — the precritical response here is one that is (arguably) socially beneficial. The whole strategy of reading for evil assumes that there really is nothing to debate — that evil must be located, brought to light, and then denounced. This is finally a profoundly antidemocratic stance, even as it dresses itself up as providing greater representation and democracy. Like Bennett's *The Book of Virtues*, reading for evil puts the critic in the role of enlightened moral guide (see William Bennett, ed., *The Book of Virtues: A Treasury of Great Moral Stories* [New York: Simon & Schuster, 1993]). It would be better for critics to first demonstrate any claims to moral wisdom, rather than making their literary analyses the vehicle for proclaiming their moral illumination. This approach also gives rise to judging the sins of the past against the standards of the present. We now often have a pinhole optic of multiculturalism, in which an ever wider array of texts is looked at through an increasingly narrow hole; multiculturalism of the content, insularity of the framework. The fruitfulness of the reading (one always succeeds in unmasking evil) substitutes for confronting the ideas of others.

25. Graff makes this argument most fully in his book *Beyond the Culture Wars: How Teaching the Conflicts Can Revitalize American Education* (New York: Norton, 1992), but the quotes that follow are from his earlier essay "Other Voices, Other Rooms." This essay (written for an academic audience) is sharper in some ways than the book, which was projected toward some imagined nonacademic audience. See Gerald Graff, "Other Voices, Other Rooms," *New Literary History* 21 (1990): 817–39; all further references will be included parenthetically in the text.

26. At issue here is the value of bad debate. Graff suggests that even poor debates can be excellent tools for helping students gain a better understanding of the issues and of the different positions that motivate academic critics. I agree — students can learn a lot from, and become engaged by, teaching that stages rather than hides the conflicts between different professorial outlooks. In contrast to Graff, I am arguing for debates of intellectual or political — rather than pedagogical — value.

7. The Poverty of Conversation

1. Catharine Stimpson, one of "a group of scholars [who] met in Chicago to answer the call of Sheldon Hackney, chairman of the National Endowment for the Humanities," defends both the NEH project and the ideal of "conversation" against what she describes as the other possibility, "unpalatable conversation-stopping monologues," in a piece entitled "A Conversation, Not a Monologue," in the *Chronicle of Higher Education*, 16 March 1994, B1–B2. Typically but implausibly, she uses her allegiance to conversation to fend off critics and position herself as speaking for "those of us in the evolving center," against the extremes of Left and Right. I will have more to say about the NEH project later in the chapter.

2. Paul Mann begins his essay on "masocriticism" with an injunction that both mimics and mocks Beckett: "It would be excellent if the farce called criticism could be brought to an end." See Paul Mann, "Masocriticism," *SubStance* 75 (1994): 3. He immediately concludes, of course, that this cannot be done, but he does a good job of exposing the farcical impulses of criticism.

3. Frank Rich, "Cheney Dumbs Down," *New York Times*, 26 February 1995, E15. Rich makes similar appeals for "genuine debate" in other op-ed pieces defending the arts and attacking the Republicans.

4. The ellipsis appears on the book jacket. See Gerald Graff, *Beyond the Culture Wars: How Teaching the Conflicts Can Revitalize American Education* (New York: Norton, 1992). Graff has also blurbed Gates's book *Loose Canons: Notes on the Culture Wars* (New York: Oxford University Press, 1992), and he also uses the word "readable" (a code word for "to be read by others, outside academia"), implying that what we write principally for each other is "unreadable." Graff's full blurb is: "In these incisive and readable essays, Henry Louis Gates, Jr., is at once sympathetic, funny, and cautionary in making the case for cultural pluralism and the revision of the literary canon."

5. Gates, *Loose Canons*, 118.

6. An example of the postures that preclude any reasoning together is Jonathan Culler's remarks at the beginning of his essay "Lace, Lance, and Pair" (in *Profession 94* [New York: Modern Language Association, 1994]), a piece written in response to an invitation by MLA president Elaine Marks to speak at the presidential forum on the topic "*Amo, Amas, Amat:* Literature." Culler writes: "Was this forum, I asked myself, an attempt to recapture the terrain of love of literature from the cultural Right? But

when I read Elaine Marks's remarks on the subject in the MLA *Newsletter*, I began to wonder whether this was her goal, for instead of contesting or undoing the opposition between love of literature and theory, she seemed to restate it as an opposition between a love of literature and a preoccupation with social and political relevance. . . . I fear to deploy an opposition between love and literature and its other—whether it is called 'theory' or 'social relevance'—is to support rather than contest the discourse of the Right and to simplify, in a fashion that can only be called wishful, the complex problem of what 'love' may entail here" (5). If the starting point and fundamental test for literary criticism is to contest the cultural Right, there is not much hope for any meaningful dialogue between honored members of the academic literary establishment and adherents of the "cultural Right." Culler, in a very typical gesture, links the political agenda ("contest the discourse of the Right") with the intellectual one (explore "the complex problem of what 'love' may entail here"). For many critics, such a linkage is taken for granted: anything intellectually rigorous will necessarily "contest the discourse of the Right." This is also typical for an MLA presidential forum, where the hierarchy defends itself against those who challenge or mock the MLA.

7. I mention Kimball and Baker since they have vehemently attacked each other. Offering anything other than a complete condemnation of Kimball's *Tenured Radicals: How Politics Has Corrupted Our Higher Education* (New York: Harper, 1990) is usually seen as a sign of collaboration with the radical Right. Christopher Lasch writes, however, in *The Revolt of the Elites and the Betrayal of Democracy* (New York: Norton, 1995): "Roger Kimball is not particularly interested in the fate of social criticism, but his attack on academic radicalism, *Tenured Radicals*, can be read with a good deal of profit by anyone who is. . . . But anyone who reads Kimball's book with an open mind will recognize the accuracy of many of his observations" (182–83).

8. Graff, *Beyond the Culture Wars*, 193; all further references are given parenthetically in the text.

9. Only a tenured professor could admit not having an original passion for literature. The 1993 MLA presidential forum "*Amo, Amas, Amat*: Literature" (referred to in note 6) presents the more usual posture: stories of an early love of literature, which certify that any ensuing analysis, criticism, or theory (and which may seem to disfigure the cherished object) is at least grounded in an earlier experience of love.

10. Graff states: "That is why teachers in modern periods need nonmodernists (and vice versa) in order to make their subjects intelligible to their students, just as teachers who defend the culture of the West need the teachers who criticize it (and vice versa). . . . Insofar as neither a defense nor a critique of tradition makes sense apart from the dialogue these positions are engaged in, a curriculum which removes that dialogue from view defeats the goals of traditionalists and revisionists alike" (109).

11. Russell Jacoby, *Dogmatic Wisdom: How the Culture Wars Divert Education and Distract America* (New York: Doubleday, 1994), 184, 188.

12. Graff is very aware of the weakness of much academic debate, and when he writes for the profession rather than for a popular, public audience (*Beyond the Culture Wars*, published by Norton, is addressed to a nonacademic audience) he adopts a harsher tone, such as in his English Institute piece "Preaching to the Converted" (in *English Inside and Out: The Place of Literary Criticism*, ed. Susan Gubar and Jonathan Kamholtz [New York: Routledge, 1993], 109–21). Nevertheless, one of Graff's main proposals for educational reform is to introduce symposia into the curriculum. I have found some symposia and conferences to be intellectually rewarding, but never to showcase the kinds of enlightened and illuminating conflicts that Graff calls for.

13. Cornel West, *Race Matters* (Boston: Beacon, 1993), 12, 14. On the pages cited, West offers the very grounds for debate: which suppositions must be accepted and rejected and what the starting point should be. He writes: "This debate must go far beyond the liberal and conservative positions in three fundamental ways. First, we must acknowledge that structures and behavior are inseparable, that institutions and values go hand in hand.... Second, we should reject the idea that structures are primarily economic and political creatures — an idea that sees culture as an ephemeral set of behavioral attitudes and values.... Third, and most important, we must delve into the depths where neither liberals nor conservatives dare to tread, namely, into the murky waters of despair and dread that now flood the streets of black America.... The proper starting point for the crucial debate about the prospects for black America is an examination of the nihilism that increasingly pervades black communities." Having this "crucial debate" depends on already agreeing with West about much of what is to be discussed.

14. Carl Schmitt, *The Crisis of Parliamentary Democracy*, trans. Ellen Kennedy (Cambridge, Mass.: MIT Press, 1985), 5; all further references are given parenthetically in the text.

15. In contemporary American ideology, democracy and liberal individualism are usually taken to be almost synonymous. Schmitt argues differently: "Bolshevism and Fascism by contrast are, like all dictatorships, certainly antiliberal but not necessarily antidemocratic. In the history of democracy there have been numerous dictatorships, Caesarisms, and other more striking forms that have tried to create homogeneity and to shape the will of the people with methods uncommon in the liberal tradition of the past century.... Compared to a democracy that is direct, not only in the technical sense but also in a vital sense, parliament appears an artificial machinery, produced by liberal reasoning" (16–17). He concludes that the crisis of contemporary parliamentarism "springs from the consequences of modern mass democracy and in the final analysis from the contradiction of a liberal individualism burdened by moral pathos and a democratic sentiment governed essentially by political ideals." Schmitt was writing in 1926, well before the defeat of fascism and the collapse of bolshevism. Yet similar contradictions still haunt our liberal, democratic regimes, even if they do not appear to be in crisis. In her introduction to Schmitt's book, Ellen Kennedy provides an excellent description of how "discussion is central to liberalism": "The necessity for discussion is no less epistemological than it is political; in liberalism, the search for truth goes on as a conversation from which force is absent and where reason and persuasion prevail. Liberal political theory thus depends on an assumption that political conflict can be transformed into a matter of opinion; the better informed and more 'enlightened' the public is, the closer it will come to the truth, and on this reading, parliament becomes the greatest force for the political education not only of leaders but also of the public. Parliament's job, performed through debate and questioning, is to sort out conflicting opinions and evidence, so that parliamentary government can govern not just by dint of holding power or through authority but because it comes closest to the truth" (xix). The United States Congress fails miserably in performing this job.

16. Such were the reactions to a speech by President Clinton calling for "a new common ground" and to his joint appearance in New Hampshire with Newt Gingrich a couple weeks earlier when they both called for a new conversation and a new civility in political discourse. Clinton's speech began: "Today I want to have more of a conversation than deliver a formal speech, about the great debate now raging in

our nation, not so much over what we should do, but over how we should resolve the great questions of our time here in Washington and in communities all across our country" (*New York Times*, 7 July 1995, A14). The *Times* editorial the next day begins: "Republicans have a right to their suspicions about President Clinton's calls for an end to harsh partisanship," and goes on to analyze the political conditions that motivated this plea for civility (*New York Times*, 7 July 1995, A18). A similar set of reactions was provoked by Clinton's speech (in June 1997) calling for a national conversation on race.

17. In universities, only a few issues are adjudicated by rational-critical debate. The proliferation of departments, programs, and other somewhat autonomous administrative structures has worked to keep disagreements from spilling beyond narrow disciplinary boundaries. Administrators seek at all costs to avoid open conflicts and prefer a disengaged pluralism, with the tenured members allowed largely to do their own thing, to an energetic debate. They see themselves as control rods (making sure that the reaction never gets too hot) rather than as catalysts for debate. Important decisions about the use and allocation of power (for example, reappointment and funding) are tightly controlled and rarely open to scrutiny; the operating model is closer to a private corporation than a political democracy.

18. Jürgen Habermas, *The Structural Transformation of the Public Sphere: An Inquiry into a Category of Bourgeois Society*, trans. Thomas Burger (Cambridge, Mass.: MIT Press, 1989), 82.

19. Any theory of dialogue would have to confront the challenges and rethinking of dialogue and communication by Derrida, Adorno, Blanchot, Lyotard, and others, and also examine the models of dialogue proposed by Gadamer, Jauss, Habermas, Rorty, Benhabib, and so on.

20. See the brochure "Special Competition: A National Conversation on American Pluralism and Identity" (National Endowment for the Humanities, 5).

21. The language here echoes leftist pedagogical jargon in which "competition" is bad and a threat to self-esteem. It would be interesting to watch Hackney attempt to reconcile this view with the promotion of competition and capitalism by other branches of the Clinton administration.

22. Hans-Georg Gadamer writes: "In fact the horizon of the present is continually in the process of being formed because we are continually having to test all our prejudices. An important part of this testing occurs in encountering the past and in understanding the tradition from which we come. Hence the horizon of the present cannot be formed without the past. There is no more an isolated horizon of the present in itself than there are historical horizons which have to be acquired. *Rather, understanding is always the fusion of these horizons supposedly existing by themselves. . . .* If, however, there is no such thing as these distinct horizons, why do we speak of the fusion of horizons and not simply of the formation of the one horizon, whose bounds are set in the depths of tradition? . . . Every encounter with tradition that takes place within historical consciousness involves the experience of a tension between the text and the present. The hermeneutic task consists in not covering up this tension by attempting a naive assimilation of the two but in consciously bringing it out" (*Truth and Method*, 2d rev. ed., trans. Joel Weinsheimer and Donald G. Marshall [New York: Continuum, 1989], 306). Conversation is a key concept for Gadamer, but the different horizons he speaks of are that of the past and the present, not, say, Latino culture and Japanese American culture (Charles Taylor, borrowing the notion from Gadamer, speaks of a "fusion of horizons" in the cross-cultural sense and argues for

"a willingness to be open to comparative cultural study of the kind that must *displace* our horizons in the resulting fusions" [*Multiculturalism*, ed. Amy Gutmann (Princeton, N.J.: Princeton University Press, 1994), 67, 73]). I mention Gadamer here because what is lacking in the NEH project and in many multicultural proposals is any serious reflection on the dynamics of understanding and mediating differences. Contact with the other, in a proper (state-sanctioned) conversation, will somehow automatically enable participants to "expand their own horizons" and achieve "greater understanding of perspectives different from their own." The *hermeneutics* of any such understanding need to be fully explained and defended.

23. Lasch, *Revolt of the Elites*, 117.

24. In *Revolt of the Elites*, Lasch discusses at length the decay of civic institutions and emphasizes the decline of "third places" ("a meeting ground midway between the workplace and the family circle") and of public debate. Lasch does not record the structural changes in society; he blames the elites for their abandonment of broader communities. He argues: "Elites, who define the issues, have lost touch with the people. The unreal, artificial character of our politics reflects their insulation from the common life, together with a secret conviction that the real problems are insoluble" (3–4).

25. In *Specters of Marx: The State of Debt, the Work of Mourning, and the New International*, trans. Peggy Kamuf (New York: Routledge, 1994), Jacques Derrida writes: "[I]s it still necessary to point out that liberal democracy of the parliamentary form has never been so much in the minority and so isolated in the world? That it has never been in such a state of dysfunction in what we call the Western democracies? Electoral representativity or parliamentary life is not only distorted, as was always the case, by a great number of socio-economic mechanisms, but it is exercised with more and more difficulty in a public space profoundly upset by techno-tele-media apparatuses and by new rhythms of information and communication, by the devices and the speed of forces represented by the latter, but also and consequently by the new modes of appropriation they put to work, by the new structure of the event and of its spectrality that they *produce*" (78–79). While I disagree with Derrida's pronouncements about Western democracies, and especially with this mode of argument (phrasing questions in a manner that makes anyone who disagrees appear stupid, rather than offering any support at all for these claims), I think the issues he raises need to be confronted in any project for new conversations.

26. Stanley Fish, *There's No Such Thing as Free Speech* (New York: Oxford University Press, 1994), 97.

27. A good example of this is Fish's essay "Rhetoric," in *Doing What Comes Naturally: Change, Rhetoric, and the Practice of Theory in Literary and Legal Studies* (Durham, N.C.: Duke University Press, 1989), 471–502, where he employs the terms Serious Man and Rhetorical Man (borrowed from Richard Lanham), but Fish employs this tactic in almost all his essays.

28. D'Souza's book *The End of Racism* (New York: Free Press, 1995) precipitated a falling out with his black conservative colleagues at the American Enterprise Institute. Robert Woodson and Glenn Loury both quit the think tank, angry that AEI heavily promoted a book they viewed as racist.

29. Of all the people I know in academia, Stanley Fish, with whom I studied in graduate school, is one of the people most interested in genuinely arguing his ideas. I have met D'Souza twice, and neither occasion provided the opportunity for much discussion. But I have met many other conservatives who, at least among themselves (for

instance, a seminar at the Heritage Foundation), are wonderfully capable of participating in "the back and forth of argument." Debates among academics or politicians in a public setting, where the adversary is not at all the person to be convinced, produce a different discussion. I discuss my experience at the Heritage Foundation in the "Afterword."

30. See Michael Lerner and Cornel West, *Jews and Blacks: Let the Healing Begin* (New York: G. P. Putnam's Sons, 1995).

31. For Michael Oakeshott, "acknowledgment" and "accommodation" are central to civilization and education. He writes in *Rationalism and Politics* (New York: Basic Books, 1962): "[A] civilization (and particularly ours) may be regarded as a conversation being carried on between a variety of human activities, each speaking with a voice, or in a language of its own.... And I call the manifold which these different manners of thinking and speaking compose, a conversation, because the relations between them are not those of assertion and denial but the conversational relationships of acknowledgment and accommodation" (304). He also writes, "[T]here appears in a university what cannot (or cannot so easily) appear elsewhere, the images of civilization as a manifold of different intellectual activities, a conversation between different modes of thinking and this determines the character of the education it offers" (312). Oakeshott contrasts "acknowledgment and accommodation" with "assertion and denial." This seems to describe the difference between debate and conversation. My use primarily of "dialogue," as a middle term, is meant to include the conflictual aspects of debate with the accommodationist ones of conversation; the possibility of this middle ground is what is in question.

32. Gilles Deleuze and Félix Guattari, *What Is Philosophy?* trans. Hugh Tomlinson and Graham Burchell (New York: Columbia University Press, 1994), 80. This passage is a bit less opaque if one has read the definitions of "concept," "the plane of immanence," and "conceptual personae" earlier in the book.

33. Graff, *Beyond the Culture Wars*, 15.

34. Socratic dialogue has nothing to do with an equal *exchange* of opinion. What then is the role of the people other than Socrates? Each dialogue is an inquiry — usually an inquiry into a notion that, with the passage of time and the change in language, is itself unanswerable to a modern audience. What is *technē* or *sophrosyne*? The dialogue proceeds by questioning in turn several definitions, or suppositions, about who or what embodies the qualities under investigation. The procedure is not primarily to ascertain someone else's ideas in order to see whose ideas are better; rather, someone else is required to put forth the preliminary notions that will be tested and contested. The other people in the dialogue serve to put forward a type of conventional wisdom or first response that is *not* philosophic precisely because it is untested and is not the product of philosophic inquiry and scrutiny.

Dialogue, then, is necessary to move from the common understanding, the untested notion, the preliminary definition, to philosophy: to a knowledge that can be attained through inquiry, scrutiny, criticism, questioning, and testing an idea from several angles. As the dialogue proceeds, several further ideas will be put forth and scrutinized and rejected in turn. Socrates requires dialogue in order to think, since what he is most interested in is less a new series of definitions, less a more sophisticated definition of *sophrosyne* than any put forward by others, than the process of inquiry and scrutiny, the process by which these ideas are challenged and tested. Yet this testing does not take place by an exchange of "viewpoints" in any personal sense or in any way that depends essentially on the "identity" of the speakers. It is not by

looking at the ideas from Charmides's perspective, or by considering a different political viewpoint, or by adopting the perspective of someone with a different set of
"interests" that Socrates moves the inquiry forward. He never operates in a vacuum,
and others are always required, but not to achieve a "critical exchange of ideas."
   35. Michael Bérubé, *Public Access: Literary Theory and American Cultural Politics*
(New York: Verso, 1994), 175–76.
   36. John Leo, "The Professors of Dogmatism," *U.S. News and World Report*, 18
January 1993, 25. I was one of the other speakers on the panel with Bérubé, but
Leo did not mention me (the panel was chaired by Gerald Graff, and I presented a
much earlier version of chapter 3, "Forging a Public Voice for Academic Critics").
Leo describes Bérubé: "a black-shirt male who is answering an earnest question from
the floor: Is it OK, in college English classes, to teach music videos instead of literature? Black-shirt thinks it's just fine, though he says, derisively, that it might upset
some 'traditionalists'; the audience chuckles appreciatively at the put-down." Bérubé
responds at length in his essay, but his elaborations are no less simpleminded. He
describes a questioner who "voiced her alarm that we'd spoken as if teaching music
video were *better* than teaching traditional periods in literary history, and this disturbed her because her work was in Romanticism and she resented being treated
as a second-class critic next to all these theory hotshots. Realizing that I'd already
raised a traditionalist's hackles..." (173). He is just as patronizing, condescending,
and unwilling to listen to others as Leo; the alarm, disturbance, and resentment are
Bérubé's projections and a means to avoid the issues raised (the concerns are only
those of a backward, worried, semicompetent traditionalist, not hip enough to make
it on the current scene). The person who asked the question (a friend of mine) does
not conform to Bérubé's categories: she is certainly a "theory hotshot" if that means
having studied with the leading literary theorists (Jacques Derrida, Werner Hamacher,
Philippe Lacoue-Labarthe, among many others), having published in leading journals,
and teaching literary theory at an Ivy League university, but not if it means simply
teaching music videos rather than romantic poetry (and there are always choices, always value judgments being made, despite Bérubé's disclaimer that "I would never
consider teaching music video *better* than doing Romanticism"). The safety of such
categories as "traditionalists" and "theory hotshots" allows Bérubé to hear what he
wants to hear, to offer his own "contestation" rather than address the ideas of others,
and to avoid any deeper consideration of the actual choices and problems in literary
studies.
   37. At a conference, I would much rather hear Nancy Vickers analyzing George
Michael videos (as I did at the English Institute several years ago) than listen to yet
another typical analysis of a Shakespeare play or a Wordsworth poem; the former
would more likely be capable "of generating serious reflection." But using this criterion for what should be taught in the classroom ignores the processes and purposes of
education: for students, the experience of reading Shakespeare is very different from
watching George Michael videos in class, even if they generate similar discussions.
The insularity of both Leo and Bérubé, each secure in his defenses and condemna-
tions, sidesteps any discussion of what a university education can and ought to do.
Michael Oakeshott's essay "The Study of Politics in a University" (from *Rationalism in
Politics*) brings up the crucial point that university professors are "engaged in learning
something other than what they undertake to teach." He continues: "Nevertheless,
what they teach is not what they themselves are in process of learning, nor is it what
they may have learned or discovered yesterday. As scholars they may live on what

are called the 'frontiers of knowledge,' but as teachers they must be something other than frontiersmen. Nor, again, is what they teach exactly the activity in which they are themselves engaged; their pupils are not apprentices to an activity.... What a university has to offer is not information but practice in thinking" (312–13). Oakeshott's claims are now heavily disputed, and his essay might form the basis of a productive debate between a "Bérubé" and a "Leo."

38. Attending (for at least a few sessions, if not the whole semester) a "traditional" class on Shakespeare, another Shakespeare class in which the professor used music videos and films such as My Own Private Idaho (which lifts whole passages from Henry IV, part 1) alongside the plays, and a third class that focused solely on popular culture, could provide the basis for an edifying discussion, with Bérubé and with the students, about the aims of education, about how learning takes place, and about whether the classroom has become "politicized." In most debates, what actually happens in the classroom, beyond discreet anecdotes, is usually ignored.

39. I am borrowing the notion of "enlarged thought" from Seyla Benhabib, who in turn borrows it from Hannah Arendt, who borrows it from Kant (see Arendt's "The Crisis in Culture," in Between Past and Future: Six Exercises in Political Thought [New York: Viking, 1961], where she speaks of Kant's notion of "eine erweiterte Denkungsart" from the Critique of Judgment). Benhabib, in Situating the Self: Gender, Community and Postmodernism in Contemporary Ethics (New York: Routledge, 1992), writes: "Perhaps the most valuable outcome of such authentic processes of public dialogue when compared to the mere exchange of information or the mere circulation of images is that, when and if they occur, such public conversations result in the cultivation of the faculty of judgment and the formation of an 'enlarged mentality'" (121). Benhabib (and Arendt) uses the terms "enlarged thought" and "enlarged mentality" to translate Kant's idea.

40. This invocation comes from another column from Frank Rich ("Who Lost the Arts," New York Times, 9 August 1995, A19): "The dispirited Mr. Luers [president of the Metropolitan Museum], like others I spoke to, also soon discovered that the endowments' fate was not tied to 'a rational, intelligent debate over what the arts and humanities do' in any case. No argument — esthetic, economic, educational or even patriotic — could save the N.E.A. as long as it was on the religious right's hit list." Which programs do have their fate tied to "a rational, intelligent debate" in the Congress?

41. Ernesto Laclau and Chantal Mouffe, Hegemony and Socialist Strategy: Towards a Radical Democratic Politics (London: Verso, 1985).

42. See my epigraph, which is from Jane Tompkins, "Me and My Shadow," New Literary History 18 (1987): 172.

43. John Leo, in his dismissal of the MLA and Bérubé, describes his attempts to listen simultaneously to two sessions: to Catharine Stimpson speaking in the next room, as well as to Bérubé and the others on our panel.

Afterword

1. Bill Readings concludes The University in Ruins (Cambridge, Mass.: Harvard University Press, 1996) with the chapter "The Community of Dissensus." He argues that it is time to let go of the story that the "University is supposed to be the potential model for free and rational discussion, a site where the community is founded in the sharing of a commitment to a rational abstraction" (180–81), and sketches

out an alternative notion of a "dissensual community." Readings draws heavily on Ly-otard's critique of Habermas and of consensus in developing his thoughts on dissensus. Near the end of *The Postmodern Condition*, Jean-François Lyotard states: "Consensus has become an outmoded and suspect value" (*The Postmodern Condition: A Report on Knowledge*, trans. Geoff Bennington and Brian Massumi [Minneapolis: University of Minnesota Press, 1984], 66).

    2. In "The University without Culture" (*New Literary History* 26 [1995]), Bill Readings writes: "If my preference is for a thought of dissensus over that of consensus, it is necessary to realize that dissensus cannot be institutionalized, because the precon-dition for such institutionalization would be a second-order consensus that dissensus is a good thing. . . . Something like this latter tendency is what makes me dissatisfied with Gerald Graff's powerful arguments in *Teaching the Conflicts*" (484). In his "Re-sponse to Bill Readings" in the same issue of *New Literary History*, Graff replies: "But then, it does not seem so unreasonable to expect such a consensus in a culture that has let the present noisy level of dissensus become established. *Somebody* must think dissensus is a pretty good thing, or why have contemporary universities come to har-bor so much of it?" (496). Graff goes on to make a distinction between approaching "these problems pedagogically and pragmatically, as problems of administrative and curricular strategy, or theoretically (as I think Bill does), as problems of philosophical incommensurability." Peggy Kamuf, in *The Division of Literature: Or the University in Deconstruction* (Chicago: University of Chicago Press, 1997), offers a similar critique of Graff: "Literary study, Graff argues, has been instituted only at the price of a denial of the conflicts that divide its understanding. On his own analysis, then, must not the vision of institutionalizing 'the conflicts of interpretations and overviews itself' partic-ipate in this denial even as Graff proposes to overturn it or correct it? Does it not, in other words, put forward a notion of consensual neutrality that masks a conflict of another order?" (18).

    3. Readings, *University in Ruins*, 182.

    4. Readings argues somewhat opaquely that "[t]he University's ruins offer us an institution in which the incomplete and interminable nature of the pedagogic relation can remind us that 'thinking together' is a dissensual process; it belongs to dialogism rather than dialogue" (ibid., 192). For an interesting use of this distinction, see Paul de Man's essay on Bakhtin, "Dialogue and Dialogism," in *The Resistance to Theory* (Minneapolis: University of Minnesota Press, 1986), 106–14.

    5. Readings, *University in Ruins*, 183.

    6. Hannah Arendt, "The Crisis in Culture: Its Social and Its Political Signifi-cance," in *Between Past and Future: Six Exercises in Political Thought* (New York: Viking, 1961), 220.

    7. Immanuel Kant, *The Critique of Judgment*, trans. James Creed Meredith (Oxford: Oxford University Press, 1952), 151.

    8. Arendt, "Crisis in Culture," 222. "Woo the consent of everyone else" is Arendt's translation of Kant's "Man wirbt um jedes andern Beistimmung" (*Kritik der Urteilskraft* [Frankfurt am Main: Suhrkamp Taschenbuch Wissenschaft, 1981], 156). This is much better than Meredith's translation, "We are suitors for agreement from every one else" (82). Arendt goes on to make a distinction between persuasion and philosophical dialogue: "This 'wooing' or persuading corresponds closely to what the Greeks called πείθειν, the convincing and persuading speech which they regarded as the typically political form of people talking with one another. Persuasion ruled the intercourse of the citizens of the polis because it excluded physical violence; but

the philosophers knew that it was also distinguished from another non-violent form of coercion, the coercion by truth. Persuasion appears in Aristotle as the opposite to διαλέγεσθαι, the philosophical form of speaking, precisely because this type of dialogue was concerned with knowledge and the finding of truth and therefore demanded a process of compelling proof" (222–23). Seyla Benhabib, in *Situating the Self: Gender, Community and Postmodernism in Contemporary Ethics* (New York: Routledge, 1992), interprets Arendt as providing the groundwork for "a dialogic or discursive ethic": "To 'think from the perspective of everyone else' is to know 'how to listen' to what the other is saying, or when the voices of others are absent, to imagine to oneself a conversation with the other as my dialogue partner. 'Enlarged thought' is best realized through a dialogic or discursive ethic" (137).

9. Arendt, "Crisis in Culture," 220; emphasis added.

10. I participated for ten days in a colloquium titled "Foundations of American Liberty" at the Salvatori Center for Academic Leadership at the Heritage Foundation. Mike Davis, in *City of Quartz: Excavating the Future of Los Angeles* (New York: Vintage Books, 1990), describes Henry Salvatori, who funded the center, as "the *éminence grise* of the most conservative camp" of California Republicans and as "godfather to Goldwater and Reagan" (122, 128).

11. On 11 November 1991, Hampshire staged an "alumni forum" at the Heritage Foundation, in which the president of Hampshire and two faculty members squared off against William Bennett and Morton Kondracke. Also participating were two alumni, one from the "Left" and one from the "Right" (a few exist), and Eleanor Clift, whose son went to Hampshire. When I called the Heritage Foundation to ask about the event, they said they knew nothing about it and that occasionally they rented their facilities to other organizations. I assume the reason for holding the event there was for the symbolism of Hampshire confronting the Heritage Foundation.

12. If the analysis of power at the Heritage Foundation was wildly askew — it's been seized by a dishonest and unprincipled elite who scorn the opinions and the lives of middle Americans (almost a mirror image of certain leftist conspiratorial views) — there was something almost refreshing about the pragmatic approach to gaining power. We were told that since we live in a political culture, the Heritage Foundation is positioned at the intersection of political and intellectual currents. The aim of the foundation is to invest in people, to maneuver the people they invest in into positions of power, and to have these investments "pay off in solid dividends."

13. While at Heritage, I learned about a whole network of conservative academic groups (such as the Institute of Humane Studies and the Intercollegiate Studies Institute) that I never knew existed.

14. Mario J. Valdés, "Introduction to Presidential Forum: Discourses of Truth," in *Profession 92* (New York: Modern Language Association, 1992), 3.

15. One might draw a sharp contrast here to St. Johns College (in Annapolis and Santa Fe), where there is a radical combination of conservatism in the content and progressivism in the form of the education; they teach the "great books," but the education proceeds almost entirely by discussions that are driven by the students, and the aim is always to explore and question, rather than protect and venerate, the ideas contained in these "great" books.

INDEX

◆

229

Jeffrey Wallen is associate professor of comparative literature at Hampshire College. In addition to writing about the current conflicts and debates in the university, he has published widely on nineteenth-century European literature. His essays have appeared in *Word and Image*, the *Yale Journal of Criticism*, *ELH*, and *diacritics*, among other journals.